ENGLISH TROUT-FLY STYLES

TOP ROW: *North-Country Wet Flies*: Brown Owl; Olive Bloa; Spring Black; Light Snipe & Yellow; Gravel Bed. SECOND ROW: *West-Country Wet Flies*: Blue Upright; Red Upright; Dark Olive Upright. THIRD ROW: Mole Fly (a); Straddlebug (Skues); Mole Fly (b). FOURTH ROW: Blue Dun; Lock's Blue Upright; Black Gnat. BOTTOM ROW: *South-Country Dry Flies*: Pale Watery Dun; Ginger Spinner (Skues); Mating Black Gnat (Deane)

English Trout Flies

W. H. LAWRIE

SOUTH BRUNSWICK
NEW YORK: A. S. BARNES AND COMPANY

ENGLISH TROUT FLIES. © 1967 by W. H. Lawrie. First American edition published 1969 by A. S. Barnes and Company, Inc., Cranbury, New Jersey 08512.

Library of Congress Catalogue Card Number: 69-14872

SBN 498-06924-9
Printed in the United States of America

To
the Master Craftsmen
of the centuries

CONTENTS

Introduction 11

PART ONE
Links in the Evolutionary Chain

The Treatyse of Fysshynge wyth an Angle, 1496	15
Thomas Barker, 1651	19
Charles Cotton, 1676	23
James Chetham, 1681	35
Richard & Charles Bowlker, 1747	44
19th. Century Authors	59
ALFRED RONALDS	60
H. C. CUTCLIFFE	89
T. E. PRITT	108
W. H. ALDAM	120
The Close of the 19th Century	132
F. M. HALFORD	133
20th. Century Authors	155
G. E. M. SKUES	156
LEONARD WEST	160
J. C. MOTTRAM	161
EDMONDS & LEE	164
M. E. MOSELY	165
J. W. DUNNE	166
E. W. HARDING	168

PART TWO
Reference lists of Trout-fly Patterns

'Arundo', 1849	175
Austin, R. S. n.d.	181
Bainbridge, Geo., 1816	191
Blacker, Wm., 1843	197

CONTENTS

'Clericus', (Rev. Wm. Cartwright), 1854	206
Dick, St. John, 1873	213
Francis, Francis, 1867	222
'Halcyon' (Henry Wade), 1861	232
Hall, H. S., n.d.	271
Hofland, T. C., 1839	276
Jackson, John, 1854	283
Mackintosh, Alexander, 1806	294
Ogden, James, 1879	300
Pulman, G. P. R., 1841	306
Salter, Robert, 1811	312
Shipley & Fitzgibbon, 1838	317
Taylor, Samuel, 1809	326
Theakston, Michael, 1853	331
Turton, John, 1836	346
Contemporary Trout-fly Patterns	359
Appendices	375
1 Feathers for fly-dressing	379
2 Bibliography	
Index	383

ILLUSTRATIONS

COLOUR

English trout-fly styles	*frontispiece*
Traditional Derbyshire trout flies	92
A plate from Halford's *Floating Flies and How to Dress Them*	93
Chalk Stream May Flies and Spent Gnats	124
Variant Dry Flies	125

BLACK AND WHITE

The implements for the making of hooks	32
The craftsmanship of the famous James Ogden	32
The second outstanding figure in fly-fishing history	33
The portly trout flies of the early 19th century	64
Fly dressing examples from Aldam's "Quaint Treatise"	65
Frederic Maurice Halford	192
George Edward Mackenzie Skues	193
The Scottish fly-design that came south	224
Chalk stream nymphs as designed by G. E. M. Skues	225

ACKNOWLEDGMENTS

Without the generous co-operation and ready courtesy of Editors and Publishers this reference work must have lost much of its usefulness and value, and grateful acknowledgment is therefore made of indebtedness to the following:

Messrs. Sampson Low, Marston & Co. Ltd., the original publishers of F. M. Halford's first classic: *Floating Flies*.

Messrs. William Blackwood & Sons, Ltd., publishers of David Webster's *Angler and the Loop-Rod*.

Messrs. Routledge & Kegan Paul, publishers of Martin E. Mosely's *Dry-Fly Entomology*.

Miss Penelope Turing, Editor of the *Salmon and Trout Magazine*.

A. Norman Marston, Esq.

All these have shown great generosity in making available material of historic interest in one form or another, and to them sincere thanks are tendered.

Acknowledgment must be made also of the craftsmanship of Messrs. Hardy Bros. (Alnwick) Ltd. as exemplified by the North-Country wet flies, the Baigent Variant dry flies, and the Mayflies reproduced in the various colour plates. Warm appreciation of the skill and artistry of Peter Deane, Esq., revealed in his dressings of wet flies in true West-Country style, chalk-stream nymphs, and fine examples of South-Country dry flies, must also be expressed.

Tribute must, in addition, be paid to Messrs. Halksworth Wheeler for the infinite pains taken to secure the very best photographic results.

INTRODUCTION

Above all other nations, England is rich in the traditions of sport; and in no field is this wealth more marked than in that of angling. For nearly five centuries, Englishmen have plied both rod and pen to such purpose than an unrivalled heritage of knowledge and literature has been passed down to us from the late 15th. century onwards. Particularly is this the case with the literature of fly-fishing for game fish, the pursuit of trout and salmon with the artificial fly having fascinated sportsmen of all times as the highest form of the entire art of angling.

It is thanks to this rich treasury of fly-fishing literature that it is possible to trace the evolution of the English trout fly from the time of the *Treatyse*, ascribed to Dame Juliana Berners, down to the present day. It is a fascinating history, and it is only by reading of it that a true appreciation may be obtained of the enduring interest in the art of trout-fly dressing. For nigh on five-hundred years, neither plague, war, civil strife nor any crisis could do more than interrupt or temporarily retard evolutionary progress. The development of the trout fly has never been halted.

In this present, tumultuous 20th. century, with all its rapid changes, it may be said with full confidence that interest in fly-fishing and trout flies has never been keener or more widespread. Such a volume of angling literature has poured from the presses that it is all but impossible to keep abreast of the torrent. One unfortunate result of this flood of contemporary literature, much of which is tautological, may be that of confusion, and obscuring of fascinating works of the past, in which the art of fly-dressing is deeply rooted, is a very real danger. When such a situation arises, art, whatever its nature, either stagnates or retrogresses; and there can be little doubt that the art of fly-making is very much in a rut today. In an age of stereotyping and uninspired standardisation of trout-fly patterns, there is a real need for a renaissance of the art of fly-dressing based, as it must be, on time-tested principles and the proven wisdom of the past.

INTRODUCTION

New generations of fly-fishermen are finding it increasingly difficult to obtain older books for reference, and apart from a source such as the British Museum, or, perhaps, odd purchases of scarce secondhand books from dealers or at sales at auction, the majority are unable to satisfy a desire for knowledge and information from original works. There is, therefore, a definite need today for convenient and concise books of reference, embodying as far as possible the best of the tremendous mass of invaluable data. It is precisely with this object that this present work has been prepared and compiled; and though it is manifestly beyond the capacity of any single volume to be completely exhaustive of its subject, it is hoped that what is offered will afford a very fair outline of trout-fly evolution and provide useful and adequate reference service.

W. H. L.

PART ONE
Links in the Evolutionary Chain

The Treatyse of Fysshynge Wyth an Angle

1496

THYSE ben the xij. flyes wyth whyche ye shall angle to the trought & grayllyng, and dubbe lyke as ye shall now here me tell.

Marche

The donne flye. the body of the donne woll & the wyngis of the pertryche. A nother doone flye the body of blacke woll: the wynges of the blackyst drake: and the lay vnder the wynge & vnder the tayle.

Apryll

The stone flye. the body of blacke wull: & yelowe vnder the wynge. & vnder the tayle & the wynges of the drake. In the begynnynge of May a good flye. the body of roddyd wull and lappid abowte wyth blacke sylke: the wynges of the drake & of the redde capons hakyll.

May

The yelow flye. the body of yelow wull: the wynges of the redde cocke hakyll & of the drake lyttyd below. The blacke louper. the body of blacke wull & lappyd abowte wyth the herle of the pecok tayle: & the wynges of the redde capon with a blewe heed.

Iune

The donne cutte: the body of blacke wull & a yelow lyste after eyther syde: the wynges of the bosarde bounde on with barkyd hempe. The maure flye. the body of doske wull the

wynges of the blackest mayle of the wylde drake. The tandy flye at saynt Wyllyams daye. the body of tandy wull & the wynges contrary eyther ayenst other of the whitest mayle of the wylde drake.

Iuyll

The waspe flye. the body of black wull & lappid abowte with yelow threde: the winges of the bosarde. The shell flye at saynt Thomas daye. the body of grene wull & lappyd abowte wyth the herle of the pecoks tayle: wynges of the bosarde.

August

The drake flye. the body of blacke wull & lappyd abowte wyth blacke sylke: wynges of the mayle of the blacke drake wyth a blacke heed.

Thus the *Treatyse of Fysshynge wyth an Angle* as contained in the *Boke of St. Albans* and as first printed in 1496 by Wynkyn de Worde, successor to Caxton at Westminster. The first edition of the *Boke of St. Albans was* printed in 1486 but did not contain the *Treatyse* which was added ten years later to the second edition. The *Treatyse* itself, according to authorities, is almost certainly drawn from earlier sources, and probably dates back to the beginning of the 15th. century. The source or sources and the identity of the author are obscure. Originally it may have been French. Over these matters Time has drawn her veil, and we must remain content with the realisation that we are fortunate enough to possess a valuable work dating back at least five and a half centuries.

The importance and interest of the *Treatyse* in the eyes of the scholarly angler rest on the fact that it is the first work on angling in the English language. And for those who, in particular, delight in the study of trout flies this same *Treatyse* symbolises the dawn of the art of trout-fly dressing in these ancient Isles. Since this work is devoted to the trout fly and its evolution, concern as to authorship and origin of the *Treatyse* is purely of secondary interest, and attention may be pleasantly concentrated on these first examples of trout-fly dressing.

It is impossible to consider the twelve listed flies to have been the original inventions of the author of the *Treatyse*. They are

obviously something more than first efforts of representation, and it is equally obvious that any form of art does not spring into being at one sudden stroke. It is much more probable that the evolution of the trout fly had its dawn very much earlier than may be suspected.

The limitation of the number of patterns to a round dozen has not escaped comment; and in this enlightened age we who have an incredible number of patterns in every form of permutation and combination at our disposal, are apt to misconstrue such simplicity. We forget that, in such early times, if *Homo sapiens* was simpler than we consider ourselves to be, so, and much more probably, was *salmo fario* much less sapient than the acute and extremely wary descendants against whom we pit our wits today. Indeed, this must have been so, for otherwise how could the *Treatyse* validly recommend lines—*cables* would be a more accurate description—composed of nine hairs for trout and twelve hairs for the great trout? It is quite reasonable to suppose that the twelve patterns would be quite sufficient in variety to enable the angler to obtain reasonable sport.

It is equally obvious that the twelve flies given are no mere fanciful products. They are, in fact, definite attempts to represent natural insects in form and colour. The matter of identifying eight of the twelve patterns is easy, the other four providing puzzles. The first fly on the list is almost certainly the March Brown. The second is most likely an Olive Dun. The third, as stated, is the Stonefly. The fourth, the Great Red Spinner. The fifth, either May fly or the Yellow May Dun. The sixth, not easily identified. The seventh, a sedge fly. The eighth, the Alder fly. The ninth, either a Dung fly or possibly the Oak fly. The tenth, may be either a wasp or one of the Crane flies. The eleventh, definitely the Grannom or an insect very similar.*
The twelfth, cannot be identified with certainty.

Assuming these identifications to be correct, there is still no certainty that the patterns were evolved in England. The March Brown, for example, does not appear on the streams of the South, excepting the West-Country districts. On the other hand, this fly does hatch out in the rivers of Normandy. Then again, some of the flies are common to both the Continent and England. So there is no ground for any definite attitude towards the question of source. That is a question of academic interest only: the important fact is that this first printed list of trout flies marks the point from which, down through the

*The Shell fly of Alfred Ronalds.

centuries, the art of trout-fly dressing has progressed and continued.

Yet the fame of this list of flies persisted for long. It was used by Leonard Mascall for the purposes of his work, styled: *A Booke of Fishing with Hooke and Line* which he published in 1590. And even Walton scrupled not to borrow the list from Mascall, although for his second edition of *The Compleat Angler* he turned to Thomas Barker for a more up-to-date list. And so with very many lesser authors, including the unscrupulous Markham.

The *Treatyse* is silent in regard to fly-dressing instructions: only the materials are indicated and a plate illustrating the necessary hooks is given. Too much reliance need not be placed on such early plates, and it is questionable if hooks, constructed out of needles, were actually so coarse as those depicted.

It must be admitted that, as the first English work on angling, the *Treatyse* is impressive. It shows that the essentials of the representation of natural insects were understood and applied in practice. It shows appreciation of the importance of choice and colour of materials; and the materials—silk, feather and wool—are identical with those which we still employ to-day. And the *Treatyse* besides these particular references to trout flies, contains much other fishing lore that is surprisingly modern.

Thomas Barker
1651

A century and a half passed after the Treatyse before fly-fishermen received a book containing the first instructions on trout-fly dressing. In the interim, Leonard Mascall had published his book in 1590; John Taverner his *Certaine Experiments concerning Fish and Fruite* in 1600; John Dennys his poem *Secrets of Angling* in 1606; Gervase Markham his *Discourse of the generall art of fishing with the angle* in 1614; and in 1617-20 William Lauson issued his Comments on John Dennys' *Secrets of Angling*. All of these books, though silent in regard to the matter of fly dressing, are noteworthy and of rare interest.

The first book on angling to give instructions on fly-dressing was written by Thomas Barker. He entitled it: *The Art of Angling;* and it was first published in 1651. Barker was a Shropshire man, a Cromwellian, a seasoned angler, and, perhaps, above all, a cook. In the "Epistle to the Reader" he writes: "For I am grown old; and therefore am willing to set forth my true experience, that I have been gathering these fifty years, and the true grounds of Angling, having spent many pounds in the gaining thereof, as is well known where I was born and educated, which is Brac-meal in the libertie of Salop, being there a Free-man, and Burgesse of the same Citie." "I live in Henry the sevenths gifts, the next door to the Gate-house in Westminster . . ." He apologises "for not writing Scholler like"; yet, so excellent is his book, he need not have done so. His modesty has the true ring.

Here is what Barker says of fly-dressing:

"Now to shew how to make Flies: learn to make two Flies, and make all; that is, the Palmer ribbed with silver or gold, and the May Flie; these are the ground of all Flies.

"Wee will begin to make the Palmer Flie: You must arm

your Line on the inside of the hook; take your Scisers and cut so much of the brown of the Mallards feather, as in your own reason shall make the wings, then lay the outmost part of the feather next the hook, and the poynt of the feather towards the shank of the hook, then whip it three or four times about the hook with the same silk you armed the hook; then make your silk fast; then you must take the hackle of the neck of a Cock or Capon, or a Plovers top, which is the best; take off the one side of the feather; then you must take the hackle silk, or cruell, gold, or silver, thred; make all these fast at the bent of the hook, then you must begin with cruell, and silver, or gold, and work it up to the wings, every bout shifting your fingers and making a stop, then the gold will fall right, then make fast; then work up the hackle to the same place, then make the hackle fast; then you must take the hook betwixt your finger and thumb, in the left hand, with a neeld or pin, part the wings in two; then with the arming silk, as you have fastened all hitherto, whip about as it falleth crosse betwixt the wings, then with your thumb you must turn the poynt of the feather towards the bent of the hook; then work three or four times about the shank; so fasten; then view the proportion.

"For the other Flies; If you make the grounds of Hogs wooll, sandy black or white; or the wooll of a Bear; or of a two year old red Bullock: you must work all these grounds upon a waxed silk, then you must arm and set on the wings, as I have shewed you before: For the May Flie, you work the bodie with some of these grounds, which is very good, ribbed with a black hair; you may work the bodie with Cruells, imitating the colour; or with silver, with suiting the wings. For the Oake Flie, you must make him with Orenge tauny and black, for the body; and the brown of the Mallards feather for the wings. If you doe after my directions, they will kill Fish, observing the times fitting, and follow my former directions"

Thus does Barker give the earliest known recorded instructions on fly dressing. He wings his flies in the style favoured still by many amateur fly dressers who give to it the description of the "reverse-wing" method. And he is choice in his preference of body materials.

As to patterns of flies, Barker gives the following, and writes:

"Let us begin to Angle in March with the Flie; If the weather prove Windie, or Cloudie, there are severall kinds of Palmers that are good for that time.

First, a black Palmer ribbed with silver; the second, a black Palmer with an Orenge-taunie body; thirdly, a black Palmer with the bodie made all of black: fourthly, a red Palmer ribbed with gold, and a red hackle mixed with Orenge cruel; these Flies serve all the year long morning and evening, windie and cloudie. Then if the Aire prove bright and clear, you must imitate the Hauthorn Flie, which is all black and very small, and the smaller the better. In May take the may Flie: imitate that, which is made severall wayes; some make them with a shammie body, ribbed with a black hair: another way made with Sandy-Hogs wooll, ribbed with black silk, and winged with a Mallards feather, according to the fancie of the Angler. There is another called the Oak-Flie, which is made of Orenge colour Cruel and black, with a brown wing; imitate that: Another Flie, the body made with the strain of a Pea-Cocks feather, which is very good in a bright day; The Grasshopper which is green, imitate that; the smaller the Flies be made, and of indifferent small hooks, they are the better; these sorts I have set down, will serve all the yeer long, observing the times and seasons: Note, the lightest of your Flies for cloudie and darknesse, and the darkest of your Flies for lightnesse, and the rest for indifferent times; that a mans own Judgement, with some experience and discretion must guide him: If he mean to kill Fish, he must alter his Flies according to these directions. Now, of late, I have found that Hogs wooll, of severall colours, makes good grounds; and the wooll of a red Hayfer makes a good body; And Bears wooll makes a good ground; so I now work much of them, and it procureth very much sport."

Such is the selection which sufficed Thomas Barker; and the soundness of his observations regarding materials, hook sizes, and the factor of conditions of light in making a choice of fly, is beyond question.

In other respects *The Art of Angling* shows Barker to have been a competent fisherman. He states plainly that: "If you can attain to Angle with one hair, you shall have the more rises and kill more Fish." And in addition to this advice to fish fine,

Barker is the first to mention the reel or "barrell" as it is quaintly termed. He knew all the lore of "doping" (dapping) for trout with natural insects; did not scorn night fishing with the artificial fly; and shows himself to have been a competent bait fisher. In his references to salmon fishing, Barker again, mentions the reel or "winder," but the figure describing it is something of a mystery. Nevertheless this reel carried a line of "twenty six yards of length," and the salmon was ultimately grassed with the aid of "a good large landing hook" (a gaff). Of salmon flies he states that: "the flie must be made of a large hook, which hook must carry six wings, or four at least; there is judgement in making those flyes."

Of Barker's trout flies, it may be observed that while some of them are in the nature of "general" patterns, yet all are based on natural insects. What he called "Palmers" are in fact winged flies of small size. And his dressing of the May-fly body "with a shammie body, ribbed with a black hair" is very good indeed.

Charles Cotton
1676

FOLLOWING Thomas Barker's *Art of Angling*, published in 1651, and reprinted in 1657 under the title: *Barker's Delight*, the next outstanding author treating of fly-fishing is undoubtedly the royalist, Charles Cotton. Yet prior to Cotton's work there were three other writers, all of whom contributed something of interest to the literature of sport with the rod. These were, first, Richard Franck who wrote his *Northern Memoirs* in 1658, though the work was not published until 1694, and the turgidity of whose style can scarcely be excelled in literature. Secondly, in 1653 Izaak Walton published the first edition of his *Compleat Angler*. And, thirdly, in 1662 there came from the pen of the irascible Cromwellian, Colonel Robert Venables, a work entitled: *The Experienced Angler*. The latter of these three works is certainly that of greatest interest from the practical fly-fisherman's point of view.

Charles Cotton's contribution formed the second part of Walton's *Compleat Angler* in the edition of the latter work published in 1676. And, in the practical sense, an outstanding contribution it was. For Cotton, in addition to much excellent all-round advice, gives a list of no less than sixty-five patterns of trout and grayling flies, all of which appear to have been original and many designed on the principle of close representation of natural insects. These are:-

January

1. A RED BROWN with wings of the male of a mallard almost white; the dubbing of the tail of a black long-coated cur, such as they commonly make muffs of; for the hair on the tail of such a dog dyes, and turns to a red brown, but the hair of a smooth-coated dog of the same colour will not do, but retains

its natural colour. And this fly is taken, in a warm sun, this whole month through.

2. There is also a very little BRIGHT DUN GNAT, as little as can possibly be made, so little as never to be fished with, with above one hair next the hook; and this is to be made of a mixed dubbing of marten's fur, and the white of a hare's scut, with a very white and small wing; and it is no great matter how fine you fish, for nothing will rise in this month but a Grayling; and of them I never, at this season, saw any taken with a fly, of above a foot long, in my life: but of little ones about the bigness of a smelt, in a warm day and a glowing sun, you may take enough with these two flies; and they are both taken the whole month through.

February

1. Where the RED BROWN of the last month ends, another, almost of the same colour, begins with this; saving that the dubbing of this must be of something a blacker colour, and both of them wrapt on with red silk. The dubbing that should make this fly, and that is the truest colour, is to be got off the black spot of a hog's ear: not that a black spot in any part of the hog will not afford the same colour, but that the hair in that place is, by many degrees, softer, and more fit for the purpose. His wing must be as the other; and this kills all this month, and is called the LESSER RED BROWN.

2. This month, also, a PLAIN HACKLE, or palmer-fly, made with a rough black body, either of black spaniel's fur, or the whirl of an ostrich feather, and the red hackle of a capon over all, will kill, and if the weather be right, make very good sport.

3. Also a LESSER HACKLE, with a black body, also silver twist over that, and a red feather over all, will fill your pannier, if the month be open, and not bound up in ice and snow, with very good fish; but in case of a frost and snow, you are to angle only with the smallest gnats, browns, and duns you can make; and with those are only to expect Graylings no bigger than sprats.

4. In this month, upon a whirling-round water, we have a GREAT HACKLE, the body black, and wrapt with a red feather of a capon untrimmed; that is, the whole length of the hackle

staring out (for we sometimes barb the hackle-feather short all over; sometimes barb it only a little, and sometimes barb it close underneath), leaving the whole length of the feather on the top or back of the fly, which makes it swim better, and, as occasion serves, kills very great fish.

5. We make use also, in this month, of another GREAT HACKLE, the body black, and ribbed over with gold twist, and a red feather over all; which does great execution.

6. Also a GREAT DUN, made with dun bear's hair, and the wings, of the grey feather of a mallard near unto the tail; which is absolutely the best fly can be thrown upon a river this month, and with which an angler shall have admirable sport.

7. We have also this month the GREAT BLUE DUN, the dubbing of the bottom of bear's hair next to the roots, mixt with a little blue camlet; the wings, of the dark grey feather of a mallard.

8. We have also this month a DARK BROWN, the dubbing of the brown hair off the flank of a brended cow; and the wings, of the grey drake's feather.

March

For this month you are to use all the same hackles and flies with the other; but you are to make them less.

1. We have, besides, for this month a little Dun, called a WHIRLING DUN, though it is not the Whirling Dun, indeed, which is one of the best flies we have; and for this, the dubbing must be of the bottom fur of a squirrel's tail; and the wing of the grey feather of a drake.

2. Also a BRIGHT BROWN; the dubbing either of the brown of a spaniel, or that of a cow's flank, with a grey wing.

3. Also a WHITISH DUN; made of the roots of camel's hair; and the wings, of the grey feather of a mallard.

4. There is also for this month a fly called the THORN-TREE FLY; the dubbing an absolute black, mixed with eight or ten hairs of Isabella-coloured mohair; the body as little as can be made, and the wings of a bright mallard's feather. An admirable fly, and in great repute amongst us for a killer.

5. There is, besides this, another BLUE DUN; the dubbing of which it is made being thus to be got. Take a small toothcomb, and with it comb the neck of a black greyhound, and the down

that sticks in the teeth will be the finest blue that ever you saw. The wings of this fly can hardly be too white; and he is taken about the tenth of this month, and lasteth till the four-and-twentieth.

6. From the tenth of this month also, till towards the end, is taken a little BLACK GNAT. The dubbing, either of the fur of a black water-dog, or the down of a young black water-coot; the wings, of the male of a Mallard as white as may be; the body as little as you can possibly make it, and the wings as short as his body.

7. From the sixteenth of this month also, to the end of it, we use a BRIGHT BROWN; the dubbing for which is to be had out of a skinner's lime-pits, and of the hair of an abortive calf, which the lime will turn to be so bright, as to shine like gold; for the wings of this fly, the feather of a brown hen is best. Which fly is also taken till the tenth of April.

April

All the same hackles and flies that were taken in March will be taken in this month also, with this distinction only concerning the flies, that all the browns be lapt with red silk, and the duns with yellow.

1. To these a SMALL BRIGHT BROWN made of spaniel's fur, with a light-grey wing, in a bright day, and a clear water, is very well taken.

2. We have, too, a little DARK BROWN; the dubbing of that colour, and some violet camlet mixt; and the wing of a grey feather of a mallard.

3. From the sixth of this month to the tenth we have also a fly called the VIOLET-FLY; made of a dark violet stuff; with the wings, of a grey feather of a mallard.

4. About the twelfth of this month comes in the fly called the WHIRLING DUN, which is taken every day, about the mid-time of day, all this month through, and, by fits, from thence to the end of June; and is commonly made of the down of a fox-cub, which is of an ash colour at the roots next the skin, and ribbed about with yellow silk; the wings, of the pale grey feather of a mallard.

5. There is also a YELLOW DUN, the dubbing of camel's hair, and yellow camlet, or wool, mixt, and a white-grey wing.

6. There is also this month another LITTLE BROWN, besides that mentioned before, made with a very slender body; the dubbing of dark brown and violet camlet, mixt, and a grey wing; which, though the direction for the making be near the other, is yet another fly, and will take when the other will not, especially in a bright day and a clear water.

7. About the twentieth of this month comes in a fly called the HORSE-FLESH FLY; the dubbing of which is a blue mohair, with pink-coloured and red tammy mixt, a light coloured wing, and a dark brown head. This fly is taken best in an evening, and kills from two hours before sunset till twilight, and is taken the month through.

May

1. The TURKEY-FLY; the dubbing ravelled out of some blue stuff, and lapt about with yellow silk; the wings of a grey mallard's feather.

2. Next, a GREAT HACKLE, or PALMER-FLY, with a yellow body, ribbed with gold twist, and large wings of a mallard's feather dyed yellow, with a red capon's hackle over all.

3. Then a BLACK-FLY; the dubbing of a black spaniel's fur, and the wings of a grey mallard's feather.

4. After that, a LIGHT BROWN, with a slender body, the dubbing twirled upon small red silk, and raised with the point of a needle, that the ribs or rows of silk may appear through the wings of the grey feather of a mallard.

5. Next a LITTLE DUN; the dubbing of a bear's dun whirled upon yellow silk; the wings of a grey feather of a mallard.

6. Then a WHITE GNAT, with a pale wing, and a black head.

7. There is also in this month a fly called the PEACOCK-FLY; the body made of a whirl of a peacock's feather, with a red head, and wings of a mallard's feather.

8. We have then another very killing fly, known by the name of the DUN-CUT; the dubbing of which is a bear's dun, with a little blue and yellow mixt with it, a large dun wing, and two horns at the head, made of the hairs of a squirrel's tail.

9. The next is a COW-LADY, a little fly; the body of a peacock's feather, the wing of a red feather, or strips of the red hackle of a cock.

10. We have then the COW-DUNG fly; the dubbing light brown and yellow mixt; the wing, the dark grey feather of a mallard.

11. The artificial Green-Drake then is made upon a large hook, the dubbing camel's hair, bright bear's hair, the soft down that is combed from a hog's bristles, and yellow camlet, well mixt together; the body long, and ribbed about with green silk, or rather yellow, waxed with green wax, the whisks of the tail of the long hairs of sables, or fitchet, and the wings of the white-grey feather of the mallard, dyed yellow, which also is to be dyed thus:-

Take the root of a barbary-tree, and shave it, and put to it woody viss, with as much alum as a walnut, and boil your feathers in it with rain-water; and they will be a very fine yellow.

12. ... the GREY-DRAKE, which in all shapes and dimensions is perfectly the same with the other, but quite almost of another colour, being of a paler, and more livid yellow, and green, and ribbed with black quite down his body, with black shining wings ...; which fly is thus made: the dubbing of the down of a hog's bristles and black spaniel's fur mixt, and ribbed down the body with black silk, the whisks of the hairs of the beard of a black cat, and the wings of the black-grey feather of a mallard.

13. ... This same STONE-FLY ... which is to be made thus: the dubbing of bear's dun with a little brown and yellow camlet very well mixt, but so placed that your fly may be more yellow on the belly and towards the tail, underneath, than in any other part; and you are to place two or three hairs of a black cat's beard on the top of the hook, in your arming, so as to be turned up when you warp on your dubbing, and to stand almost upright, and staring one from another; and note, that your fly is to be ribbed with yellow silk; and the wings long, and very large, of the dark grey feather of a mallard.

14. The next May-fly is the BLACK-FLY; made with a black body, of the whirl of an ostrich feather, ribbed with silver twist, and the black hackle of a cock over all; and is a killing fly, but not to be named with either of the other.

15. The last May-fly, that is, of the four pretenders, is the LITTLE YELLOW MAY-FLY; in shape exactly the same with the Green-Drake, but a very little one, and of as bright a yellow as

can be seen: which is made of a bright yellow camlet, and the wings of a white-grey feather dyed yellow.

16. The last fly for this month, and which continues all June, though it comes in the middle of May, is the fly called the CAMLET-FLY, in shape like a moth, with fine diapered or water wings, and with which, as I told you before, I sometimes used to dibble; and Grayling will rise mightily at it. But the artificial fly, which is only in use amongst our anglers, is made of a dark brown shining camlet ribbed over with a very small light green silk; the wings of the double-grey feather of a mallard; and 'tis a killing fly for small fish. And so much for May.

June

From the first to the four-and-twentieth, the Green-Drake and Stone-Fly are taken, as I told you before.

1. From the twelfth to the four-and-twentieth, late at night, is taken a fly called the OWL-FLY: the dubbing of a white weasel's tail; and a white-grey wing.

2. We have then another dun, called the BARM-FLY, from its yeasty colour. The dubbing of the fur of a yellow-dun cat, and a grey wing of a mallard's feather.

3. We have also a HACKLE with a purple body, whipt about with a red capon's feather.

4. As also a GOLD-TWIST HACKLE with a purple body, whipt about with a red capon's feather.

5. To these we have this month, a FLESH-FLY. The dubbing of a black spaniel's fur and blue wool mixt, and a grey wing.

6. Also another little FLESH-FLY, the body made of the whirl of a peacock's feather, and the wings of the grey feather of a drake.

7. We have, then, the PEACOCK-FLY, the body and wing, both made of the feather of that bird.

8. There is also the flying-ant, or ANT-FLY, the dubbing of brown and red camlet mixt, with a light grey wing.

9. We have likewise a BROWN-GNAT, with a very slender body of brown and violet camlet well mixt, and a light grey wing.

10. And another little BLACK GNAT, the dubbing of black mohair, and a white-grey wing.

11. As also a GREEN GRASSHOPPER, the dubbing of green and

yellow wool mixt, ribbed over with green silk, and a red capon's feather over all.

12. And, lastly, a little DUN GRASSHOPPER, the body slender, made of a dun camlet and a dun hackle at the top.

July

First, all the small flies that were taken in June are also taken in this month.

1. We have then the ORANGE FLY, the dubbing of orange wool, and the wing of a black feather.
2. Also a little WHITE DUN, the body made of white mohair, and the wings, blue, of a heron's feather.
3. We have likewise this month a WASP-FLY, made either of a dark brown dubbing, or else the fur of a black cat's tail, ribbed about with yellow silk, and the wing of the grey feather of a mallard.
4. Another fly taken this month is a BLACK HACKLE, the body made of the whirl of a peacock's feather, and a black hackle feather on the top.
5. We have also another, made of a peacock's whirl without wings.
6. Another fly also is taken this month, called the SHELL-FLY, the dubbing of the yellow-green Jersey wool, and a little white hog's hair mixt, which I call the palm-fly, and do believe it is taken for a palm, that drops off the willows into the water; for this fly I have seen Trouts take little pieces of moss, as they have swam down the river; by which I conclude that the best way to hit the right colour is to compare your dubbing with the moss, and mix the colours as near as you can.
7. There is also taken, this month, a BLACK-BLUE DUN, the dubbing of the fur of a black rabbit mixt with a little yellow, the wings of the feather of a blue pigeon's wing.

August

The same flies with July.

1. Then another ANT-FLY, the dubbing of the black-brown hair of a cow, some red warpt in for the tag of his tail, and a dark wing. A killing fly.

The second outstanding figure in fly-fishing history, the first being the unknown author of the *Treatyse*

THE IMPLEMENTS FOR THE MAKING OF HOOKS

Left to right: 'Hamour, Knyfe, Pynsons, Clamm, Fyle, Wreste, Anuelde', *Treatyse, 1496*

The craftsmanship of the famous James Ogden of Cheltenham: said to be the earliest example extant of a floating mayfly

And as to the making of a winged fly, Cotton gives his directions thus:-

"In making a fly, then, which is not a hackle or palmer fly (for of those, and their several kinds, we shall have occasion to speak every month in the year), you are, first, to hold your hook fast betwixt the forefinger and thumb of your left hand, with the back of the shank upwards, and the point towards your fingers' ends; then take a strong small silk of the colour of the fly you intend to make, wax it well with wax of the same colour too, to which end you are always, by the way, to have wax of all colours about you, and draw it betwixt your finger and thumb to the head of the shank; and then whip it twice or thrice about the bare hook, which, you must know, is done, both to prevent slipping, and also that the shank of the hook may not cut the hairs of your towght, which sometimes it will otherwise do. Which being done, take your line, and draw it likewise betwixt your finger and thumb, holding the hook so fast as only to suffer it to pass by, until you have the knot of your towght almost to the middle of the shank of your hook, on the inside of it; then whip your silk twice or thrice about both hook and line as hard as the strength of the silk will permit. Which being done, strip the feather for the wings proportionable to the bigness of your fly, placing that side downwards which grew uppermost before upon the back of the hook, leaving so much only as to serve for the length of the wing of the point of the plume lying reversed from the end of the shank upwards: then whip your silk twice or thrice about the root-end of the feather, hook, and towght; which being done, clip off the root-end of the feather close by the arming, and then whip the silk fast and firm about the hook and towght, until you come to the bend of the hook, but not farther, as you do at London, and so make a very unhandsome, and, in plain English, a very unnatural and shapeless fly. Which being done, cut away the end of your towght and fasten it. And then take your dubbing which is to make the body of your fly, as much as you think convenient, and holding it lightly, with your hook, betwixt the finger and thumb of your left hand, take your silk with the right, and twisting it betwixt the finger and thumb of that hand, the dubbing will spin itself about the silk, which when it has

2. Next, a fly called the FERN-FLY, the dubbing of the fur of a hare's neck, that is, of the colour of fern or bracken, with a darkish grey wing of a mallard's feather. A killer too.

3. Besides these we have a WHITE HACKLE, the body of white mohair, and warpt about with a white hackle feather; and this is, asuredly, taken for thistle-down.

4. We have also, this month, a HARRY LONG-LEGS; the body made of bear's dun and blue wool mixt, and a brown hackle feather over all.

September

This month the same flies are taken that are taken in April.

1. To which I shall only add a CAMEL-BROWN fly, the dubbing pulled out of the lime of a wall, whipt about with red silk; and a darkish grey mallard's feather for the wing.

2. And one other for which we have no name; but it is made of the black hair of a badger's skin, mixt with the yellow softest down of a sanded hog.

October

The same flies are taken this month that were taken in March.

November

The same flies that were taken in February are taken this month also.

December

Few men angle with the fly this month, no more than they do in January; but yet, if the weather be warm, as I have known it sometimes in my life to be, even in this cold country, where it is least expected, then a brown, that looks red in the hand, and yellowish betwixt your eye and the sun, will both raise and kill in a clear water and free from snow-broth: but, at the best, it is hardly worth a man's labour.

done, whip it about the armed hook backward, till you come to the setting-on of the wings. And then take the feather for the wings, and divide it equally into two parts; and turn them back towards the bend of the hook, the one on the one side, and the other on the other of the shank; holding them fast in that posture betwixt the forefinger and thumb of your left hand: which done, warp them so down as to stand and slope towards the bend of the hook; and having warped up to the end of the shank, hold the fly fast betwixt the finger and thumb of your right hand; and where the warping ends pinch or nip it with your thumb nail against your finger, and strip away the remainder of your dubbing from the silk; and then with the bare silk whip it once or twice about; make the wings to stand in due order; fasten, and cut it off. After which, with the point of a needle, raise up the dubbing gently from the warp; twitch off the superfluous hairs of your dubbing; leave the wings of an equal length, your fly will never else swim true; and the work is done."

So the North-country pen of Charles Cotton not only furnishes a list of sixty-five patterns, some of which are fancy flies but most of the patterns being based on natural insects, but describes very lucidly precisely how to dress a winged fly. He is insistent upon the slender North-country body for his flies, and particular both as to the colour of tying silk and the dubbing which is to be spun about it, counselling that flies are best dressed on "a bright sunshine day" when the true colour of dubbing may be determined by holding it up to strong light. Of waxes too, there is shown the same nicety, and waxes of all colours are to be carried for the waxing of silks of different colours. The wings, it is to be noted, are still made from a single slip of feather, divided and dressed in the "reverse-wing" style. There is no certainty, of course, that the list of trout and grayling flies is original i.e. the inventions of Cotton himself; much more probably Cotton had gathered together the best of those patterns then in general local use, and if that is so, they are almost certain to have been established for many years before their incorporation in Part 2 of the 1676 edition of the "The Compleat Angler." However that may be, certain it is that many of these same sixty-five patterns would still prove to be effective to-day; while many of the names by which some of the patterns were known two hundred and seventy years ago remain, and are likely to continue evergreen.

Dissolute, and perhaps a better poet, despite his lapses of bawdiness, than a prose writer, yet Charles Cotton, by this one work, has ensured that so long as rivers run, and so long as Man seeks to match his wit and cunning against those of the fishes which inhabit them, his name will never be forgotten. His writing shows him to have been an all-round angler of ability, and some of his advice is remarkably up-to-date and modern. But then that is precisely why his work was a great one: otherwise it would not have endured.

James Chetham
1681

THE contributions of Thomas Barker and Charles Cotton towards the development of the trout fly were followed by a work from the pen of a Lancastrian, one James Chetham of Smedley. This book was first published in 1681, and was styled: *The Angler's Vade Mecum*. As a manual for practical anglers, it is undoubtedly a sound work and a sensible. Chetham's writing has a dry caustic quality, and the tone of the book, set in the very Preface thereto, is at least a refreshing change from the slightly tedious piety and righteousness of so many of the earlier works.

Yet James Chetham is something of a plagiarist, for he not only employs for the purpose of his *Vade Mecum* without acknowledgment, the list of flies given by Cotton, but also purloins the latter's instructions on the dressing of flies. Fortunately, Chetham includes: "Another Catalogue of Flies, practised by a very good Angler, and useful to be known by the young Anglers in clear, Stony Rivers." It is this second list which is of interest, and the patterns are not only original work but are a definite advance on those of Cotton. These patterns are as under:-

Dub-flies for February

Prime Dun

1. Dubbing of the Down of a Fox Cub, dub'd with sad Ash-coloured Silk, Wings of the Feather got from the Quill of a Shepstares Wing. This Fly is made little, but there is another made of the same Dubbing but larger by far.

Dub-flies for March

The same Flies taken in February, will be taken in March, and also the subsequent.

Moorish Brown

1. Dub'd of the Wooll of a Black Sheep, and Red Silk, Wings of the Feather got from a Partridge Wings.

Palm-fly

2. Made of Hair of a Brown Spaniel got on the outside of the Ear, and a little Sea-green Wooll mixt, Dub'd with Brown Cloth-coloured Silk, Wings of the Feather of a Shepstare Quill got out of the Wing.

Green Tail

3. Made of the Brown Hair of a Spaniel, got on the outside of the Ear, but a little in the end of the Tail, must be all of Sea-green Wooll without mixture, Wings as the last.

Dub-flies for April

Bright Bear

1. Made of Bright Bears Hair, Dubb'd with sad Cloth coloured Silk, Wings of the Feather of a Shepstares Quill; others Dub the Body with Yellow Silk, which is better.

Yellow Dun

2. Made of Yellow Wooll, and Ash coloured Fox Cub Down mixt together, Dub'd with Yellow Silk, Wings of the Feather of a Shepstares Quill; others Dub it with Dun Bears Hair, and the Yellow Fur got from a Martern's Skin mixt together, and with Yellow Silk, Wings of the Feather of a Shepstares Quill. Make two other Flies their Bodies Dub'd as the last, but in the one mingle sanded Hogs Down, and in the other Black Hogs Down,

and the Wings of the Feather of a Shepstares Quill. And there is also taken an excellent Fly made of Dun Bears Hair, Yellow Marterns Fur, sanded Hogs Down, and Black Hogs Down, all mixt in an equal proportion together Dub'd with Yellow Silk, and the Wings of the Feather of a Shepstares Quill got out of the Wing: These Flies mentioned for April are very good, and will be taken almost all the Spring and Summer.

Note once for all, That the Yellow Fur got from a Marterns Skin, is absolutely the very best Yellow of any whatsoever, either to Dub with, or mingle with other Dubbing.

Dub-flies for May

Thorn fly

1. Dubbing of Black Lambs Wooll, and Dub'd with Black Silk, Wings of a Mallards light Grey; Note that all the Feathers got from Mallards for Wings, ought to be got from a wild Mallard, and not from a tame one.

Knop-fly

2. Made of the Down of an Otter Cub, warpt about with the Herle of a Peacock, and Dub'd with Black Silk, Wings of the light Grey Feather of a Mallard.

Fern Bud

3. This Fly is got on Fern, and the natural one is a very good Fly to dib with; it is but of a short thick Body, of a very sad Greenish colour, and hath two pair of Wings; the uppermost are hard, and sometimes taken off, but the undermost are diaphanous and tender; it's Dub'd with the Herle of a Peacock, and very sad Green-colour'd Silk, Wings of the Feather of a Felfare Quill got out of the Wing.

Little-Dun

4. Dubbing of an Otters Fur, Dub'd with Ash-coloured Silk, Wings of the Feather of a Shepstares Quill.

Yellow May Fly

5. The Body made of Yellow Wooll mixt with Yellow Fur of a Martern, Dub'd with Yellow Silk, Wings of the lightest colour'd Feather of a Throstle.

Dub-flies for June

Black Midge, or Gnat

1. Made of the Down of a Mole, Dub'd with Black Silk, Wings of the light Grey Feather of a Shepstares Quill.

Grey Midge, or Gnat

2. Dubbing of the Down of a sad Grey Cat, or sad Grey Camels Hair, Dub'd with Grey Silk, Wings of the Grey Feather of a Mallard.

Purple-fly

3. Made of Purple Wooll, and a little Bears Hair mixt with it, and sometimes no Bears Hair at all; Wings of the Feather of a Shepstares Quill, Dub'd with Purple Silk.

Sandy-fly

4. Made of the Wooll gotten off the Flank of a Black Sheep, Dub'd with Black Silk, Wings of the sad coloured Feather of a Throstle Quill; others make the Body of the Feather of a Herons Neck.

Mackerill

Dubbing of light Brown Camels Hair, Dub'd with Black Silk, Wings of a Red Cocks Feather.

Dub-flies for July

Blue Dun

1. Made of the Down of a Water-Mouse, and the Blewish Dun of an Old Fox mixt together, Dub'd with sad Ash-coloured Silk; Wings of the Feather of a Shepstare Quill.

August Flies
Buss Brown

1. Made of the light Brown Hair of the Ear of a Cur, the Head Black, Wings of the Feather of a Red Hen whipt with Orange coloured Silk.

Hearth-fly

2. Made of the Wooll of an Old Black Sheep with some Grey Hairs in it for the Body and Head, Dub'd with Black Silk, Wings of the light Feather of a Shepstares Quill.

Pismire-fly

3. Make the Body of bright Brown Bears Hair twirl'd upon Red Silk, Wings of the saddest colour'd Feather got from the Quill of a Shepstares Wing, a good Fly.

September's Fly
Little Blue Dun

1. Made of the Down of a Mouse for Body and Head, dub'd with sad Ash-coloured Silk; Wings of the sad coloured Feather of a Shepstares Quill.

Note, that the Feather got from the Quills, or Pens of Shepstares Wings, Throstle Wings, Fieldfare Wings are generally better, (the 2 first especially) to use for Dub-fly Wings, than those got from a wild Mallard, or Drake.

It will be noted that all these, twenty-one in number, are winged flies, and that, for the first time in angling literature, the Shepstare, or starling, quill feather is recommended for the winging of trout flies and is preferred to the Mallard feather upon which Cotton largely relied. The dubbing from which the bodies are made are selected and blended with a care revealing the trouble taken over the accurate representation of the colour of the natural insects. It is interesting to note, also, that the neck feather of a Heron is used as a body-material, for heron herl is still used to-day in the dressing of one of our best patterns of the Large Dark Olive of spring.

Chetham goes very fully into the variety of materials necessary for fly dressing, and insists that the angler's "Budget" be "plentifully furnished" with the following materials: Viz.

Bears Hair

1. Bears Hair of diverse Colours and Shades, are most excellent Dubbing; as Gray, Dun, light Coloured, sad Coloured, and bright shining Bears Hair, and bright Brown Bears Hair.

Camels Hair

2. Camels Hair sad, light, and of a middle, or indifferent Colour.

Badger Hair

3. Badgers Skin Hair, that is, the brownish soft Fur, which is on some part of the Badgers Skin, is very good Dubbing, after the Skin is tewed in the Skinners Lime-pits, and so is the Blackish.

Spaniels Hair

4. Spaniels soft Fur and Hair of diverse Colours, and parts of the Spaniel, as on the Ear etc. as Brown, sad Brown, light Brown, Blackish, and perfect Black.

Dogs Hair

5. Get the like Colours from a Water Dog, and from a long-coated Cur, and a smooth-coated Cur.

Hogs Down

6. Be sure to procure from Butchers, or others, Black, Red, Whitish and Sanded Hogs Down, such as is combed from the Roots of the Hair, or Bristles of Hogs of those Colours. And you may get the Dyer to dye the White Hogs Down of any Colour you judge convenient, and it's excellent; because it both shines well, and is stiff, and proper for the Water, and lively.

Sheeps Wooll

7. Sheeps Wooll of all colours both Natural and Artificial, get the coursest Sheeps Wooll, and the Dyer (especially the Silk-Dyer) will make it you of any colour you judge convenient, and such as will best abide in the Water; for all your colours should have that property.

Mohairs

8. Mohairs of all colours, especially the following, viz. Black, Blew, Purple, White, Violet coloured, Isabella, and Philomot, coloured Mohairs, Yellow, Tawny, etc.

Cow Hairs

9. Get soft Hair and Furs from the Flanks and other soft parts of a Black Cow, Red Cow, and Brended Cow, and of these have Brown, sad Brown, light Brown, and perfect Black Hair and Furs.

Camlets

10. Get pieces of Calmets both Hair and Worsted of all colours, especially the following, viz. Blew, Yellow, Dun, Brown, dark Brown, light Brown, Red, Violet, Purple, Black, dark Brown, shining Camlet, dark Violet, Horse-Flesh, Pink and Orange colour'd.

Abortive Colts, and Calves Hair

11. Resort to a Skinners Lime-pit, and there get Hair of various colours, and you may get most excellent Dubbing of Castling Skins of Calves, and Colts that are Tewed; and several colours and shades of one Skin: so of Cushions made of such Skins that have been neatly Tewed in the Skinners Lime-pit: so of Abortive Skins of Colts and Calves, at Skinners Lime-pits Tewed, etc.

Furs

12. Furs of the ensuing Animals, viz. Furs of Squirrels, and squirrels Tail, Black Cats-Tail, Yellow dun Cat, Hares Neck Fern Colour, White Weasels-Tail, Mole, Black Rabbet, Yellow Rabbet, Down of a Fox Cub, Ash coloured at the Roots, Fur of an Old Fox, Fur of an Old Otter, and Fur of an Otter Cub, Blackish and Brown soft Fur, and Hair of a Badgers Skin, that has been Tewed in a Skinners Lime-pit, Marterns Yellow Fur, Filmerts Fur, Ferrets Fur.

Hackles

13. Hackles (which are Feathers about a Cock or Capons Neck, and such as hanging down on each side, next a Cock or Capons Tail) of all colours, as the Red Dun, Yellowish, White Orange coloured, and perfect Black, these are of especial use to make the Palmer-fly, or Insect called by some Wool-beds.

Feathers

14. Feathers of all sort of Fowls, and of all colours, as Feathers on the Back, and other parts of the wild Mallard, or Drake, and Feathers of a Partridge, and of a Partridge-Tail, and Feathers of a Brown Hen, Throstle-wing, and Feathers got from the Quills and Pens of the wings of Shepstares, Stares or Starling, Fieldfare, and Throstle. The Peacocks Herle, Feathers of a Herons Neck, the top or Cop of a Plover, or Lapwing, which will make the Black Gnat, the Black Feather of an Ostridge or Estridge, and those of various Dyed colours, which Children and others wear in Caps, Feathers from Quills in a Blackbirds Wing and Tail, the Black Down of a Water-coot, and Feathers of all other Colours and Birds, etc.

Cadows and Blanckets

15. Of Outlandish Cadows, and Blanckets of diverse colours, are very often got excellent Dubbing, so of Cushions made of Abortive Skins of Colts, and Calves, and of Badgers Skins Tewed, etc.

Silks

16. Silk of all colours, small, but very strong.

Wire and Twist

17. Silver-Twist, Gold-Twist, Silver-Wire, Gold-Wire.
18. A sharp and neat pair of Scissars.

All these were necessary items in the "Budget" of the angler of Chetham's day, and virtually all of them are still indispensable to the fly dresser of today.

A curious mixture is James Chetham of Smedley, at once hard-headed, practical and shrewd, and yet revealing himself as capable of plagiarism and something grim and credulous in his belief in the efficacy of ointments containing ingredients more suited for a witch's kettle—"Man's Fat" or "the powdered Bones or Scull of a dead Man"—than calculated to render irresistible to fish any bait annointed therewith.

Richard and Charles Bowlker
1747

OF the numerous eighteenth-century authors of works on angling none is distinguished in the literary sense. Indeed, notice need only be taken of one book, and that solely for its practical excellence. The book is: *The Art of Angling* by Richard and Charles Bowlker of Ludlow in Shropshire. There is some uncertainty about the date of the first edition of this book, but in the catalogue of the Bodleian Library it is dated 1747. Of the twain Richard is the father and Charles the son, and in the second and all subsequent editions of the book, it is the latter, perhaps the foremost fly-fisherman of his time, who is named as the author.

The book, which is written in a simple and direct style, is eminent, in addition to its general directions, particularly in respect of its instructions on fly dressing, the patterns advocated, and entomological knowledge. The popularity of this manual is shown by the number of editions published.

In addition to furnishing an up-to-date list of trout flies, twenty-nine in all, and listing these others: the Dragon Fly, the King's Fisher or Peacock Fly, the Brown and White Night Flies, and four Palmer-Worms, as additions, Bowlker has no hesitation in disposing of many of the earlier patterns in these terms:-

"First I shall give you a catalogue more out of curiosity than use, of those flies that are not worth the angler's notice, and so proceed to those that are more useful." He then proceeds to name nineteen flies, many of them being those described in the Treatyse, and some of them being those given by Cotton, as under:-

A Catalogue of Flies seldom found useful to fish with.

1. The Dun Fly.
2. Ruddy Fly.
3. Black Fly.
4. Sandy-yellow Fly.
5. Moorish Fly.
6. Twine Fly.
7. Wasp Fly.
8. Shell Fly.
9. Dark Drake Fly.
10. Dark Brown Fly.
11. Prime Dun Fly.
12. Black May Palmer Worm.
13. Calmet Fly.
14. Oak Fly.
15. Owl Fly.
16. Brown Gnat.
17. Green Flesh Fly.
18. Harry Long Legs.
19. Badger Fly.

Then follows:
The most useful Flies throughout the Year, and their proper Season.

1. The Red Fly.
2. Blue Dun Fly.
3. Brown Fly.
4. Cowdung Fly.
5. Stone Fly.
6. Granam Fly.
7. Spider or Gravel Fly.
8. Black Gnat.
9. Black Caterpiller, or Hawthorn Fly.
10. Iron-blue Fly.
11. Sally Fly.
12. Canon, or Down-hill Fly.
13. Shorn Fly.
14. Green Drake.
15. Grey Drake.
16. Orl Fly.
17. Sky-colour'd Blue.
18. Cadis Fly.
19. Fern Fly.
20. Red Spinner.
21. Blue Gnat.
22. Large Red Ant.
23. Large Black Ant.
24. Welsham's Button.
25. Little Red Ant.
26. Little Black Ant.
27. Little Whirl Blue.
28. Little Pale Blue.
29. Willow Fly.

The *Red Fly*

Comes down about the middle of February, and continues till the latter end of March. He is made artificially of a dark drake's feather, the body of a red part of a squirrel's fur, with the red hackle of a cock wrapt twice or thrice under the but of

the wing; has four wings, and generally flutters upon the surface of the water, which tempts the fish, and makes them take him the more eagerly: The size of the hook, No. 6.

The *Blue Dun Fly*

Comes down the beginning of March, and continues till the middle of April: His wings are made of a feather out of the Starling's wing, or the blue feathers that grow under the wing of a duck widgeon; the body is made with the blue fur of a fox, or the blue part of a squirrel's fur, mixed with a little yellow mohair, and a fine blue cock's hackle wrapt over the body, in imitation of the legs: As he swims down the water his wings stand upright on his back; his tail forked, and of the same colour of his wings. He appears on the water about ten o'clock in the forenoon, and continues till about three in the afternoon but the principal time of the day is from twelve till two; the flies then come down in great quantities, and are always more plentiful in dark, cold, gloomy days, than in bright sun-shine weather. Your morning's fishing, till the flies come on, should be with the worm or minnow; the size of the hook this fly is made of, is No. 7; but if the water is very low and fine, No. 8.

The *Brown Fly* or *Dun Drake*

Comes down the beginning of March, and continues till the middle of April: His wings are made of the feather of a pheasant's wing, which is full of fine shade, and exactly resembles the wing of the fly: The body is made of the bright part of hare's fur, mixed with a little of the red part of squirrel's fur, ribbed with yellow silk, and a partridge's hackle wrapt twice or thrice under the but of the wing: As he swims down the water, his wings stand upright upon his back, his tail is forked, the colour of his wings: He comes upon the water about eleven o'clock, and continues till two, appearing upon the water in shoals or great quantities; in dark gloomy days, at the approach of the least gleam of sun, it is amazing to see, in a moment's time, the surface of the water almost covered over with ten thousand of these pretty little flying insects, and the fish rising and sporting at them, insomuch that you would think the whole river was

alive; a pleasant sight to the angler, and affords him great diversion; in this manner they appear upon the water every successive day, till the end of their duration. The Blue Dun, and the Brown, are both on at the same time, the blues are most plentiful in cold and dark days, and the browns in warm and gloomy days, tho' I have often seen blues, browns and granams on at the same time, when they have refused the other two sorts, and have taken the browns only. There cannot be too much said in commendation of this fly, both for its duration, and the sport he affords the angler: The size of the hook he is made on, is No. 6.

The *Cowdung Fly*

Comes down about the middle of March, and continues till the latter end of April: When upon the water his wings lie flat upon his back. He is to be used in cold stormy days; is seldom seen upon the water but when drove there by high winds. His wings are made of a feather out of the wing of a landrail; his body is of a dirty lemon-coloured mohair, with a hackle the same colour, wrapt under the but of the wings, and to be made somewhat in resemblance of the large horse ant: The size of the hook, No. 7.

The *Stone Fly*

Comes down about the middle of April, and continues till the latter end of May. He is a large four-winged fly; bred from an insect in the water, called the water cricket; to be found in stony, gravelly brooks, or rivers; his belly is of a dirty yellow, his wings of a fine blue colour, full of small veins, so that he is best made with a fine blue grizzle cock's hackle; the body with dark brown mohair, mixed with a dirty yellow. He is to be fished with at any time of the day, but does best in small brooks, or in the most rapid streams in rivers: The size of the hook, No. 3.

The *Granam Fly,* or *Green Tail*

Comes about the beginning of April, if the weather be warm, being a very tender fly, and cannot endure the cold. When they

first appear upon the water, they come in great quantities, in bright mornings: you may begin to fish with them from six o'clock in the morning till eleven, then you will find the browns come on, which you must use, as you will find they will not touch the Granams as long as the browns continue. About five o'clock in the evening you may use the Granams again with success; the browns then having totally disappeared for that day. This Granam is a four-winged fly; as he swims down the water his wings lie flat upon his back, has a small bunch of eggs of a green colour which gives him the name of the Green Tail Fly, for as soon as he lights upon the water he drops his eggs; is of short duration, not lasting above a week, and then totally disappears for that year. His wings are made of a feather out of the wing of a partridge, or pheasant, which is shaded like the wing of the fly; his body is made of the fur of the hare's face, or ear, and a grizzled hackle of a cock, wrapt under the but of the wing: The hook, No. 8.

The *Spider Fly*

Comes about the twentieth of April, if the weather be warm, and continues about a fortnight: They are bred in beds of gravel by the water side, where you may find them in bunches engendering, in order for their production the next season. In cold and stormy days they hide themselves in the gravel, not being able to endure the cold. You may fish with him from sun-rise, till sun-set, being a very killing fly, therefore cannot say too much in praise of him. His wings are made of a woodcock's feather, out of the but of the wing; the body of a lead coloured silk, with a black cock's hackle, wrapt twice or thrice under the but of the wings. This fly cannot be made too fine: The hook, No. 8, or 9.

The *Black Gnat*

Comes about the same time as the Spider fly, and continues till the latter end of May; to be fished with in cold stormy days, seldom to be seen in warm weather. His wings are made of a dark blue hackle, and the body of an ostrich's feather: The hook, No. 9.

The *Black Caterpillar*

Comes about the beginning of May, and continues about a fortnight, and is to be fished with after hot sunshine mornings; if winds and clouds appear, they then grow weak for loss of the sun, and fall upon the waters in great quantities. His wings are made of the feather out of a jay's wing, the body of an ostrich's feather, which I think far preferable to the plover's, with a fine black cock's hackle over the body. He is a very killing fly in small rivers and brooks: The hook, No. 7.

The *Little Iron-Blue Fly*

Comes about a week in May, and continues till the middle of June: In cold and stormy days they come down the waters in great quantities, but in warm days there are few to be seen. As he swims down the water his wings stand upright upon his back; his tail is forked, the colour of his wings. He is a neat curious little fly, and cannot be made too fine; to be fished with from about eleven o'clock in the forenoon, till three in the afternoon. When these flies are on, the fish refuse every other sort, and take these only; every sort of fish being fond of them. His wings are made of a cormorant's feather that grows under the wings, or the feather of a dark blue hen that grows on the body under the wings, the body of water-rats fur, ribbed with yellow silk, with a sutty blue hackle of a cock wrapt over the body: The hook, No. 8, or 9.

The *Yellow Sally Fly*

Comes about the twentieth of May, and continues till about the tenth or twelfth of June, and is a four-winged fly. As he swims down the water his wings lie flat on his back. His wings are made with a yellow cock's hackle, his body is made with yellow dubbing only. He is one of the flies that prepare the fish to look for the May Fly, or Green Drake: The hook, No. 7.

The *Canon*, or *Down-Hill Fly*

Comes about the sixteenth of May, and continues about a week in June; to be found on the buts of trees, with his head

always downwards, which gives him the name of the Down-hill Fly. He is bred in the oak-apples; and is best of all flies for bobbing at the bush, in the natural way, and a good fly for the long line, when made artificially: His wings are made with a feather out of the wing of a partridge; his body with a bittern's feather, the head with a little of the brown part of hare's fur: The hook, No. 7.

The *Shorn Fly*

Comes about the same time as the Canon Fly, and continues till the latter end of July. They are for the most part found in mowing grass; he is of the caterpillar kind, his husky wings of a dark brown colour, with fine clear blue wings under them, which he makes use of in his flight: Is in his greatest perfection in June, and, for the time of his continuance upon the water, is as killing a fly as any I know of, in rivers, or brooks: There are three sorts of them; the one I have before-mentioned, as to his colour; there is another with a dull red wing; and the third with a dark blue wing, all which sorts the fish take very well, but the preference must be given to the red sort. To be fished with any time of the day, from sun-rise to sun-set: His wings are made of a red cock's hackle, with a black list up the middle; the body with a peacock's harle: The hook, No. 6, if for a river; but if for a dead, heavy, running brook, the fly must be made larger: The hook, No. 4, or 5.

The *May Fly,* or *Yellow Cadow*

Comes down the water about the twentieth of May, is of short duration, not lasting above nine or ten days. He is a large and beautiful fly, which both fish and birds are very fond of: They are most plentiful in gravelly, sandy, stoney rivers or brooks; but in some dead, heavy, dull waters, there are few to be seen. As he swims down the water his wings stand upright on his back; has a three-forked tail, is about an inch long, and is to be fished with from about ten o'clock in the morning, till sun-setting; being a fly the fish are remarkably fond of, they not only take them very eagerly at the top of the water, but feed on them as they rise from the bottom, where they are bred in

husks, which they quit when they come to the surface of the water, and are so short-lived, that they are almost instantly devoured by fish or birds. It is an excellent fly for bobbing at the bush, as well as the long line, and is as killing upon standing waters, as in streams. When these flys are in perfection, the fish refuse all other sorts, and take these only. His wings are made of the feather of a grey drake, or rather the grey feathers of a wild mallard dyed yellow; the body is made of the yellow wool of a ram, or wether; his body is ribbed with a dark brown, for which no feather does so well as the hackle of a bittern; it likewise makes the legs very artificially; his head is of a dark brown, made of a peacock's harle, and his tail with the hair of a fitchew's tail: The hook, No. 6.

The *Grey Drake*

Comes about the twenty-seventh, or twenty-eighth of May; he is a large and beautiful fly, in shape and make very much resembles the Yellow Cadow; seldom appearing on the water till about six or seven o'clock in the evening, and to be fished with from that time till sun-setting: All the former part of the day the fish take the Yellow Cadow very freely, but in the evenings, when the grey ones appear in great quantities, they will not touch the yellow ones. In fishing with this fly, you must endeavour to imitate the rising and falling of him on the water, being always in motion, striking up and down, for which reason, in some places, he is called the Tilt-up Fly: He is not a difficult fly to make, but more difficult to fish with after he is made, and therefore, if possible, cast your line, so that your fly may drop directly over the fish's head, which resembles the manner of these flies, dropping on the water; which method must be observed in fishing with these flies upon standing waters, as well as streams: But all other flies ought to be thrown about half a yard above the head of the fish, as they all swim gradually down the water. There are three sorts of Grey Cadows, and but only one of the sorts to be made artificially; the other two sorts seldom appearing upon the water, but are generally playing and striking by the sides of hedges near the water side, and are much darker and smaller than those that frequent the water, therefore are not worth the angler's notice. The wings of

this fly are made with a grey feather of the wild millard, the widgeon being too dark; the body, of goat's hair, which makes it the best of any thing I know of, the silver twist being too heavy, and too glaring in the water; the legs of a dark grizzle cock's hackle, which I find far preferable to the bittern's hackle; the head of a dark brown, made with a peacock's harle; his tail is three-forked, about an inch and an half long, which is made of the hairs or whisks out of the tail of a fitchew: The hook, No. 5.

[There follows here an "ingenious account of this fly . . . very justly described by a gentleman, a very accurate observer of nature's productions . . ." describing the nymph, subimago and imago, and, indeed, revealing a remarkable amount of entomological knowledge.]

The *Orl Fly*

Comes down the latter end of May, and continues till the latter end of June: He is a four-winged fly, generally flutters along the surface of the water; and is a fly the fish are remarkably fond of; you may fish with him with success after the May Fly is gone, from four o'clock in the morning till about seven in the evening, at which time the Sky Blue comes on, then leave off the Orl and take the Sky Blue only. The wings of the Orl Fly are made with a dark grizzle cock's hackle, the body of a peacock's harle, worked with dark red silk: The hook, No. 6.

The *Sky-Coloured Blue*

Comes about the same time as the Orl Fly, and continues till the middle of July: It is a neat, curious, and beautiful Fly; his wings stand upright on his back, and are of a fine transparent blue colour; his body of a pale yellow, with a forked tail, the colour of his wing. It is a fly the fish take extremely well from seven o'clock in the evening till sunset. His wings are made with a light blue feather of a hen; the body is made with a pale yellow mohair, mixed with a light blue fur, ribbed with a fine cock's hackle, dyed yellow: The hook, No. 8.

The *Cadis Fly*

Comes about the tenth of June: It is a large four-winged fly, of a buff-colour; his body the same colour of his wings: He continues on the water till about the beginning of July; he is bred from the cod-bait, a curious little creature: While in the state of a grub, he is greatly to be admired, the out-side husk he lives in being curiously wrought with gravel or sand. This fly does best at the clearing of the water; though I think him a fly worth the least notice of any in the catalogue, there being many sorts on at the same time far preferable to him. His wings are made of a feather taken from the body of a buff-coloured hen; the body is made of buff-coloured mohair, with a pale yellow hackle for the legs: The hook, No. 6.

The *Fern Fly*

Comes about the middle of June, and continues till about the middle of July: He is a four-winged fly; his body very slender and of an orange colour; he is to be fished with at any time of the day, from sun-rise till sun-set, being a very killing fly. His wings are made with a woodcock's feather, his body with orange-colour'd silk: The hook, No. 5.

The *Red Spinners*

Come about the middle of June, and continue till the latter end of August: To be fished with only in the evenings after very hot days, from seven o'clock as long as you can see. There are two sorts of Spinners; the one is made with the grey feather of a drake, tinged with a copper-coloured gloss; his body with the red part of the squirrel's fur, ribbed with gold twist, and a fine red cock's hackle for the legs; with a long forked tail, made with the harles of a red hackle: The wings of the other Spinner is made with the feather out of the wing of a starling; the body of a dull red mohair, ribbed with gold twist, with a fine red cock's hackle over the body, the tail long and forked, and made as the former. These are both very killing flies, particularly upon rivers: The hook, No. 7, or 8, according to the water you fish in.

The *Blue Gnat*

Comes down about the same time as the Spinner, and continues about a fortnight: If the water be low and fine the fish take them very well, as long as they last upon the water: The wings of this Gnat are made with a small pale blue cock's hackle, the body with a light blue fur, mixed with a little yellow mohair: The hook, No. 8, or 9.

The *Large Red Ant Fly*

Comes about the middle of June, if it be hot and sultry weather, and continues till about the fifteenth or sixteenth of July, appearing mostly in hot, close, gloomy days. To be fished with from about eleven o'clock in the forenoon, till about six in the evening; then make use of the evening flies, as described before. The Ant Flies, when in perfection, are amazingly killing; and all sorts of fish that rise at flies are very fond of them; indeed you may take fish with them in dead heavy waters, as well as in streams. The wings of this fly are made with a feather out of the wing of a starling, the body of a peacock's harle, made pretty large at the tail, and fine towards the wing, with a fine ginger-coloured cock's hackle, wrapt twice or thrice under the but of the wing: The hook, No. 8.

The *Large Black Ant Fly*

Comes at the same time with the red, and to be fished with at the same time, and after the same manner. The wings of this fly are made with the lightest sky-coloured blue feather you can get, and with the greatest gloss; but it is difficult to find any that can come up to the glossiness of the natural wing, except the thistle, which makes it the best of any thing I know of, but is not lasting; the body is made with a black ostrich's feather, with a black cock's hackle wrapt under the but of the wing, and to be made in the same form as the red one: The hook, No. 8.

The *Welshman's Button* or *Hazle Fly*

Comes about the latter end of July, and continues about nine or ten days; is in form like a round button, from which he

derives his name; he has four wings, the uppermost husky and hard, the undermost of a fine blue colour, soft and transparent; to be found upon hazle trees or fern bushes. He is an excellent fly for bobbing at the bush, or long line, being rather difficult to make, upon account of his shape and form. His wings are made with the red feather that grows upon the rump or tail of a partridge; the body is made with a peacock's harle and an ostrich's feather mixed, with a fine black cock's hackle for the legs. The hook, No. 7.

The *Little Red* and *Black Ant Flies*

Come about the tenth or twelfth of August, and are to be seen in warm gloomy days till the latter end of September; to be fished with from about twelve o'clock till four in the evening; to be made in the same form as the large one, and with the same materials, but very small: The hook, No. 9.

The *Little Whirling Blue*

Comes down about the tenth or twelfth of August, and contines about three weeks. As he swims down the water his wings stand upright on his back: has a forked tail the colour of his wings; to be fished with from eleven o'clock in the forenoon till three in the afternoon. His wings are made with a feather out of the wing of a starling; his body is made with squirrel's fur, mixed with a little yellow, with a fine red hackle over the body: The hook, No. 8.

The *Little Pale Blue*

Comes down about the same time as the Whirling Blue, and continues till the latter end of September: As he swims down the water his wings stand upright on his back; has a forked tail the colour of his wings. It is a neat curious little fly, which the greylings are very fond of. To be fished with from about ten o'clock in the morning till three in the afternoon, and generally affords the angler great diversion. His wings are made of the feather of a sea-swallow, the body is made of the lightest blue fur you can get, mixed with a very little yellow mohair, with a fine pale blue hackle over the body: The hook, No. 8.

The *Willow Fly*

Comes down the beginning of September, and continues till the latter end of October. He is a four-winged fly, and generally flutters upon the surface of the water: To be fished with in cold stormy days, being then most plentiful upon the water; but in warm gloomy days make use of the Pale Blue. His wings are made of a blue grizzled cock's hackle, the body of the blue part of squirrel's fur, mixed with a little yellow mohair: The hook, No. 7. The three last mentioned flies carry out the season for fly-fishing.

[The dressings of the Dragon Fly and of the King's Fisher, or Peacock Fly, are then given as patterns for salmon fishing.]

The *Brown* and *White Night Flies*

Are a couple of Moths, which come about the beginning of June, and continue till the middle of July; seldom to be seen at any time but in the night; and to be fished with in a dark gloomy night, after a bright sun-shine day, from eleven o'clock at night till break of day, with success: But if it be a moon-shine, or star-light night, there are no fish to be taken. Your line for this method of fishing must be about a yard longer than your rod, putting two or three maggots, or a worm, at the point of your hook, for the smelling part; and you may hear them rise in as much perfection, as if you were fishing by day; and will take them in standing waters as well as in streams. The brown one is made of a feather of a brown owl, the body of a light mohair, with a dark grizzle cock's hackle for the legs. The white one's wings are made of the feather out of the wing of a white owl; the body of white cotton, and the white hackle of a cock for the legs: The hook, No. 3.

Palmer-Worms

First, the *Golden Palmer*.

His body is made of orange-coloured silk, ribbed down with a peacock's harle and gold twist, with the red hackle of a cock wrapt over the body: the hook, No. 5, or 6, according to the water you fish in.

The *Brown Palmer*

The body is made with hog's down, dyed of an amber colour, ribbed with silver and gold twist, with a red cock's hackle wrapt over the body.

The *Black Palmer*

The body is made with the black ostrich's feather, ribbed with silver twist, with a black cock's hackle over the body.

The *Red Palmer*

The body is made with a dark reddish-coloured mohair, ribbed with gold twist, and a blood-red cock's hackle over the body: The hooks the same size as the golden one.

The Manner of Making the *Artificial Fly*

When you make an artificial Fly, you must, in the first place, make choice of a hook of a size proportionable to the Fly you intend to make, which must be whipped on to your gut or hair in the same manner you would whip on a worm-hook, only with this difference, that instead of fastening near the bend of the hook, you must fasten your silk near the top of the shank, and let your silk remain; then taking as much feather as is necessary for the wings, lay it as even as you can upon the upper side of the shank, with the but end of the feather downward, towards the bend of the hook, and tye it fast three or four times with the silk, and fasten it; then, with a needle or pin, divide the wings as equal as you can; then take your silk and cross it three or four times between the wings, bringing the silk still downward, towards the bend of the hook, then taking your hackle feather, tye it fast at the bend with the point of the hackle upwards; next, your fur or dubbing being ready, which is to make the body of the Fly, take a little of it and twist it gently round your silk, and work it upwards to the but of the wings, and there fasten it; then take your hackle and rib it neatly over your dubbing, and fasten it; then bending the wings and putting them into the form you design, bring on the but end of your hackle towards the head, and there fasten it firm; then taking a bit of dubbing or fur, as near to the colour

of the head of the Fly as you can, whip it twice or thrice round with your silk, and then fasten it just above the wings; so your Fly is completed.

The above method of dressing trout and grayling flies, it will be observed, still adheres to the reverse-wing method of the earlier writers, and the wing itself is still made of a single slip of feather divided equally by the tying silk. The dubbed bodies are ribbed in some, but not all, instances, with a hackle feather, and seem to have been carried well down the hookshank close to the bend. This is, doubtless, the kind of body which inspired North-Country Charles Cotton to professed risibility anent the long and unduly heavy bodies of South-Country flies, and, indeed, the contrast with the slim Yorkshire tie must have been striking.

Yet these twenty-nine patterns, and especially the advice and comments which accompany them individually, show the degree to which close and accurate observation of natural river flies had advanced, and there is still the principle of representing the natural insect in form, shape, colour and size. And the detailed enumeration of the sizes of hooks to be used shows that the matter of proportion was well appreciated as being of importance.

The Bowlkers did two desirable things: first, they disposed of those hoary and ancient patterns, such as a few which continued from the time of the *Treatyse* in 1496, which had long outlived their day of usefulness; and, second, they provided a sound and up-to-date list of very real service to fly-fishermen in the eighteenth century, and, indeed, it would seem from the popularity of the book, for long after.

Nineteenth-Century Authors

QUITE undistinguished as was the literature of the eighteenth century, the nineteenth was to witness a sudden renaissance from the very dawn of the century. First, in 1800, there came from the pen of one, George Scotcher, a little book published at Chepstow entitled: *The Fly-Fisher's Legacy*. It is notable, perhaps, because it is the first book to give illustrations in colour of natural insects, and also because of its reference to the use of a floating fly. This was followed in 1816 by *The Fly-Fisher's Guide* written by George C. Bainbridge, and published at Liverpool—a sound manual containing five reasonably good colour plates of natural insects. In turn, this was followed by W. Carroll's *The Angler's Vade Mecum* published in Edinburgh in 1818, also containing colour plates of flies, but of such crudity and inferiority as to be all but worthless. Then in 1836 there was published in London the book for which the whole fly-fishing world had been waiting. This was: *The Fly Fisher's Entomology* by Alfred Ronalds—an entirely original work and so magnificently illustrated that the coloured copperplates remain unsurpassed to this day. At once the standard of illustration was raised and the new school of the angler-naturalist was founded at last.

Following Ronalds, there were published several notable books. In 1849, Hewett Wheatley's work: *The Rod and Line* was published in London—a good book and one with good illustrations. In this year, also, John Beever's *Practical Fly-fishing* was published in London under his *nom-de-plume* of "Arundo"—a modest but interesting little book. Then, in 1853, there was published at Ripon, Michael Theakston's book entitled: *A List of Natural Flies*—an outstanding contribution which would have earned greater distinction had the author adhered to more orthodox nomenclature, but which, nevertheless, is worthy of genuine respect. In the following year, 1854, John Jackson's work: *The Practical Fly-fisher* was published, and

here, again, was another sound and well-illustrated book by a North-Country man. From the North Country also, in 1861, came Henry Wade's *Halcyon*—yet another good work. Two years later, in 1863, there was published an intensely practical little volume dealing with fishing in the streams of North Devon entitled: *Trout Fishing in Rapid Streams* by H. C. Cutcliffe. In 1876 the publication of *A Quaint Treatise on Flees, and the Art a Artyfichall Flee Making* by W. H. Aldam, gave fly-fishermen not only a list of highly interesting patterns, but also the actual materials employed as well as some of the most exquisitely dressed flies one could hope to see. The book is, perhaps, the gem of all the attractive books on the fly-fisher's shelves. And, finally, to round off the progressive nineteenth century, in 1885 there was published in Leeds another sound work dealing with North-Country flies, and well-illustrated with colour plates: *Yorkshire Trout Flies* by T. E. Pritt.

So if the eighteenth century was barren, the nineteenth proved to be another golden age of angling literature. South of the Tweed, the North-Country, the South-Country, and the South-West-Country all made eminent contributions; north of Tweed, too, men were beginning to write about angling—first, in 1835, came Thomas Tod Stoddart's: *The Art of Angling as practised in Scotland;* then John Younger's little work: *On River Angling for Salmon and Trout* in 1840; in 1857 there was published W. C. Stewart's famous work: *The Practical Angler;* and finally, in 1857, David Webster's book: *The Angler and the Looprod* was published.

All the foregoing literature concerns the wet fly, its making and its use. Yet the latter part of the nineteenth century was to witness a great development in the form of a *floating* as distinct from a sunk or wet fly, and this advent is so important as to demand notice by itself.

Of the wet-fly school, it will perhaps be sufficient to reproduce extracts from the following four writers as representing the best English contributions: Alfred Ronalds; H. C. Cutcliffe; T. E. Pritt; and W. H. Aldam.

ALFRED RONALDS

No. 1. *Red Fly*
Order, *Neuroptera*.
Family, *Perlidae*.
Genus, *Nemoura*.

No. 2. *Blue Dun* (Cock Wing, Cock Tail).
Order, *Neuroptera*.
Family, *Ephemeridae*.
Genus, *Baetis*.

No. 3. *Red Spinner*
Order, *Neuroptera*.
Family, *Ephemeridae*.
Genus, *Baetis*.

No. 1. *Red Fly*

In a forward spring this fly comes out about the middle of February, it is in season until the end of March, and may be used on fine but rather windy days, until the Blue Dun (see No. 2) and other flies come in. I have taken very large Grayling with it.

Imitation

Body. The dubbing is composed of the dark red part of squirrel's fur, mixed with an equal quantity of claret-coloured mohair, shewing the most claret colour at the tail of the fly. This is spun on and warped with brown silk thread.

Wings. From a ginger dun covert feather of the mallard's wing. The pea hen has also feather of the exact tint.

Legs. Of a claret-coloured *stained* hackle. No feather of its *natural* colour, that I know of, is of the proper shade.

To make it buzz a copper tinged dun hackle is wound upon the above body.

No. 2. *Blue Dun*

This fly lives three or four days in the state represented; then becomes the Red Spinner, (see No. 3.) It begins to be plentiful in the early part of March, or a little sooner, should the weather be mild. When in full season it will be found on the water, chiefly on rather cold windy days. It endeavours to take flight in three or four seconds after it leaves its Nympha. On

cold days it seems to have rather more difficulty in rising from the water than in warm weather, and consequently becomes very frequently food for fishes at the moment of its new birth.

Imitation

Body. Fur of a hare's ear, or face, spun on yellow silk. When this dubbing is warped on, some of the longest part of the dubbing is left out to form legs.
Tail. Two small whiskers of a rabbit.
Wings. From a feather of the starling's wing, stained in onion dye.
Legs. If a sufficient quantity of dubbing was not left out for the legs, whilst the body was made, more must be picked out out of it with a needle.

No. 3. *Red Spinner*

This is the name given to the Blue Dun (see No. 2) after it has cast off its olive brown coat. It now appears of a bright red brown, and its wings, which were before rather opaque, are transparent. It lives four or five days. It sports in the sunshine, and will be more successfully used in warm than in cold weather; but when the sun becomes too powerful, this delicate insect seems to be disabled from continuing abroad in the middle of the day, and is to be considered more as an evening fly. Several of the other spinners (or perfect Ephemeridae) resemble it so nearly, that it may be kept as a model; the tint only varying, (as will be subsequently shewn).

Imitation

Body. Brown silk, ribbed with fine gold twist.
Tail. Two whisks of a red cock's hackle.
Wings. From a mottled grey feather of the mallard, stained to match the colour of the natural wings.
Legs. Plain red cock's hackle.

* * *

No. 4. *Water Cricket*
Order, *Hemiptera*.
Family, *Hydrometridae*.
Genus, *Velia*.
Species, *Currens*.

No. 5. *Great Dark Drone* (Saw Fly, Great Dark Dun)
Order, *Hymenoptera*.
Family, *Tenthredinidae*.
Genus, *Dolerus*.

No. 6. *Cow Dung Fly*
Order, *Diptera*.
Family, *Muscidae*.
Genus, *Scatophaga*.
Species, *Stercoraria*.

No. 4. *Water Cricket*

This insect lives upon small flies, etc. whose blood it sucks in a manner similar to that of the land spider. It runs upon the water, and darts upon its prey whilst struggling on the surface, and is one amongst the first insects which the Trout finds there. In the hot summer months it is provided with wings. It may be fished with throughout this month, and the next, on all sorts of days, but principally when the Blue Dun is *not* very abundant upon the water.

Imitation

Body. Orange floss silk, tied on with black silk thread.
Legs. Are made best of one of the two longest feathers of a peawit's topping. If this cannot be easily procured, a black cock's hackle will answer the purpose. Either of these must be wound all down the body, and the fibres then *snipped* off, as far up as is shewn in the figure.

No. 5. *Great Dark Drone*

This fly is found upon the grass in a *very dull* (almost torpid) state, until nine or ten o'clock in the morning; (whence its name of Drone) but when the sun begins to warm the air, it takes wing; and afterwards, if there be a slight breeze, it will be found upon the water.

There is a great variety of colour in the family. A bright orange is sometimes seen all over the body, a lemon colour sometimes pervades only the middle part of the body, the knee joints are sometimes tipped with orange, sometimes orange

veins appear in the wings; but the black body is by far the most frequently met with, and therefore the fly with this colour is usually fished with.

Imitation

Body. Mole fur, or black ostrich feather, warped with black silk.

Wings & Legs. Made buzz with a dun hackle, the tint lighter than that of the natural wings.

When this fly is made with wings and legs not buzz, the dun feather of the wing of the mallard is used, and a grizzle hackle for legs, upon the same body.

No. 6. *Cow Dung Fly*

This fly lives throughout the year. In the young state it is very abundant about the middle of March, when vast quantities are seen upon the water if there be a high wind. The colour of the male, when newly hatched, is a very bright tawny yellow, that of the female a greenish brown; she is rather smaller than the male, is found in as great numbers on the water, and is as good a fly to imitate. This insect is not in full season after the end of April, but in very blustering days may be used all the year round.

Imitation

Body. Yellow worsted, mohair, or camlet, mixed with a little dingy brown fur from the bear, and left rather rough, spun upon light brown silk.

Wings. From the landrail.

Legs. Of a ginger coloured hackle.

The female is made buzz thus:

Body. Olive-coloured mohair, or worsted, spun on silk of the same colour.

Wings & Legs. Of a red cock's hackle, changed to a brown colour by putting it into a solution of copperas.

* * *

No. 7. *Peacock Fly*
Order, *Coleoptera*.
Family, *Staphylinidae*.
Genus, *Lathrobium*.
Species, *Elongatum*.

The portly trout flies of the early 19th century, probably dressed in London

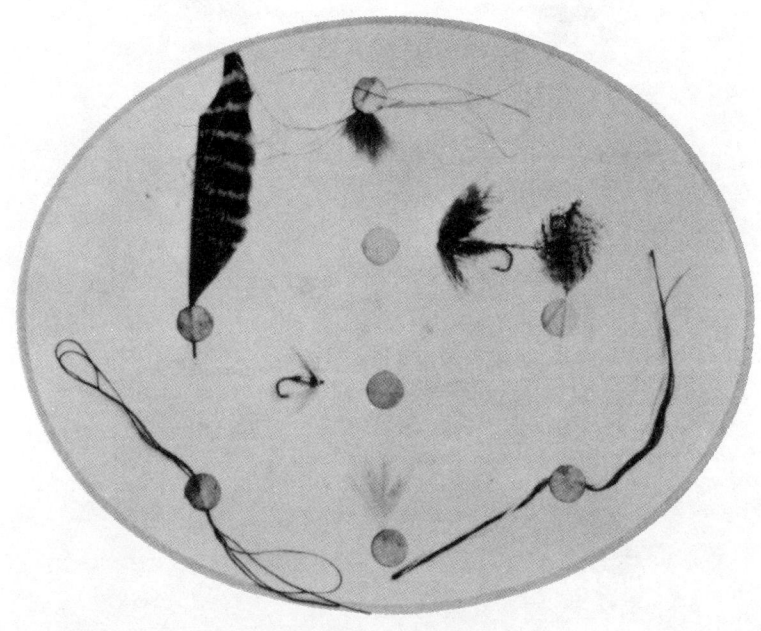

FLY-DRESSING EXAMPLES FROM ALDAM'S 'QUAINT TREATISE'
Upper fly: the March Brown of Britain; *lower fly:* the Jenny Spinner

No. 8. *Dun Drake* (March Brown, called in Wales the Cob Fly.)
Order, *Neuroptera*.
Family, *Ephemeridae*.
Genus, *Baetis*.

No. 9. *Great Red Spinner* (or Light Mackerel.)
Order, *Neuroptera*.
Family, *Ephemeridae*.
Genus, *Baetis*.

No. 7. *Peacock Fly*

This small beetle is extremely abundant on warm sunny days. Its usual habit on alighting is to gather up the wings under its short wing scales, a habit like that of the earwig, which flies about in Autumn; but when it falls upon the water, it cannot always succeed in doing so; then therefore the wings lie nearly flat upon its back. However fine the day may be, and however clear the water, some sport may still be expected with this fly, until the end of May, but it is most successfully used on a hot gloomy day.

Imitation

Body.   Brown peacock's herl, dressed with mulberry-coloured silk.
Wings.   The darkest part of a wing feather of the starling.
Legs.   A hackle stained dark purple; appearing black when looked down upon; but when held up to the light, having a most beautiful dark tortoise-shell hue.

No. 8. *Dun Drake*

The pupa or nympha of this fly seems to require a warmer day to enable it to rise to the surface of the water, and to change to a fly, than is required for the similar rise and metamorphosis of the Blue Dun's nympha (No. 2); the fly lives three days in the state represented in the figure, then changes into the Great Red Spinner. The male has a chocolate hue, and the female a green brown; it generally appears in great

numbers upon the streams, where it is found towards the latter end of March, and is very eagerly devoured by the Trout. It continues in season until the beginning of May; and although it may occasionally be found later, I do not recommend the use of it after that time.

Imitation

Body. Fur of the hare's face ribbed over with olive silk, and tied with brown.
Tail. Two strands of a partridge feather.
Wings. Feather of the pheasant's wing, which may be found of the exact shade.
Legs. A feather from the back of a partridge.

No. 9. *Great Red Spinner*

The Dun Drake changes into this spinner, and enjoys for three or four days its newest state and title. It seems to be in season much longer than the Dun Drake, and may even be used on warm evenings during most of the summer months; yet although the Dun Drake is not seen on the water after the middle of May, it would seem that it must still continue to come into existence afterwards, otherwise the Great Red Spinner could be in season only three or four days longer than the Dun Drake. (Note by Ronalds: Although I have spoken of this Spinner as appearing throughout most of the summer months, I am by no means certain that the individuals which are produced later than the middle of May, may not be a distinct although very similar species of *Baetis*.)

Imitation

Body. Hog's down dyed red-brown, (or orange and brown floss silk mixed), spun on brown silk. It is ribbed with fine gold twist.
Tail. Two long whisks of a bright amber red stained hackle.
Wings. From a feather of the starling's wing.
Legs. A bright amber red stained hackle.

* * *

Flies for April

No. 10. *Golden Dun Midge*
Order, *Diptera*.
Family, *Tipulidae*.
Genus, *Chironomus*.
Species, *Plumosus*.

No. 11. *Sand Fly*
Order, *Trichoptera*.
Family, *Phryganidae*.
Genus, *Phryganea*.

No. 12. *Stone Fly*
Order, *Neuroptera*.
Family, *Perlidae*.
Genus, *Perla*.
Species, *Bicaudata*.

No. 10. *Golden Dun Midge*

The male has two feathered horns which the female has not. It seems to require a warm day to disengage itself from its water nympha. On such days very great sport may be had with it until the end of May.

Imitation

Body. Olive floss silk ribbed with gold twist, and tied with dun silk thread.
Wings. From the palest feather of a young starling.
Legs. A plain dun hackle.

No. 11. *Sand Fly*

This fly comes from a water larva. It is highly extolled by Mr. Bainbridge, who says, "that it may be reckoned as one of the best flies for affording diversion which can possibly be selected, for it may be used successfully at all hours of the day, from April to the end of September, and is equally alluring to the Trout and Grayling." (Fly Fisher's Guide, p. 143). My own experience leads me to recommend the use of it during April

and May, on days when there is no abundance of any particular insect on the water. A fly very like it is used in September and October, called the Cinnamon Fly.

Imitation

Body.   Of the sandy coloured fur from the hare's neck, spun on silk of the same colour.
Wings.   From the landrail's wing made full.
Legs.   From a light ginger feather from the neck of a hen.

This fly is made buzz with a feather from the under side of the wing of the throstle, wound upon and above body.

No. 12. *Stone Fly*

This fly comes from a water larva. It is heavy in its flight, but uses its legs with extreme activity, and is generally found amongst the stones, or close to the sides of the water. I have kept an individual alive for three weeks, during which time it drank much water. It is in season from the beginning of April until the end of May, and should be used in the rapid parts of streams, and on windy days where the water is rough.

Imitation

Body.   Fur of hare's ear mixed with yellow worsted or camlet, ribbed over with yellow silk leaving most yellow at the tail.
Tail.   A mottled strand or two of a partridge feather.
Wings.   Feather from the pheasant's wing.
Legs.   A hackle stained greenish-brown.
Horns.   Two rabbit's whiskers.

* * *

No. 13. *Gravel Bed* (Spider Fly)
Order, *Diptera*.
Family, *Tipulidae*.
Genus, *Anisomera*.
Species, *Obscura*.

No. 14. *Grannom* (Greentail.)
Order, *Trichoptera*.
Family, *Phryganidae*.
Genus, *Tinodes*.

No. 15. *Yellow Dun*
Order, *Neuroptera*.
Family, *Ephemeridae*.
Genus, *Baetis*.

No. 13. Gravel Bed

This fly is not upon all waters: upon those where it is found it is extremely numerous on fine days; but in cold weather it seeks shelter amongst the larger stones of the gravel. It may be used all the day. It comes in about the middle of April and lasts about three weeks.

Imitation
Body. Dark dun, or lead-coloured silk thread dressed very fine.
Wings. From the underside of a feather of the woodcock's wing.
Legs. A black cock's hackle rather long, wound twice, only, round the body.

To make it buzz, a dark dun cock's hackle tinged brown may be used.

No. 14. Grannom

This fly comes from a water larva, and is upon the surface at about the same season as the Gravel Bed (No. 13), and chiefly in the morning and evening. It lasts a little longer. The green tint of its body is derived from the colour of the eggs. It lays these upon the water. There are several varieties, and I have taken many of these flies out of the stomachs of Trout, even in August, which had a green colour at the tail of their bodies, and were as nearly as possible of the same size and general tint as those of April.

Imitation
Body. Fur of hare's face left rough, spun on brown silk. A little green floss silk may be worked in at the tail to represent the bunch of eggs there.
Wings. Feather from the partridge's wing, and made very full.
Legs. A pale ginger hen's hackle.

Made buzz with a feather from the back of the partridge's neck, wound upon the above body.

No. 15. *Yellow Dun*

This fly proceeding from a water nympha, lives in the form shewn about three days. It is on the water generally from ten o'clock until three.

Imitation

Body. Yellow mohair, mixed with a little pale blue fur from a mouse. Or yellow silk thread well waxed with cobbler's wax to give it an olive tint.
Wings. The lightest part of a feather from a young starling's wing.
Legs. A light yellow dun hackle.

To make it buzz, a lighter dun hackle than is represented in the figure, is wound upon the same body.

This Yellow Dun changes to a Spinner of rather a lighter and yellower brown, than that which the Blue Dun (No. 2) turns to, is very nearly of the same size, and lives nine days. It is to be used on warm evenings. Its imitation may consequently be made of the same materials as that of the Red Spinner (see No. 3), only choosing lighter tints.

* * *

No. 16. *Iron Blue Dun*
Order, *Neuroptera*.
Family, *Ephemeridae*.
Genus, *Baetis*.

No. 17. *Jenny Spinner* (Spinning Jenny)
Order, *Neuroptera*.
Family, *Ephemeridae*.
Genus, *Baetis*.

No. 18. *Hawthorn Fly*
Order, *Diptera*.
Family, *Tipulidae*.
Genus, *Bibio*.
Species, *Marci*.

No. 16. *Iron Blue Dun*

After emerging from its water nympha, this fly remains about two days in the state shewn, and then changes to the Jenny Spinner, (see No. 17). It is one of the smallest flies worth the Angler's notice, but not the least useful. The male has a brownish red crown or cap on his head. The female is also crowned, but her cap is too small to be easily seen. It is in season from the latter end of April until the middle of June, and is on the water chiefly on cold days; influenced by effects similar to those which act upon the Blue Dun, (see No. 2).

Imitation

Body. Blue fur from a mole. A little reddish brown floss silk may be tied on with dun silk for the head.
Tail. A whisk or two out of a dun hackle.
Wings. From a feather of the underside of the cormorant's wing; but as this bird is scarce, and has only a few feathers under the wing, a very good substitute may be found in a feather from the breast of the water hen; the tip of which must be used.
Legs. A very useful small dun hackle, or some of the dubbing picked out of the body.

It is difficult to find a hackle feather of the tint proper to make this fly buzz.

No. 17. *Jenny Spinner*

This is the name given to the Iron Blue (No. 16) in his new dress, and it lives four or five days after the metamorphosis, sporting in the still summer atmosphere. The Iron Blue must be coming out of its nympha at the same time that this fly is in season; the Iron Blue is however found on the water chiefly on cold days, from the end of April until the middle of June. (Ronalds' note: A little dark dun with a brown head, not exactly similar to, but very much like the Iron Blue, is found in August, and then a Spinner like the Jenny Spinner, has an orange coloured head, and the extremity of its body a lighter colour.) The Jenny Spinner lasts all the Summer, is out on mild days, particularly towards the evening, and is a killing fly even when the water is extremely fine.

Imitation

Body. White floss silk wound round the shank of the hook, etc. and tied on at the head and tail with brown silk, which must be shewn.
Tail. A whisk or two of a light dun hackle.
Wings & Legs. Are best imitated by making them buzz; for which purpose the lightest dun hackle that can be procured should be used.

No. 18. *Hawthorn Fly*

This fly is by some called the black caterpillar. It has good wings, and makes good use of them. It may be seen about the last week in April, when the air is warm, sporting up and down by the sides of hedges, and may then be used. There are three very common species, one of the size represented, another much larger, and another much smaller. The female of each has dark wings (almost black); whereas those of the male are a very pale blue, (almost white). Her head is very much smaller than that of the male, and her body thicker. The male is most abundant.

Imitation

Body. Black ostrich herl.
Wings. From a feather of the sea swallow, or dotterel.
Legs. A black cock's hackle; or one of the two largest feathers from a peewit's top-knot.

The fly cannot very easily be made buzz, unless the female is imitated, in which case a black hackle wound over the above mentioned black ostrich herl will answer the purpose.

* * *

Flies for May

No. 19. *Little Yellow May Dun*
Order, *Neuroptera*.
Family, *Ephemeridae*.
Genus, *Baetis*.

No. 20. *Black Gnat*
Order, *Diptera*.
Family, *Empidae*.
Genus, *Ramphamyia*.

No. 21. *Downhill Fly* (Oak Fly, Ash Fly, Cannon Fly, Downlooker, Woodcock Fly, Downhead Fly)
Order, *Diptera*.
Family, *Rhagionidae*.
Genus, *Rhagio*.
Species, *Scolopaceus*.

No. 19. *Little Yellow May Dun*

This fly proceeding from a water nympha remains in the state represented about three days, then changes to a very light red, or amber-coloured, spinner. It lasts (as shewn) in season until the Green Drake (No. 28) comes in at the end of May, or beginning of June.

Imitation

Body. Pale ginger-coloured fur from behind the hare's ear, ribbed over with yellow silk thread.
Tail. One or two whisks from a dun hackle.
Wings. Mottled feather from the mallard, stained olive.
Legs. A light dun hackle also stained yellowish in the same dye.

To make it buzz, the mottled feather of the mallard stained olive, may be used and tied on in the manner shewn in the imitation of the Green Drake, (No. 28).

The Light Amber Spinner, to which this fly changes, lives in its new state about four days. It is used successfully on the evenings of warm days.

No. 20. *Black Gnat*

(Ronalds' note: This is not a Gnat, although commonly called one by fishermen.)

This insect skims the brook all the day long in immense crowds, flying at great speed for about ten yards up and down the stream. When night approaches, or on cold wet days, it may be found on the grass at the water side. The stomachs of Trout have been found nearly gorged with this fly. It is in season from the beginning of May until the end of June.

Imitation
Body. Black ostrich herl.
Wings. The dark part of a feather from the starling.
Legs. A black hackle.

To make it buzz, a light dun hackle tinged with brown may be wound upon the above body.

No. 21. *Downhill Fly*

This fly may be found upon the trunks of any kind of trees or post near the water side. As soon as it alights, it turns its head downward. It is in season throughout May and June, and may be used with most success on windy days.

Imitation
Body. Orange floss silk tied with ash-coloured silk thread, which may be shewn at the tail and shoulders.
Wings. From a feather of the woodcock.
Legs. A furnace hackle, (i.e. a red cock's hackle, with a black list upon the middle, and tinged with black also at the extremities of the fibres). This should be warped all down the body, and the fibres snipped off again nearly up to where the wings are set on, leaving a sufficient quantity for the legs uncut.

* * *

No. 22. *Little Brown Dun* (Turkey Brown.)
Order, *Neuroptera*.
Family, *Ephemeridae*.
Genus, *Ephemera*.

No. 23. *Little Dark Spinner*
Order, *Neuroptera*.
Family, *Ephemeridae*.
Genus, *Ephemera*.

No. 24. *Yellow Sally*
Order, *Neuroptera*.
Family, *Perlidae*.
Genus, *Perla*.
Species, *Lutea*.

No. 22. *Little Brown Dun*

This fly comes from a water larva, lives two days as shewn, and then turns to the Little Dark Spinner, (see No. 23). It is to be used on cold days; is a very good fly upon some waters; and is in season from about the time that the March Brown becomes scarce, until the end of June.

Imitation

Body. Dark brown floss silk ribbed with purple silk thread.
Tail. A whisk or two of a red cock's hackle, stained as for the legs.
Wings. Tip of the brownest feather from a partridge's tail.
Legs. Red cock's hackle stained a good brown with copperas.

To make it buzz, a feather from the grouse may be tied on, in the manner shewn in the imitation of the Green Drake, No. 28.

No. 23. *Little Dark Spinner*

This is the metamorphosis of the Turkey Brown, (No. 22.) It is a most killing fly just at the beginning of dusk.

Imitation

Body. Mulberry-coloured floss silk ribbed over with purple silk thread.
Tail. Three or four whisks out the stained hackle feather which is used for the legs.
Wings. From a feather of the starling's wing.
Legs. From a purple stained hackle which shines with a dark tortoiseshell tint, when held up between the eye and the light.

No. 24. *Yellow Sally*

This fly comes from a water nympha. It has been believed by some persons to last in season only six days, but it continues for six weeks or more, and may be used profitably on very hot days when it is busily employed laying its eggs upon the water.

Imitation

Body. Any yellow fur ribbed with fawn coloured silk.
Wings. From a wing feather of a white hen stained yellow.
Legs. From an extremely pale ginger hackle, or a white feather dyed of a yellowish ginger tint.

* * *

No. 25. *Sky Blue*
Order, *Neuroptera*.
Family, *Ephemeridae*.
Genus, *Baetis*.

No. 26. *Fern Fly* (Soldier)
Order, *Coleoptera*.
Family, *Telephoridae*.
Genus, *Telephorus*.
Species, *Livaidus*.

No. 27. *Alder Fly* (Orl Fly)
Order, *Neuroptera*.
Family, *Sialidae*.
Genus, *Sialis*.
Species, *Niger*.

No. 25. *Sky Blue*

This fly comes from a water nympha, maintains its present state of existence two or three days, and then changes to a much lighter fly or spinner, which lives three or four days.

Imitation

Body. Pale ginger mohair mixed with light blue fur.
Tail. A whisk or two of the hackle used for the legs.
Wings. From a feather of the sea swallow, or of a very light blue dun hen.
Legs. Hackle stained a pale yellow.

The body of the above mentioned spinner is more brilliant than that of the Sky Blue; the wings perfectly transparent, and almost colourless: it is very little used.

No. 26. *Fern Fly*

Two of the most common varieties of this genus are known by the appellations of the soldier and the sailor, one wears a red the other a blue coat, both are much admired by fish, and taken until the end of July, principally on hot days. They live upon other insects, such as the aphides, or plant-lice.

Imitation
Body. Orange floss silk.
Wings. The darkest part of a feather from the starling's wing.
Legs. A red cock's hackle.

To make it buzz, a furnace-hackle is wound upon the above body. It kills well thus made.

No. 27. *Alder Fly*

This fly comes from a water nympha. It is earlier on some waters than on others. It lays its eggs upon the leaves of trees which overhang the water, and delights to skim the brook, but it may also be found at some distance from it. It is in season from about the last week in May until the end of June.

Imitation
Body. Dark mulberry floss silk, or peacock's herl, tied with black silk.
Wings. From a feather of a brown hen's wing.
Legs. Dark amber stained hackle, or in case of need a black cock's hackle will answer the purpose.

To make it buzz, a dark dun hackle tinged brown may be wound upon the above body.

* * *

Flies for June

No. 28. *Green Drake* (May Fly, Cadow)
Order, *Neuroptera*.
Family, *Ephemeridae*.
Genus, *Ephemera*.
Species, *Vulgata*.

No. 29. *Grey Drake* (Glossy-winged Drake)
Order, *Neuroptera*.
Family, *Ephemeridae*.
Genus, *Ephemera*.
Species, *Vulgata*.

No. 28. *Green Drake*

This fly proceeding from a water nympha lives three or four days as shewn; then the female changes to the Grey Drake, (No. 29) and the male to the Black Drake. The Green Drake cannot be said to be in season quite three weeks on an average. Its season depends greatly upon the state of the weather; and it will be found earlier upon the slowly running parts of the stream, (such as mill dams) than on the rapid places.

Imitation

Body. The middle part is of pale straw-coloured floss silk, ribbed with silver twist. The extremities are of a brown peacock's herl, tied with light brown silk thread.

Tail. Three rabbit's whiskers.

Wings & Legs. Made buzz from a mottled feather of the mallard, stained olive.

To make it with wings in their state of rest, part of a feather similarly stained must be used, and a pale brown partridge feather must be wrapped round the same body under the wings.

No. 29. *Grey Drake*

This is the metamorphosis of the female Green Drake. She lives three or four days, and is caught by the fish whilst laying her eggs on the water. She lasts a few days longer than the Green Drake, and is to be fished with in the evening. Some fishermen prefer other flies in season to this; when well made, it will however furnish excellent sport especially towards the evening. The buzz form is intended to imitate it when struggling and half drowned.

Imitation

Body. The middle part is of white floss silk, ribbed over neatly with silver twist. The extremities are of a brown peacock's herl tied with brown silk thread.
Tails. Three rabbit's whiskers.
Wings & Legs. Made buzz from a mottled feather of the mallard, stained a faint purple.

To make it with wings at rest, the same pale purple feather may be used for them, and a dark purple stained hackle for the legs, upon the above body.

The *Black Drake*

Is the male Green Drake metamorphosed. Its term of existence is about the same as that of the female above mentioned. It is smaller than the female, and is erroneously supposed by some, who call him the Death Drake, to kill her. He is never in season without her; but is not here represented because he is not so fat and tempting a bait.

* * *

No. 30. *Marlow Buzz*. (Hazel Fly, Coch-a-bonddu, Shorn Fly)
Order, *Coleoptera*.
Family, *Chrysomelidae*.
Genus, *Vhrysomela*.
Species, *Populi*.

No. 31. *Dark Mackerel*
Order, *Neuroptera*.
Family, *Ephemeridae*.
Genus, *Ephemera*.

No. 30. *Marlow Buzz*

This insect comes from a pupa which inhabits the earth. It is very abundant in hot weather at the water side, from the beginning until the middle of June, flying about amongst poplar trees, and feeding upon the leaves.

Imitation

Body.   Black ostrich herl twisted with peacock herl and black silk thread.
Wings & Legs.   Made buzz with a dark furnace cock's hackle.

There are other varieties of the Red Beetle, and Lady Bird, which may be imitated in a similar manner, and used when numerous.

To make it with wings at rest, the darkest part of the starling's wing, and a red cock's hackle may be wound upon the above body in the same way as for the Fern Fly, No. 26.

No. 31. *Dark Mackerel*

This is the name given to the insect after it has changed from a dark kind of Green Drake. Both the male and female change to the dark brown, but the former is the smallest fly. Their habits are similar in every respect to the Green and the Grey Drake, (Nos. 28 and 29). Sir H. Davy says, that "the Green Ephemera, or May Fly, lays her eggs sitting on the water." (Salmonia, p. 249.) My observations lead to the conviction that the Green Ephemera lays no eggs, (being an imperfect insect) but that her metamorphosis, the Dark Mackerel, lays eggs (whilst rising and falling, etc.) This fly continues in season until the end of June, or for a few days in July.

Imitation

Body.   Dark mulberry floss silk, ribbed with gold twist.
Tail.   Three rabbit's whiskers.
Wings.   From a brown mottled feather of the mallard, which hangs from the back over a part of the wing.
Legs.   A purple dyed hackle, appearing a dark tortoise-shell hue, when held between the eye and the light.

* * *

Flies for July

No. 32. *Pale Evening Dun*
Order, *Neuroptera*.
Family, *Ephemeridae*.
Genus, *Cloeon*.

No. 33. *July Dun*
Order, *Neuroptera*.
Family, *Ephemeridae*.
Genus, *Ephemera*.

No. 34. *Gold Eyed Gauze Wing*
Order, *Neuroptera*.
Family, *Hemerobilidae*.
Genus, *Hemerobius*.
Species, *Perla*.

No. 32. *Pale Evening Dun*

This fly comes from a water nympha, lives two or three days as shewn, and then changes to a brighter yellow bodied fly. It may be strongly recommended as a fly which can be used when the water is fine.

Imitation
Body. Yellow martin's fur spun on pale fawn-coloured silk thread.
Wings. From a very fine grained feather of the starling's wing, stained rather lighter than that which is used for the Green Drake, No. 28.
Legs. Pale dun hackle.

The brighter yellow bodied fly to which this changes lives four or five days, is fainter coloured, and more transparent in the wing. The change is not given, as the Dark Mackerel (No. 31) is very much preferable for the evening.

No. 33. *July Dun*

This fly comes from a water nympha, lives three or four days as shewn, and then changes to a very small Dark Spinner. It affords a great treat to the Trout and Grayling, and lasts until the August Dun takes its place, in the beginning of August.

Imitation
Body. Mole's fur, and pale yellow mohair mixed and spun on yellow silk.
Tail. Two or three whisks of a dark dun hackle.
Wings. Dark part of a feather from the starling's wing, stained darker in strong onion dye.
Legs. Dark dun hackle.

To make it buzz, a lighter hackle may be wound upon the above body.

The tint of its metamorphosis is the same as that of the Dark Mackerel, No. 31. It will catch well late in the evening.

No. 34. *Gold Eyed Gauze Wing*

This is rather a scarce insect upon some waters, but where it is found affords great sport on windy days. Both larger and smaller individuals than that represented of this green sort are to be found, and also a brown kind much larger and with dark round spots upon it. The eye possesses wonderful brilliancy. It may be used as soon as the Green Drake goes out, for about three weeks, (i.e.) towards the middle or end of this month.

Imitation

Body. Very pale green floss silk, tied on with silk thread of the same colour.

Wings & Legs. The palest blue dun hackle which can be procured.

* * *

No. 35. *Frog Hopper* (Pale Brown Bent Hopper, Wren Tail)
Order, *Hemoptera*.
Family, *Cercopidae*.
Genus, *Cercopis*.
Species, *Spumaria*.

No. 36. *Red Ant*
Order, *Hymenoptera*.
Family, *Formicidae*.
Genus, *Formica*.
Species, *Rufa*.

No. 37. *Silver Horns* (Black Silver Twist)
Order, *Trichoptera*.
Family, *Leptoceridae*.
Genus, *Leptocerus*.

No. 35. *Frog Hopper*

There are many varieties of this insect; the pale brown, the dark brown, and the greenish blue, are the most common. It is very busy on hot days hopping about and taking flights of about twenty yards, and this is the time to use it, for it sometimes drops short and falls upon the water. In colder weather it is found upon the long grass principally; not much on the water. On very cold days it seems to seek shelter near the roots of the grass.

Imitation
Body. Ginger-coloured fur ribbed with gold twist.
Wings & Legs. Feather from a wren's tail.

No. 36. *Red Ant*

This insect is very abundant on the water after a swarm or flight of Ants and Emmets, the time of which is uncertain. There are two sorts; the black and the red of the size shewn, and two sorts much smaller which are used later in the season.

Imitation
Body. Peacock's herl tied with red-brown silk.
Wings. From a feather of the light part of a starling's wing.
Legs. A red cock's hackle.

The *Black Ant* is made of peacock's herl, and black ostrich mixed, for the body. Wings from the darkest part of the starling's wing, and legs a black cock's hackle.

No. 37. *Silver Horns*

This fly is extremely abundant upon some waters, and is well taken both by the Trout and Grayling until the end of August throughout the day, and principally in showery weather. The figure represents the female. The male has black horns.

Imitation
Body. Black ostrich herl tied with black silk, and dressed off.
Wings. Feather from a wing of the cock blackbird.
Legs. Small black cock's hackle.
Horns. Grey feather of the mallard.

To make it buzz, the body is ribbed with silver twist upon the black ostrich herl, and a black hackle wrapt all down.

* * *

Flies for August

No. 38. *August Dun*
Order, *Neuroptera*.
Family, *Ephemeridae*.
Genus, *Baetis*.

No. 39. *Orange Fly*
Order, *Hymenoptera*.
Family, *Ichneumonidae*.
Genus, *Cryptis*.

No. 40. *Cinnamon Fly*
Order, *Trichoptera*.
Family, *Phryganidae*.
Genus, *Phryganea*.

No. 38. *August Dun*

This fly comes from a water nympha, lives two or three days then changes to a Red Spinner. It is quite as important a fly for this month as the March Brown is for March. It is in season from the beginning of August to the middle of September.

Imitation

Body. Brown floss silk ribbed with yellow silk thread.
Tail. Two rabbit's whiskers.
Wings. Feather of a brown hen's wing.
Legs. Plain red hackle stained brown.

It is made buzz with a grouse feather wound upon the above body.

The Red Spinner, to which it changes, is very similar to that which the Blue Dun (No. 2) turns to, and is a good fly on a mild evening.

No. 39. *Orange Fly*

This is one of the best flies that can be used both for Trout and Grayling. There are a great many varieties, some larger, some smaller than the representation. It may be used all day. Although discovered alive with difficulty, it is found abundant in the stomachs of the fish. It is furnished with an apparatus called the sting, used for the purpose of piercing the skin of caterpillars, in which it deposits its eggs, the grub from which grows in, and ultimately kills the insect in which it was hatched.

Imitation
Body. Orange floss silk tied on with black silk thread.
Wings. Dark part of the starling's wing, or feather of a hen blackbird.
Legs. A very dark furnace hackle.

No. 40. *Cinnamon Fly*

This fly comes from a water pupa. There are many varieties. The larger variety being stronger can resist the force of rain and wind better than that represented, and are therefore not so well known to the fish. It should be used in a heavy shower, and also on a windy day. In both cases very great diversion may be expected with it.

Imitation
Body. Pale ginger or fawn-coloured floss silk, tied on with thread of the same colour.
Wings. Feather of a yellow brown hen's wing.
Legs. A very pale ginger hackle.

It is made buzz with a grouse feather or a red brown hackle stained with copperas, and tied on the same body.

* * *

Flies for September

No. 41. *Blue Bottle*
Order, *Diptera*.
Family, *Muscidae*.
Genus, *Musca*.
Species, *Vomitoria*.

No. 42. *Whirling Blue Dun*
Order, *Neuroptera*.
Family, *Ephemeridae*.
Genus, *Baetis*.

No. 43. *Little Pale Blue Dun*
Order, *Neuroptera*.
Family, *Ephemeridae*.
Genus, *Cloeon*.

No. 44. *Willow Fly*
Order, *Neuroptera*.
Family, *Perlidae*.
Genus, *Nemoura*.
Species, *Nebulosa*.

No. 41. *Blue Bottle*

This and the house fly become blind and weak in this month, and are therefore frequently driven on to the water on windy days, when very good sport may be expected with them. The Blue Bottle is perhaps to be preferred. It may be used until cold weather sets in.

Imitation

Body.   Bright blue floss silk tied with light brown silk thread.
Wings.   Feather of the starling's wing.
Legs.   Black hackle from a cock wrapped down the principal part of the body.

To make it buzz, a dun hackle may be wound upon the above body.

No. 42. *Whirling Blue Dun*

This fly comes from a water nympha, lives about three days as shewn, then turns to a Light Red Spinner. It is in season until the middle of October, and on the water chiefly in blustering cold weather. It has been supposed to be a second edition of the Yellow Dun of April. If compared with that it will be found rather smaller and more of a ginger colour.

Imitation

Body. Squirrel's red brown fur mixed with yellow mohair, tied with yellow silk thread well waxed.
Tail. One or two whisks of a pale ginger hackle.
Wings. Feather from a starling's wing.
Legs. Pale ginger hackle.

The *Red Spinner* lives three or four days.

No. 43. *Little Pale Blue Dun*

This fly comes from a water nympha, lives two or three days as shewn, then changes to a more delicate fly than that represented. It is upon the water at the same time as the Whirling Blue, (No. 42) and lasts until the end of the fishing season. It is very abundant, and taken equally well by both Trout and Grayling.

Imitation

Body. Very pale blue fur mixed with a very little yellow mohair.
Wings. Feather from the dotterel or sea swallow.
Legs. The palest blue hackle to be had.

To make it buzz, a dotterel feather only may be wound upon the same body.

The metamorphosis of this fly has very transparent wings. It is too delicate to be imitated.

No. 44. *Willow (or Withy) Fly*

This fly comes from a water pupa. It is extremely abundant during this month and the next, and even later in the season. On very fine days it may even be found on the water in February. It generally flutters across the stream, and is best imitated buzz fashion.

Imitation

Body. Mole's fur spun upon yellow silk.
Wings & Legs. A dark dun cock's hackle strongly tinged a copper hue.

* * *

No. 45. *Red Palmer*

This is the caterpillar of the Artica caga or Tiger Moth. I have found this palmer more abundantly than any other early in the Spring, and can recommend use of it to be made as soon as the water is fit for fishing after a flood, also on windy days.

Imitation
Peacock herl with a red hackle from a cock wrapped over it, and tied with dark brown silk thread.

No. 46. *Brown Palmer*

This is the caterpillar of the Spilosoma lubricepeda, or common Ermine Moth.

It will catch fish throughout the fishing season, and may be used with most success after a flood and on windy days.

Imitation
Mulberry-coloured worsted spun on brown silk thread, and a brown stained hackle of a cock wrapped over the whole of it.

No. 47. *Black Palmer*

This is the caterpillar of the Laciocampa rubi, or Fox Moth. It is used at the same times as the Brown Palmer.

Imitation
Black ostrich herl ribbed with gold twist, and a red cock's hackle wrapped over it.

These forty-seven patterns, each pictorially represented in colour, comprise Alfred Ronalds' contribution to the literature of fly fishing. And such magnificent plates as these, which created a sensation on their first publication, have not been equalled to this day, and are rivalled in excellence by one twentieth century work only. True, there may be slight inaccuracies, and alterations of scientific names, but this work of Ronalds stands by itself for sheer excellence and artistry. It is the beacon which set and illumined the course to be followed by succeeding angler-entomologists. And it still stands as a beacon in our own day, and the only British work which can be said to rank in excellence with it is Martin E. Mosely's beautifully illustrated *Dry-fly Fisherman's Entomology*, which was published in 1921—85 years after

Ronalds. In honesty, however, it is but fair to state that the honours for superb illustration of insects must pass to France, for, in 1927, Antoine Vavon published *La Truite et ses Mœurs et l'Art de sa Pêcher* a work which contains the most exquisite plates, again, however, the better part of a century after Ronalds. So it cannot be questioned that, though he was by no means the first to attempt the illustration of river flies in colour, Ronalds was the first to raise and establish a very high standard of illustration, and that he was much in advance of his time with his art. His achievement seems to be all the more worthy since Ronalds himself could hardly have been more modest. In his Preface, he begins: "The Author of this little work entreats that it may be considered and judged of as the labour, or rather the amusement, of an amateur . . ." And the tone of the whole book is equally modest and sincerely so.

Ronalds seems to have collected his specimens from the river Blythe, near Uttoxeter, in Staffordshire; and he tells us that it was here that he studied the ways and habits of trout. The models from which Ronalds drew his figures, according to Martin E. Mosely, are stated to form part of the collection in the Hope Department in the Oxford University Museum.

The various types of "imitations" may be usefully compared with the patterns and style of dressing of the North Country. For the winging of his flies, Ronalds uses two pieces of feather and binds these on with the butt-ends towards the top of the hook-shank. And he recommends that where a pattern is to be made "buzz," the hackle or feather used should be of a lighter tint than that of the natural wings. Of hooks, which, oddly enough, seem to be a weak point of his drawings, the Kirby, the Limerick, and the Carlisle hooks are recommended.

H. C. CUTCLIFFE

Devonshire produces many good things, and not the least of these from the piscatorial point of view is a practical little volume by H. C. Cutcliffe entitled *Trout Fishing on Rapid Streams*. It is an intensely interesting work for the student of the trout fly not only for the soundness of those remarks concerning fly-dressing materials and method of fly-dressing but because of the entirely distinct approach to the whole question of representation and presentation of the trout fly. The work is rightly

regarded by collectors as a minor classic, and quotation at length soon reveals the expert behind the pen.

Of materials Cutcliffe writes:

"Now take out the books. Here is one with furs—a squirrel's white-tipped tail peeps already at us; and hare's flax, rabbit's flax, and water rat's we are sure cannot be far off. Here is another containing similar treasures; but now comes the most valuable, the highest treasured of all—the book with hackles, oh these precious beauties! Does one project beyond its especial case? Take it gently, handle it respectfully, and place it tenderly where no harm can reach it; where it may rest undisturbed, by the leaves turned over in search for some particular feather you know is placed in its proper and appropriate position, refresh your memory with another view of these rare feathers, and assort each and all carefully, that you may know where, at a thought, to put your hand on the very one of the exact shade you may require—yes, but the books are full, and of what—how do you know what furs and what feathers will be useful and necessary? Of the former many, of the latter, a few—for furs, we cannot well do without, for general fishing, the hare's flax, and a word about this. Hares, everybody knows, have different colours in different parts of their bodies, and all hares are not of the same colour, and we must have the flax of many of various colours, each placed separately, in convenient place by itself. Now first catch your hare, and let this one be an old Jack hare, at the end of the season—March hare if you can find one insane enough to be caught; brush or stroke his flax down very carefully over the back, and make it quite smooth, and then take a very sharp razor and shave him downwards, only over the back; you do not of course lather or even wet his hair, but shave him dry, and when you have removed all the cut hair, you will find the remaining stumps looking black and below this the fur is light fawn colour, or almost white; you have indeed removed all that portion of the flax which gives the hare its peculiar colour, which you are requiring, and have left the less desirable part or roots of the hair attached to the skin. Shave an old doe and a leveret, the younger the better; and you will find the younger flax more fawn colour, and not black or red; whilst the older flax is darker, interspersed with

some blackish hairs, and has a red or rusty shade shot as it were throughout it—be particular to have an abundance and much variety of hares' flax—no other flax equals it; skin the ears and keep the ears entire; take a pad, and cut out the forehead, the rest you do not want: get some fur from a fox's skin; the pate of some foxes makes a very rich body, the difficulty is to get a hackle to match it; and the entire skin of a very young cub. Water rat—entire skins must be kept; be sure you get water and not house rat, or at least have both; some of the latter, which have fine and silky hair, are useful; the coarser reject. A mole's skin is useful; its fur is convenient to mix with others of brighter and more lively tint. Some rabbit skin, the same parts corresponding to the hare. Some squirrel skin, the darker over the back the better, these will be found redder, the lighter ones being carroty. A field mouse, a house mouse, and a little otter's fur, with some bullock's hair, of dark almost purplish tint, which may be obtained by searching along the palings in paddocks where bullocks are kept, and you will find some little tufts appended to the numerous projecting points along the rails, rubbed off and carded as it were by the animals scratching their sides against the sharp points projecting from the timber; or, in old cob walls, often little delicate tufts of useful shade may be pulled out, having been doubtless changed in colour by the action of lime; but I prefer that which I take from the rails as it is always finer, and therefore more easily used by itself, or mixed with other furs. These constitute the essential furs for general fishing for rapid and small streams. I could be quite contented with a restriction to the hare's and squirrel's flax. Sometimes furs are dyed, and it is useful to have a rabbit's and hare's skin dyed in one's box; this is usually done by soaking the fur for a day or two in turmeric—with a little alum. A new series of shades is given the fur; the roots of the hair are bright yellow; then comes the black; and the extreme points acquire a brighter hue of their former colour, from some hairs taking a yellowish tinge, thus as it were heightening the tone of the former shades. The ends must be shorn off as before directed, and will not lose their dye by washing in water. With these furs, we must have gold and silver twist, of various sizes and thickness, and some gold and silver tinsel flattened will be often serviceable."

Continuing, Cutcliffe goes on to say of feathers:

"As regards feathers, we have for making winged flies (which I however seldom or never use in small rapid streams) the woodcock, the starling, the wren, the pheasant wing, and tail of cock and hen, blackbird and thrush, snipe, partridge, lark, and the tail feathers of a peacock, a large supply of which should be obtained, as a great variation in colour may be observed in the feathers of this bird; some have a greenish tinge and are little used by me; some are copperish, and less frequently employed; but others have a bright golden lustre, sobering down to a rich red black, and these of all others I prefer. Peacocks' feathers and woodcock's wing are the only necessary feathers here named, the others it is well to have by one in case of our going on the large quiet river, but for rapid fishing, the winged fly is seldom required."

Of hooks for fly-dressing Cutcliffe prefers the Kirby bend made by Hutchinson & Co. of Kendal; and, having expressed that preference, continues:

"There is another article of the greatest importance to the fishermen, the wax as used by cobblers and saddlers. We ought to be very particular in procuring good wax. It should not be so hard as to be friable, nor so soft as when rolled into a ball and placed on a board to spread itself into a flattened mass, but just of sufficient consistency to maintain its rotundity and globular form; and it should, moreover, stick well to the silk. Some little difference will be found in the varieties of silk, one colour or kind taking the wax better than another—the yellow I have usually found the best: if the silk be not nicely and well waxed before we commence tying our fly, we shall not get the body on well, or shall run a great risk of the gut slipping out of the splicing connecting it to the hook.

A pair of tweezers are convenient for attachment to our hackle when we are fastening off the end, but are not necessary; the back of a small pen-knife answers well, using the base of the blade when open to press upon the back spring of the handle of the knife.

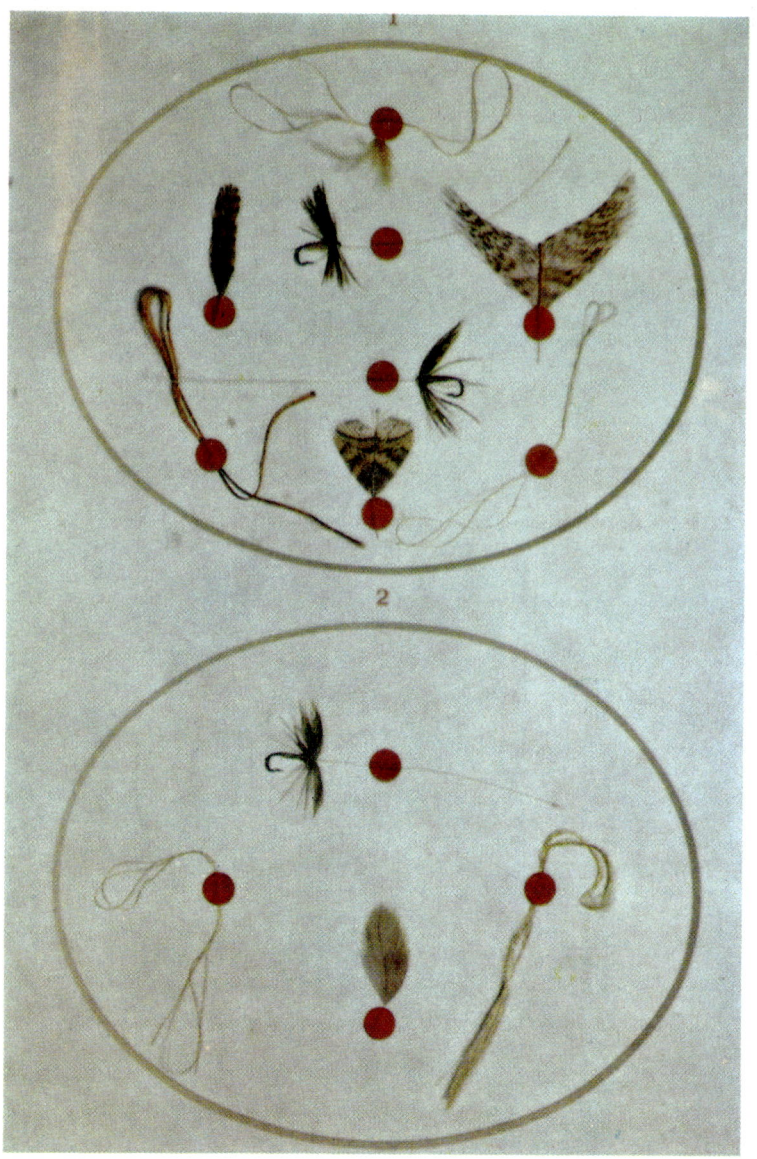

Traditional Derbyshire Trout Flies, with the materials used for their making (UPPER: the local or Derbyshire March Brown; LOWER: the Spring or Dottrill Dun). From Aldam's *Quaint Treatise*

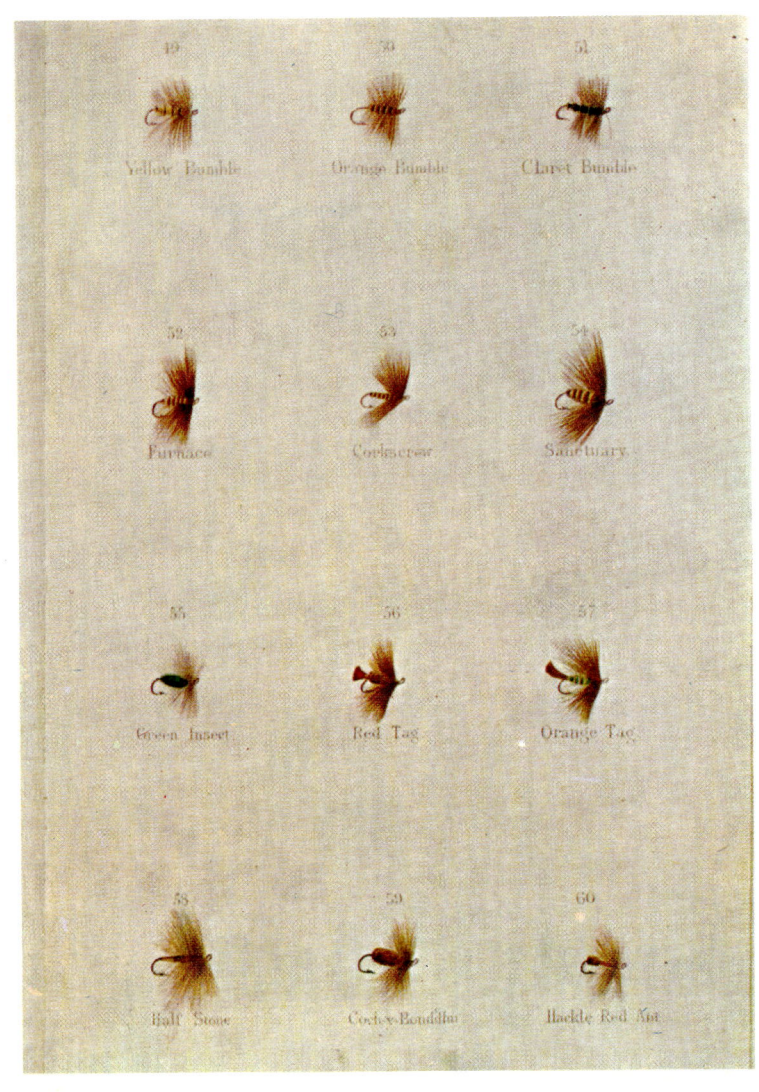

A plate from Halford's famous first work: *Floating Flies and How to Dress Them*

And now we must speak of hackles—which are very various in description and colour; and as of all the parts of a fly the hackle is the most important, much attention and care should be bestowed upon the selection and collection of these feathers. Many hackles may be obtained of good colour, but indifferent shape, or good shape and bad colour, or a colour which though good when out of the water is bad when immersed in it. A hackle then should be of a brilliant lustre, reflecting and sparkling in the light, when moved about in the finger; if the colour of the shining part of the hackle be red, the root or that part nearest the insertion of the feather should be black or nearly so, and the under side of the feather should be dark; also, if blue, (or what the fishermen calls blue, the natural living colour of such feathers) the root should be nearly black, (a little down will always be found close to the root of the feather, this must always be pulled off, as it does not form a part of what the fisherman terms the hackle—it seems an appendage, or perhaps young and undeveloped fibres) in fact in all feathers, excepting very light blues, the root should be the darkest part of the hackle. In dark hackles the tip and extreme edges of the fibres forming the feather, should be darker than the centre. All hackles should be plucked from a cock's neck; hens' hackles are worse than useless in rapid streams; they have no stiffness, cannot resist the force of the water washing on them, and consequently lie flat along the hook, lose all the little colour they have when dry, and make your fly hook more like a little oval black mass of dirt, rather than a living insect; few fish would attempt so uninviting a morsel as this represents. The shape of the feather should be an isosceles triangle, having its base at that end which is inserted into the skin, and its elongated apex, slenderly, gradually, and evenly tapering off to a fine point—many will be found suddenly ending in a rounded extremity, these are not so good, but some of them if of fine colour may be retained. Then the hackle must be stiff and elastic, the fibres standing out independently and boldly from the midrib or stalk of the feather, like so many bristles set each at exactly the same angle. A common mode of trying or examining a hackle, is after pulling or stripping off the down at the root, to take it by the stem, and with the bright side upwards, place it on the sleeve of a coat, if black, or on any dark

object, when the brilliant lustre of the feather will be displayed, and then by pressing the apex against the cloth, bend it, by which we judge of its shape, the regularity of tapering of the fibres, and its stiffness and elasticity in regaining its natural shape, after being impressed and bent in any direction.

The best of all fowls for hackles is the old English game cock, which, however is now very difficult to be obtained; no bird seems to have such lustrous, shining, stiff, and well-shaped feathers as this game fowl, such as was used in times of yore for cock fighting; if these cannot be procured, any one wishing to keep a stock of fowls for feathers, will do well to purchase a blue hen from a farm yard, where most of the fowls are either blue or red and black, where indeed the breed seems especially of a blue-red or blackish colour, and mate this hen with a well-bred dark-red or black-red bantam cock; the chicken will be of a small size, but one of the cocks of dark colour (blue or red) should be mated with a hen similar to the parent hen, all the others being destroyed, and from this generation we may perpetuate a class of fowls very similar to the old game fowl; the cross with the bantam fines down the feather, makes it more delicate, better shaped, and brighter in colour; and from this stock of fowls, reds, blues, and blacks will alone be born. By choosing a red bantam we shall ensure a richness of tinge in our hackle, and procure more rusty blues and reds than plain and sober coloured feathers. These rusty feathers are by far the most rare, and by far the best when obtained; they combine several colours, and shot as it were over the surface of a rich glossy grounding in blue and red, and on scrutinizing their surface carefully we perceive the exact similarity in tints of shading to the natural colour of various furs, as the ends of hare's flax, water rat, and mouse and fox fur, pulled out and mixed well together. There is a class of fowls generally red, of the Indian breed, which are decidedly objectionable for fly fishing; the feathers look very well and pleasing when dry, but after they have been soaked in water sometime, they become soft, flabby, and of a dull hue, as though they had been dusted over with brown sand; these fowls have a white ear, and any cross with them will show the characteristic ear, which in itself is sufficient to make one reject at once any offer of their feathers. I generally pluck my fowls twice in the year; in the

spring as soon as the bird has assumed his gay summer dress, and again, late in the autumn, before moulting season, when I find many hackles which, in the spring I would not take, because too small, now however, grown of proper size: but the best time for plucking fowls depends on the condition of their bodies; often in some adjoining yards one cock is in condition for taking his feathers long before another; we must then from time to time, catch our birds and observe the condition of their feathers, their colour and maturity of growth; and when they are most bright and regularly tapered in shape, pluck out as many as are of proper size, remembering that those which are too small nearest the head usually will grow, and if we patiently wait our time, we shall be able to take them of proper size and shape. As soon as plucked they should be placed in regular order, one over-lying another, and subjected for a time to gentle pressure, which will flatten and straighten them, and prevent their coiling up, which they have a constant tendency to do, they are thus better seen, and are less likely to get rumpled and creased, and are more easy to turn when we use them. Of the different varieties of feathers as I have said, the rusty are the most valuable in all respects, and therefore we must seek to procure a good assortment of rusty blues; a series of shades in colour resembling exactly the hare's back, these feathers are beautifully spangled in yellow and gold, on a dark blue grounding, they are very scarce, and of all feathers the best for rapid stream fishing: also rusty reds—not forgetting the blood red, the black red, or a feather whose central rib, apex, and base is black, whose back or hinder surface is shining and dark, and all the intervening part dark blood-red colour; this of red feathers next the rusty is the best: then come the browns, serviceable in the early months: and the blues, from the pale, sober blue of the heron's wing, to the dark rich spangled blue of the back of a water rat, as seen when the entire fur is smoothed down. A few black, and a few white hackles, and our assortment is complete."

Before proceeding to describe the method of fly-dressing, Cutcliffe first warns against the deficiencies of "bought flies" and counsels against the accumulation of an excessive number of patterns. He advises that the fly-fisherman should dress his

own flies, and that these should be, with one possible exception—the March Brown, hackle flies. And of these hackle patterns he writes:

"The grand point in making flies is to have every part of the correct shade, it is not that all the fly, the body and hackle, should be precisely the same colours, but there must be an harmonious blending of tints, and shading of colours; and in choice of our feathers we should strive to heighten the tones of shading above the fur of the body as much as possible, keeping within the limits of general harmony, and carefully avoiding anything approaching a contrast of colours; there should be a richness, brilliancy, and variation in the aspect of our fly, so that when immersed in water, vivid shades may spangle amongst the duller hues.

I find it impossible to convey by language to the mind of the reader the different colours, shades, and tints of hackles, it will be more easy to speak of some particular fur, whose appearances we are familiar with, and then simply state that a hackle must be found to match it, by which we mean one whose shades and tints harmonize with the different colours of the fur; a good test for which is to place the hackle upon the fur we are going to use, and then observe carefully if our feather heightens in tone the shading of the natural fur. This is not the way I make flies myself; usually I select a good brilliant hackle, which I know is nearly allied to the fur I am about to use, and then if I find the fur deficient in any of the shades which the feather possesses, I mix some other fur which has the desired shade, in conspicuity above all other shades; for example, I am about to tie a fly with the hare's flax, I select what I should call a killing hackle, a superbly attractive one, and then turn to my hare's flax; now, if I find the hackle has a reddish tinge in excess above the flax, I take a little cow's hair, (if that agrees with the red shade on the feather) and mixing that with the flax in due proportion, comparing my flax and feather frequently, I at last arrive at the precise harmony of shading I desire, and then tie my fly. Sometimes a yellow or golden tinge is excessive in the feather, I then add some hare's flax which has been dyed yellow to the natural fur, and so obtain my proper colours. The greatest care must be paid to this assortment of colours; and though I speak

of using a particular fur for a body and hackle to match it, the best rule in practice is to make the fur match the hackle—it is far better to be guided by this rule in tying flies, than to copy the prescribed receipts for making a body, and then trust to the indefinite terms of a blue or brown hackle for legs and wings; and though it may appear we are not adhering so closely in our general rule to the imitation of nature, depend upon it if we have brilliancy of colour to stimulate the trout, and harmony of shades, in copy of nature, we shall, for rapid stream fishing, find our fly of the greatest practical utility."

Cutcliffe then supplements the foregoing and other wise observations with descriptions of the method of dressing his flies. He writes:

"Well then, we will if you please, make a brown fly a blue, and a red fly—and first the brown; turn to your fox's fur and pull out some from the back, turn to your darkest squirrel fur and pull out an equal quantity from the back also, and mix them with your fingers well together. Now take your hackles and find one that precisely coincides in colour with the mixture you have made, see that it be not too dark or too light, let it be rich in shades and bright in lustre, but not differing from the fur before you.

Now select your hook which may be of the size corresponding to (if you have none of them) No. 6 or 7 Hutchinson, if the water is high and the wind boisterous, let it be 7, if quiet and calm, as we supposed, No. 6 will be best, but either will do, provided the hackle you have chosen is of the proper size for it, which you judge by measuring the fibres on one side of the hackle with the hook, and they should be just a slight degree longer than the hook from the end of the shank to the bend. Pluck off all the ragged looking down from the larger end, or, base of the hackle, till the fibres from the smaller to the larger end form by their margin or extreme points a triangle; now place the stem or midrib by which it grows in the fowl, between the fore-finger and thumb of your right hand, as low down as you can hold it in the division between the thumb and finger, keep the shining surface of the feather uppermost, having the thumb closely pressed against the fore-finger; take the apex of

the hackle between your left fore-finger and thumb, and bend the feather and pull it between the thumb and fore-finger, held as before closely together, so as to subject the fibres to pressure, and on drawing the whole length of the feather through, you will find you have turned all the fibres to one side of the midrib. Now take your gut—let it be good strong round gut, not very large in circumference, but everywhere perfectly round and transparent; bite off the length you require, and you will find the bitten end flattened, put this between your teeth and impress it in three or four places, of a distance of half the length of your hook, from the extreme end; now your gut is jagged as it were and flattened, the silk will fit into the pits made, and will not allow the gut to slip; now take some strong fly-making silk, which is only a finer description of common silk, of yellow colour, wax this well, and cut off as much as you want, say ten inches. Your tweezers are by your side, and a pair of finely-pointed, well cutting scissors; and first you take the hook in your left hand, between your fore-finger and thumb, with the bend of the hook pointing towards the hand that holds it, with the barbed point downwards, and the free extremity of the shank, on which will be formed the head of the fly, pointing to your opposite or right hand; now take your waxed silk in your right hand, and with the fore-finger and thumb bind it twice around the middle third of the shank of the bare hook; take now your gut, bitten as directed, and place it on the upper surface of the shank of the hook, and let the flattened end of the gut extend forwards as far as the point where the hook is first bent, and maintain it here, together with the hook, between the fore-finger and thumb of the left hand; now seize the silk, which is pendant from the shank of the hook, and bringing it to within four-fifths of the extreme point of the shank, begin to wind it round the gut and the hook, carrying your left hand in a direction away from your person, and evenly, regularly and firmly continue your winding towards your left hand, till you have in a perfect manner covered and concealed your gut completely. Your hook is now spliced on, and for a beginner it will be well for him to try if he can pull the gut out of the splicing, as all steps which will give firmness to the hold upon the hook are now completed; and this should be done with great caution and irresistible firmness. Now place your left fore-finger

a little lower down on the shank of the hook than it was before, so as to include in its grasp the end of the silk attaching the hook to the gut. Take now a pinch of the fur you have mixed in the fore-finger and thumb of your right hand, and lay it on the silk, which is made tense the while by seizing the free end of it between the apex of the little finger and the ball of the thumb of the right hand; having laid on a bunch of fur upon the silk, and taken care that the ends of the fur are close up to the attachment of the silk to the hook, you carry your right fore-finger and thumb down over the bunch, and spread it, as it were, down over the waxed thread, and when this is properly done, you have a tapering roll of fur just adhering to your silk, the finer end nearest the attachment of the silk, and becoming thicker and more bulky as it approaches the free end; this being done, and you being satisfied that the length of your furred portion of silk is sufficient, you place your fore-finger and thumb of the right hand upon the thicker end, and twist it round, moving your thumb over your fore-finger, in a direction towards its tip or point, and rolling the fur between them, till, after several revolutions, the fur seems to be entwisted firmly, and is regularly tapered, and lies evenly, with its points tending towards the tail of the hook; you have now to bring the silk down to the free extremity, or head of the hook, and in so doing, you will make the body and splice on the hackle; continue then to wind your silk, now covered with fur, in the same direction as you began, but of course bringing it evenly downwards to your right hand, instead of upwards to your left; as soon as you have arrived at a point in the shank of the hook corresponding to the junction of the middle with the lower third, pass the silk down, so that you may hold it firmly between the little finger and palm of the left hand; this prevents your silk unwinding, and sets your right hand free to take up the hackle, which has been prepared as directed; seize, then, the hackle by its feathered and pointed extremity, and with its root, or that portion by which it grows in the skin, lying towards the left, and its finer end towards the head of the hook, and its midrib or stem placed along the back of the hook, as you are still holding it; maintain it in this position with the fore-finger and thumb of the left hand still holding the hook, and having adjusted its length, so that the tip of the feather protrudes a little below the

head of the hook, you again take up your silk from the left little finger, and continue your winding of the fur for the body, now including, together with the hook and gut, the end of the hackle as well. And now having arrived at that point, the lower four-fifths of the shank, where you first began to splice on the gut, pull off all the fur adhering to the silk, and wax it again thoroughly, and quite close up to the hook, and then wind it twice around the projecting small end of the hackle you have spliced on. Now pass the silk, as before, between the hook and the gut, that it may not slip, and just hang the long end of the silk over the gut, to keep it out of the way whilst you cut off the protruding little end of the hackle close to the silk; trim up the body by pulling out any fur that may be bushy, and arrange the hackle for winding it on; see that all the fibres stand off at a right angle to the stem, and do not intrude upon one another, but at equal distance project in their proper direction. Now being satisfied with the body of the fly which is completed, there but remains to wind on the hackle for legs and wings, and fasten the end so that it may not slip, and in so doing, we shall have made the head to our fly. Now, still holding the hook as at first and throughout the whole process, clasp the root of the hackle between your right fore-finger and thumb, and wind the hackle in the same direction that you passed your hand in forming the body, at first over the little fur which intervenes between the point of attachment of the hackle and the bare silk below; make your turns at first more distant from one another than afterwards, but judge how close they should be by the length of your hackle, and the distance intervening between its point of attachment and the extreme end of the hook, remembering that you must leave a little of the hook at the head uncovered (about one-sixth of the whole length of the straight part of the shank.) In winding on the hackle, you must be particularly careful not to allow one pass of the feather to rumple or overlap any portion of another; the fibres should incline outwards and a little downwards, towards the tail of the fly; and to obtain the proper direction of the fibres and prevent any overlaying of the turns of the feather, you may, by a half-twist of the stalk of the feather between your right fore-finger and thumb, cause each successive layer of feather to lie smoothly up over the preceding one, which will keep also the fibres out of your way, and allow you to see

the precise position of the midrib or stalk of the hackle. Having now wound on all the feather you intend, and having brought the last turn near the free extremity of the shank of the hook, you may take the remaining bare stalk between the middle or ring finger, and compress it between its extremity and the first joint of the thumb, to prevent its becoming loose, and you must firmly hold and draw upon this, as the midrib of the feather is very stiff, and tends speedily to unwind itself when coiled up. If tweezers are at hand, you may attach them to the end of the root of the feather, or if not, you must proceed to fasten off the end, and form the head of the fly, which is done by taking the silk you left between the hook and the stalk of the feather, having by three or four turns spliced the end of the feather to the shank of the hook, you now, keeping the silk tense with the fingers of your left hand pressing on the palm, smooth down all the prominent fibres of the hackle, and include all evenly in your grasp between the thumb and fore-finger of the left hand, and this being arranged smoothly, you take again the silk, and after bestowing a little more wax close to the attachment, make several half-hitches, which are simply formed by passing the silk around the hook loosely, so as to form a bow, through which you slip the end of the silk, and draw it tight; or instead of ending and forming your head by half-hitches, you may lay the end of the silk upwards over the hackle, and grasp it with the hackle, and then taking the silk at a short distance from its attachment, splice the root of the feather to the end of the silk (now doubled back) and the gut altogether—five or six turns will suffice, when, by drawing upon the end of the silk which you find passing through the splicing you have made, you can pull all the loop you left tight, and cut the silk off close to where it appears from beneath the turns below it. The fly is now complete, and you have only to overlook it, and arrange any irregularity in the position of the fibres of the hackle or the fur forming the body of the fly. I may here mention a mode of partially curling the hackle, by which we secure a more precise regularity and order of lying: it is thus done—first you take the fly in the left hand and hold it by the hook, having the bend inclining downwards; you now, with a pin or penknife divide the fibres of the feather on either side, and press the fly between the fingers so as to make the feathers lie in the direction

now given them, that is, one half standing up and the other downwards, in the direction of the bend of the hook; now, by stroking these fibres between the thumb and the edge of a penknife held obliquely towards them, and commencing from close to the roots, we shall give them a curve which sets off a fly, gives it a more finished appearance, and so divides the fibres of the hackle, as to assume the direction of the wings and legs of a natural fly, the uppermost representing the wings, and the lower ones the legs. Whether this is of any practical advantage, I leave the reader to judge, merely stating that I do not believe that it is, so far as the representation of the natural fly is concerned; but by placing the fibres so as to maintain only two directions, I think it gives them greater firmness to resist the action of rapid current washing upon them, than when they are permitted to stand out in a circle around the hook."

Cutcliffe preferred his own patterns to the standard flies of his time, and, whatever may be thought of his theory concerning actual representation of natural insects, he did much to bring out the importance of quality of materials used for fly-dressing. He held the view—and rightly so—that a trout fly of a general character dressed with first-quality fur- and feather-material would prove more consistently effective than any precise representation dressed with inferior materials. That is the important lesson he teaches. It is one that applies with no less validity and force to-day.

The type of trout fly advocated by Cutcliffe still is extremely effective in competent hands for the fishing of the streams for which it was originally designed. The trout of North Devon have not changed, save, perhaps, in numbers and wariness, and they still respond to a well placed, bright and lively fly. The patterns which follow, therefore, are not to be written-off as old-fashioned or in any sense inferior to modern patterns: they are well-worth re-examination and re-consideration.

List of Artificial Flies

(N.B. "Wherever hare's flax is mentioned, the ends shaved off as before directed are intended to be understood, unless otherwise specially stated.

"The hooks used are Messrs. Hutchinson's, of Kendal, Westmoreland, and of their Kirby bend.
"The silk used in tying these flies should be of a straw colour.
"The yellow dye alluded to is a strong solution of turmeric, in which a lump of alum has been dissolved, and in which the furs are boiled for some minutes.")

February

No. 1. Size, No. 7.
Body: Equal parts of fox's and squirrel's fur, from the back.
Hackle: Rusty brownish blue.

No. 2. Size No. 7 or 6.
Body: Equal parts,—House rat's and light brown sable's fur, or fur taken from the tail of the brown sable alone.
Hackle: Silvery speckled brown.

No. 3. Size, No. 7 or 6.
Body: (a) Dark peacock's herl. Rib: gold twist, or (b) Cow's hair of a purple tint. Rib: gold twist.
Hackle: Black red.

No. 4.
Body: Equal parts of hare's flax dyed yellow, water rat's fur undyed, and of rabbit's flax undyed. Rib: straw-coloured silk.
Hackle: Smoky Blue.
(N.B. This is a greenish-coloured body. This fly may be made up lighter or darker, both in body and in hackle.)

No.5.
Body: The same as No. 2. Rib: gold twist.
Hackle: As positively brown or drab-coloured, as can be got.

No. 6. Size, No. 7 to 5.
Body: Equal parts of brown bullock's hair and of the ends of squirrel fur. Rib: gold twist.
Wing: Pheasant, or
Hackle: Blueish red.

No. 7. Size, No. 6 or 5.
Body: The black flax from a rabbit's tail, some flax from the eyelid, ditto from the back, all from a skin dyed in the yellow dye.
Wing: Thrush, or
Hackle: Blue to match the body.

No. 8. Size, No. 7 to 5.
Body: Finest cow's hair, such as you can pick out of a wren's nest. Rib: straw-coloured silk.
Hackle: Dark rusty blue.
(The above will all kill, particularly No. 2 & 5.)

March

No. 9. Size, No. 7 to 5.
Body: Hare's flax, and water rat's fur mixed. Rib: straw-coloured silk.
Hackle: Very rusty blue, inclining to a brown, not to a red.

No. 10. Size, No. 6.
Body: Light claret-coloured silk.
Hackle: Smoky blue.

No. 11. Size, No. 5 or 4.
Body: Yellow mohair, and the roots of the flax from a hare's back, dyed in the yellow dye.
Hackle: Light smoky blue.

No. 12. Size, No. 7 or 6.
Body: Red cow's hair.
Hackle: Lightish blue.
Wing: Woodcock.

No. 13.
Body: Red fur of a fox.
Hackle: Blood red.
Wing: Under feather of a woodcock's wing.

No. 14. Size, No. 6 or 5.
Body: The dark smoky feather of a heron.
Hackle: Of similar colour.

No. 15. Size, 7 or 6.
Body: The reddest part of a fox's brush, flax from the neck of a hare, and also some from the same part dyed yellow, in equal parts. Rib: straw-coloured silk—conspicuously.
Wing: Woodcock's—pick out the body for legs or feet—or put on
Hackle: A light rusty red.

No. 16. Size, 7 or 6.
Body: Bright red bullock's hair, flax from hare's neck, dyed yellow, and some from the reddest part of a fox's brush. Pick out the body for legs.
Wing: Woodcock's.

No. 17. Size, 7 to 5.
Body: Yellow silk, slightly waxed.
Hackle: Red.
Wing: Thrush.

No. 18. Size, 6 to 4.
Body: From the back of a water rat.
Hackle: Black red.

No. 19. Size, 6 to 4.
Body: Lightest part of the roots of the fur of a fox's back. Rib: straw-coloured silk conspicuously. Two tails taken from a blue hackle.
Hackle: Two turns of a light blue.
Wing: Starling.

No. 20. Size, No. 7 or 6.
Body: Equal parts, cow's hair, hare's flax, and fox's fur, put on abundantly and then picked out, so as to stick out roughly.
Wing: Woodcock.

April

(The foregoing flies will kill in this month. The greenish-bodied flies should be made lighter as the season advances.)

No. 21. Size, 7 to 5.
Body: Reddish fox's fur and fur from a grey cat, pick out the body to make the legs.
Wing: Blueish pheasant's feather.

No. 22. Size, No. 5 or 4.
Body: Equal parts of the fur of a rabbit's skin dyed yellow, and of one in natural colour. Rib: silver twist.
Hackle: Light silvery blue.

No. 23. Size, No. 5 or 4.
Body: Rabbit's fur. Rib: straw-coloured silk.
Hackle: Two turns of a silvery blue.
Wing: Thrush.

No. 24. Size, No. 6 to 4.
Body: Equal parts of the fur from the back of a fox, and of the roots of the fur from the back of a hare's skin, dyed yellow. Rib: straw-coloured silk.
Hackle: Light silvery blue.

No. 25. Size, No. 7 to 4.
Body: House Rat. Rib: silver twist.
Hackle: Highly speckled or grizzled blue.

No. 26.
Body: Peacock's tail. Rib: silver twist.
Hackle: Rusty blue.

No. 27. Size, 7 or 5.
Body: Hare's flax. Rib: gold twist.
Hackle: Dark rusty red.

No. 28. Size, No. 6 to 4.
Body: Hare's ear, mixed with a little dark squirrel's fur.
Hackle: Dark rusty blue.

No. 29. Size, No. 5.
Body: Hare's ear.
Hackle: Dark brown.
Wing: Dark part of a pheasant's wing.

No. 30. Size, 5 or 4.
Body: Dark squirrel. Rib: straw-coloured silk.
Hackle: Lightish rusty blue.

No. 31. Size, 6 to 4.
Body: Fur pulled out from the forehead of an old fox. Rib: gold twist.
Hackle: Blueish red.

No. 32. Size, 5 or 4.
Body: Equal parts from the ear of a hare, of a natural colour, and from one dyed yellow. Rib: bright yellow silk.
Hackle: Dark rusty red.

May

(In this month the May flies, and small winged blues of the shops may be used with advantage of the larger streams.)

No. 33. Size, 7 or 6.
Body: Equal parts, hare's flax, natural and ditto dyed yellow. Rib: gold twist.
Hackle: Yellow spangled red.

No. 34. Size, 7 or 6.
Body: Flax from a very young leveret, shaved as the hare's flax. Rib: silver twist.
Hackle: Spangled silvery blue, or spangled blue ginger.

June

(The flies here below given are for up-stream fishing in very low and bright water.)

No. 35. Size, 7 or rarely 6.
Body: Hare's flax dyed yellow. Rib: gold twist.
Hackle: The most brilliant yellowish red obtainable.

No. 36. Size, 7 or rarely 6.
Body: Bright yellow worsted, bound over lightly with strong yellow silk of the same colour as the worsted.
Hackle: The bright yellow red hackle from a bantam cock.

No. 37. Size, 7 or rarely 6.
Body: Bright red worsted. Rib: gold twist.
Hackle: The same as in No. 36.

No. 38. Size, 7 or rarely 6.
Body: Dark blood orange. Rib: gold twist.
Hackle: Black.

"In making all the flies from No. 33 to No. 38 inclusive, put on the hackle in abundance, so as to make the fly very bushy."

T. E. PRITT

The trout fly of the North Country seems always to have had individuality of design, and a character which, perhaps, reflects that of the fly-fishermen responsible for its evolution. The care shown in the choice of correct materials, the spare application of materials, and attention to details, in addition to a real insight into the art of fly-dressing, all identify the fly of the Northern Counties and permeate the literature on the subject by North-Country author-anglers.

The nineteenth century, as has been mentioned, was enriched by many books on fly-fishing, and the North made noteworthy contributions in this respect. Had it not been for Alfred Ronalds' classic, the works of men like Michael Theakston and John Jackson might well have achieved greater fame and popularity. Nevertheless, though overshadowed by a greater work, the books of Jackson and Theakston—particularly the latter—did much to advance the development of the wet fly and its effective use and are to be valued accordingly.

Some thirty years after publication of the works of Jackson and Theakston—to mention but two of many authors—T. E. Pritt wrote a book entitled *Yorkshire Trout Flies*, which was published in 1885, containing eleven plates of hand-painted

illustrations of sixty-two patterns of wet flies. So successful was this book that a second addition, restyled *North-Country Flies*, was published in 1886, the text remaining identical with that of the first edition.

T. E. Pritt, then Angling-Editor of the "Yorkshire Post," and Honorary Secretary of the Yorkshire Anglers' Association, produced a work preserving many of the best wet-fly patterns of his time and many of the old favourite flies of the Dales. The plates of illustrations, though not in any respect comparable with the masterly work of Ronalds, are accurate and good, and they do convey a correct impression of what a properly dressed North-Country wet fly should resemble. The result is a work which is of value and service to this very day for those who fish the northern rivers.

The fly-patterns listed bring out clearly the trend to the wingless or hackled type of wet fly as the preferred design, and the illustrations emphasize the importance attached to spare dressing, correct size, the avoidance of showy tinsel-material, and the attention to detail in the matter of the colour of the head of a fly.

The list of sixty-two patterns is as follows:

("The seasons are given approximately, the actual time of the appearance of each fly being dependent on the mildness of the previous winter and the prevailing spring weather.")

No. 1. *Water Cricket*. Hook No. 1.
Wings: Hackled with a feather from the Golden Plover's breast, in its summer plumage, or the wing or back of a starling.
Body: Yellow or orange silk. It is sometimes ribbed with black silk.
In its early stages the insect of which this is supposed to be an imitation, is not a fly, but an active little spider. It runs upon the surface of the water, and is often taken greedily.

No. 2. *Little Black*. Hook 0, short.
Wings: Hackled with a feather from a black cock's hackle or starling's neck.
Body: Purple silk, dubbed sparingly with Magpie herl.
Head: Purple.

This fly will kill quite as well as No. 1. On very cold dull days in March and April, and again in August and September it will be found very useful.

For the latter part of the season the following is often used:-
Wings: Hackled with a feather from the outside of a Green Plover's wing, or a Swift's back.
Body: Black silk, sparely dubbed with black Ostrich herl.

No. 3. *Winter Brown.* Hook 2.
Wings: Hackled with a feather from the inside of a Woodcock's wing.
Body: Orange silk—not too bright.
Head: Peacock herl.

A favourite early fly on all the Yorkshire rivers, killing well on wild, windy days in March and April. The wings assume a lighter shade in the course of ten days after its first appearance on the water, when it is commonly dressed as

No. 4. *Little Winter Brown;* or, *Light Woodcock.* Hook 1.
Wings: Hackled with a feather from the outside of a Woodcock's wing.
Body: Orange silk, with a spare dubbing of Hare's ear.

Jackson recommends for the later dressing a feather from a hen pheasant's wing, but the above is quite as good.

No. 5. *Brown Owl.* Hook 1.
Wings: Hackled with a reddish feather from the outside of a Brown Owl's wing.
Body: Orange silk.
Head: Peacock herl.

This is a capital killer and may be safely fished all the year round, dressed a trifle smaller as the season advances.

No. 6. *Fieldfare Bloa.* Hook 1.
Wings: From the bloa feather on a Fieldfare's rump, or failing that from the Tern, Bluetail, or Jay.
Body: Yellow silk.
Legs: From a feather from the Golden Plover.

Kills well during the latter part of March, and throughout April and May on rather warm days, with a wind.

No. 7. *Dark Moor-Game,* or *Orange Grouse,* or *Freckled Dun.* Hook 0.
Wings: Hackled with a black and orange feather from the Red Grouse, the hen bird for preference.
Body: Orange silk.
Head: Either orange silk, or Peacock herl.

A good fly during March and April, particularly in a brown water, when the river is clearing after a flood.

No. 8. *Water-Hen Bloa.* Hook 1.
Wings: Hackle feather from the inside of a Water-hen's wing.
Body: Yellow silk, dubbed with the fur of the Water-rat.

This fly is identical with the blue dun of Ronalds, and is indispensable during March and April, and again towards the latter part of the season. It is also a useful grayling fly all through the winter months.

No. 9. *Dark Bloa.* Hook 1.
Wings: From the Starling's quill.
Body: Dark claret silk.
Legs: From black feather of a black Hen's neck.

Jackson dresses this fly somewhat similarly, and adds a tail as in the real insect. It is identical with one well-known and valued in the north as Broughton's Point.

No. 10. *Dark Snipe.* Hook 1.
Wings: Hackled with a feather from the outside of a Snipe's wing.
Body: Purple silk.

A splendid killer on cold days in the early part of the season.

No. 11. *March Browns* (Great Brown, Brown Drake, Dun Drake.) Hook 3.
Wings: From the tail of a Partridge.
Body: Pale orange silk, dubbed with a little Hare's ear and yellow mohair, mixed; ribbed over with a little yellow silk.
Tail: Forked with two strands from a Partridge's tail.
Legs: From the back of a Partridge.

No. 12. Hook 2.
Wings: From a quill feather of a Hen Pheasant.
Body, Tail, and Legs as in No. 11.

No. 13. Hook 2.
Wings: Hackled with a reddish feather from the outside of a Woodcock's wing.
Body: Orange silk, dubbed over with a little fur from a Fox's ear.

No. 14. Hook 2.
Wings: From the tail of a Partridge.
Body: Orange and yellow silk twisted, dubbed with fur from a Fox's ear.
Legs: From a Wren's tail.

No. 15. Hook 2.
Wings: From the Hen Pheasant's wing.
Body and Legs: same as in No. 14.

The five dressings here given admit of little preferences as killers. The hackled fly—though comparatively rarely dressed—will be found very useful on cold, rough days, and the winged flies are indispensable on fair days through March and April, and not infrequently into May.

No. 16. *Red Clock* or *Pheasant.* Hook 1.
Wings: Hackled with a golden feather from a Cock Pheasant's neck, or from a small red cock's feather.
Body: Yellow silk, with a twist of Peacock herl next to the hackle.
Head: Peacock herl.

Kills well sometimes on bright days in March and April.

No. 17. *Red Palmer.* Hook 1.
Body: Green herl from Peacock, with a red cock's hackle wrapped over it.

This fly is best in a water which is fining after a flood, and occasionally it will be found very useful in a low clear river.

No. 18. *Little Dark Watchet* (Iron Blue Dun.) Hook 0, short.
Wings: Hackled with a feather from a Jackdaw's neck, or outside a Coot's wing.
Body: Orange and purple silk twisted, dubbed with down from a Water-rat.
Head: Orange.

No. 19. Hook o, short.
Wings: From a Water-hen.
Body: As in No. 18.
Head: Ditto.
Legs: From a Coot.

No. 20. Hook o.
Wings: From the breast of a Water-hen.
Body: Orange silk dubbed with Mole's fur.
Head: Orange.
Legs: A dirty whitish brown from a Hen's neck, or hairs from a Calf's tail, dyed yellow.

No. 21. Hook o.
Wings: Hackled with a feather from Water-hen's breast; or, if you can get it, from a feather from a Bluecap for preference.
Body: Orange silk, dubbed with Mole's fur.
Head: Orange.
 Four dressings, varying little, but by different makers. No. 20 is a fanciful imitation of the natural insect, but it is an excellent killer.

No. 22. *Dark Spanish Needle* (Needle Brown). Hook o.
Wings: Hackle with a feather from the darkest part of a Brown Owl's wing.
Body: Orange silk.
Head: Peacock herl.
 A good standard fly all through the season.

No. 23. *Light Spanish Needle*. Hook o.
Wings: Hackled with a feather from inside a Jack-Snipe's wing, or from the breast of a young Starling.
Body: Crimson silk.
Head: Peacock herl.
 Another form of No. 22, more suitable for warm days. The shades of the natural flies vary considerably.

No. 24. *Light Watchet* (Spinning Jenny, Pearl Drake.) Hook o.
Wings: From the Jay.
Body: Straw-coloured silk.
Legs: Fibres from a Yellow Plover.

This is not a good fly to imitate. It is the metamorphosis of the dark watchet or Iron Blue Dun, and both are often on the water together. It should be fished on mild days and in the evening during summer.

No. 25. *Olive Bloa.* Hook 1.
Wings: From a Starling's quill.
Body: Greenish yellow silk.
Legs: White hackle from a Hen's neck, stained to olive in onions.

No. 26. *Olive Bloa.* Hook 0.
Wings: Hackled with a feather from a Lapwing's back or rump.
Body: Yellow silk.
Head: Orange silk.
Known by a great variety of names, and always useful. Either of the forms here given will kill well on cold windy days, particularly about midday in March and April.

No. 27. *Yellow-Legged Bloa* (Yellow Dun.) Hook 1.
Wings: From a young Starling's quill feather.
Body: Yellow silk, waxed well, so as to make it nearly olive.
Legs: Ginger hackle from a Cochin-China Hen's neck.
Tail: Two strands of the above.
A first-rate killer, indispensable during its season.

No. 28. *Yellow Partridge* (Grey Gnat.) Hook 1.
Wings: Hackled with a light feather from the back of a Partridge.
Body: Yellow silk.
A good killer almost any time during April.

No. 29. *Snipe Bloa.* Hook 1.
Wings: Hackled with a feather from the inside of a Jack Snipe's wing.
Body: Straw-coloured silk.

No. 30. *Snipe Bloa.* Hook 0.
Wings: Hackled with feather from under Snipe's wing.
Body: Yellow silk, with a spare dubbing of Mole's fur, but not sufficient to hide the yellow body.

Pritt goes directly into the descriptions of the flies. Hook sizes are different from the ones we use now. In Pritt's time, hook sizes were called "new." The hook sizes we use now are called "old." The following table will translate them to the standard sizes of today:

000	00	0	1	2	3	4	5	6	7	8	9
17	16	15	14	13	12	11	10	9	8	7	6

All of the descriptions and comments including the brief note on the seasons belong to Pritt. I have added the name of the order the artificial is supposed to imitate in parentheses following the hook size. This information comes from Edmonds and Lee and is not complete for the 62 patterns. I have decided to place all of the "Bloa" patterns in the order of the mayfly, for reasons also explained later. And I have deduced the orders of some of the other patterns by studying Edmonds

Two dressings of the same fly, and practically identical. It is a splendid killer, and many anglers fish it more or less all the year round.

No. 31. *Brown Watchet* (Little Brown Dun.) Hook 1.
Wings: Hackled with a well dappled feather from a Partridge's back.
Body: Orange silk.
Head: Peacock herl.

No. 32. *Orange Partridge.* Hook 1.
Wings: Hackled as in No. 31.
Body: Orange silk.
These are practically the same flies, and are very excellent killers.

No. 33. *Greentail* (Grannom Fly) Hook 1.
Wings: Hackled with a feather from the inside of a Woodcock's wing, or from a Partridge's neck, or from under a Hen Pheasant's wing.
Body: Lead coloured silk, twisted with a little fur from a Hare's face.
Tail: Green silk, wrapped over lower part of body.

No. 34. *Sandfly.* Hook 1.
Wings: From a sandy feather from a Landrail's wing.
Body: Light brown silk, ribbed with sandy fur from a Hare.
Legs: Dark ginger hackle.
This fly is commonly dressed rather large in the wing.

No. 35. *Dotterel.* Hook 1.
Wings: Hackled with a feather from the outside of a male Dotterel's wing.
Body: Straw-coloured silk; some anglers prefer Orange silk.
Head: Straw-coloured, or orange silk.
This fly is undoubtedly a splendid killer . . . The dotterel is a good standard fly all through the season from the end of April, more especially on rather cold days.

No. 36. *Yellow Sally.* Hook 0.
Wings: From a Green Linnet's tail.

Body: Yellow silk.
Legs: White feather from a Hen's neck, dyed yellow in onions.

Nos. 37 & 38. *Poult Bloa,* or *Light Bloa.* Hook 0.
Wings: Hackled with a feather from under the wing of a young Grouse.
Body: Light yellow silk.
    A fair killer on cold days all through the season. For warm days a fancy dressing of it, as under, will sometimes be found useful:- Wings, hackled as above; Body, straw-coloured silk, with a twist of purple silk round it; and a peacock herl head.

No. 39. *Old Master.* Hook 1.
Wings: Hackled with a feather from the inside of a Woodcock's wing.
Body: Ash-coloured silk, wrapped over with Heron's herl.
    This is a capital killer from April to the end of August, on warm days or in the evenings.

No. 40. *Stone Midge.* Hook 0.
Wings: Hackled with a feather from a Pewit's neck, breast, or rump.
Body: Ash-coloured silk, dubbed sparely with Heron's herl.
Head: Magpie herl.

No. 41. *Grey Midge.* Hook 0.
Wings: Hackled with a feather from a Woodcock's breast.
Body: Yellow silk.
Head: Peacock herl.
    Kills best on warm days, and summer evenings.

No. 42. *Knotted Midge.* Hook 0.
Wings: Hackled with a feather from the back of a Swift or Martin, or from the shoulder of a Pewit's wing.
Body: Ash-coloured silk, dubbed with Heron's herl, rather more fully than in No. 40.
Head: Magpie herl.
    Does very well sometimes on hot stuffy days, when thunder is about.

No. 43. *Sandy Moorgame.* Hook 0.
Wings: Hackled with a dark reddish-brown feather from the back of a Grouse.
Body: Dark brown silk.
Head: Ditto.
   This is a very useful fly from May to the end of July, and it is not to be neglected in a brown water clearing after a flood.

No. 44. *Blue Partridge.* Hook 1.
Wings: Hackled with a feather from a Partridge's back.
Body: Blue silk dubbed with a little lead-coloured lamb's wool.
   A first-rate killer in a biggish water any time after the middle of May.

No. 45. *Red Owl* (Brown Owl.) Hook 1.
Wings: Hackled with a red feather from a Brown Owl's wing; shorter in the fibre than that used for No. 5.
Body: Orange silk.
Head: Peacock herl.
   A good killer in warm weather, particularly in the evening.

No. 46. *Stone Bloa.* Hook 0.
Wings: From a feather from under a Jack Snipe's wing.
Body: Yellow silk.
Legs: Fibres from a Jack Snipe's feather.
   This fly is useful from the beginning of June until the end of the season; it kills well occasionally about mid-day, but is best as an evening fly.

No. 47. *Small Blue Bloa.* Hook 0.
Wings: From a feather from Bluecap's tail.
Body: Orange silk.
Legs: Pale yellow fibres.

No. 48. *Greensleeves.* Hook 1.
Wings: Hackled with a feather from the inside of a Woodcock's wing, or from a hen Pheasant's neck.
Body: Bright green silk.
Head: Ditto.

No. 49. *Thornfly Dun*. Hook 1.
Wings: Hackled with a Landrail's feather, taken from under the wing.
Body: Orange silk.
Head: Peacock herl.
A very excellent fly in a good brown water on warm days in summer, from June onwards.

No. 50. *Curlew*. Hook 0.
Wings: Hackled with a small feather from the outside of a young Curlew's wing (August at latest).
Body: Orange silk for preference, but maroon or yellow will sometimes kill equally well.
It will kill amost any time, and particularly in a rather low and clear river.

No. 51. *Starling Bloa*. Hook 0.
Wings: Hackled, with the lightest feather from a young Starling's wing.
Body: Straw-coloured silk. Some anglers prefer white silk.
It will kill on cold days in May, and late in the evenings in June and July.

No. 52. *Small Ant*. Hook 0.
Wings: Hackled with a feather from a Tomtit's tail.
Body and Head: A bright brownish Peacock's herl; body dressed full.
Is best on hot days in July and August.

No. 53. *Fog Black*. Hook 0.
Wings: From a Bullfinch's wing.
Body: Dark purple silk, dubbed with Heron's herl, or, more sparingly, with black Ostrich herl.
Legs: From the Starling's neck.
Suitable for cold dark days, from June to the end of the season.

No. 54. *Cubdown Bloa*. Hook 1.
Wings: From the inside of a Swift's wing, or from a Lapwing's apron.

Body: Yellow silk, dubbed with down from a Fox cub, or fur from a Water-rat.
Legs: From a Plover's feather.
Useful towards evening through June and July.

No. 55. *Cinnamon*. Hook 1.
Wings: Hackled with a feather from a Brown Owl's wing.
Body: Yellow silk, dubbed with fur from a Water-rat.
Head: Peacock herl.
A capital summer fly, particularly in the evening.

No. 56. *Smoke Fly*. Hook 1.
Wings: Hackled with a feather from a young Grouse.
Body: Bright brown Peacock's herl. It is sometimes dressed with a twist of silver round the body.

No. 57. *Grey Partridge* (Grey Watchet.) Hook 0.
Wings: Hackled with a light feather from a Partridge's breast.
Body: Straw-coloured silk.
Head: Peacock herl.
For cold days, and in the evenings during June and July.

No. 58. *Large Ant*. Hook 0.
Wings: From a Starling's quill.
Body: Orange silk wrapped over the lower part, with three turns of a copper-coloured Peacock's herl.
Head: Peacock's herl.
Legs: Fibres from the light part of a Starling's quill feather.
Kills best on warm days towards the latter part of the season.

No. 59. *Sea Swallow*. Hook 0.
Wings: From a very light feather from the outside of a Sea Swallow's wing.
Body: White silk.
Legs: Fibres from the wing feathers.
Mainly an evening fly.

No. 60. *July Dun*. Hook 1.
Wings: From a Starling's quill.
Body: Yellow silk dubbed with a little Mole's fur.
Legs: Fibre from a bluish dun Hen's neck.

No. 61. *Black Gnat.* Hook o, short.
Wings: None.
Body: A little Ostrich herl.

No. 62. *Black Snipe.* Hook o.
Wings: Hackled with a Jack Snipe's feather from under the wing.
Body: Dark Green Peacock herl.
It will kill well almost all the year round.

W. H. ALDAM

The latter part of the 19th. century very probably merits description as the "Golden Age of Fly-Fishing." Techniques of making and using the artificial fly had been brought to a high standard, and at no time had there been greater interest shown in the matter of representation of natural insects, particularly on the chalk rivers of the South Country. The century which had contributed so lavishly to the literature of fly-fishing was to close with outstanding contributions by men genuinely devoted to the sport and all that appertained to it. In no instance, then or since, has W. H. Aldam's *Quaint Treatise on Flees and the Art a Artyfichall Flee Making,* published in 1875-1876, been equalled or surpassed in interest and attraction, and Hill, in his *History of Fly Fishing,* writing of books containing actual examples of trout flies, opines: "But best of all, for beauty and interest, is Aldam's *Quaint Treatise.* The flies in it are tied with an excellence that I have never seen beaten; and, as well as complete flies, all the materials of which they are made, silk, wool and feathers, are there displayed."

Aldam's inspiration to produce a work based on an 18th. century manuscript ("by an old man well known on the Derbyshire streams as a first-class fly-fisher . . .") contains twenty-five actual examples of the Derbyshire style of wet flies, including two floating Mayfly patterns. Most of these are the work of Mary Ogden-Smith, a daughter of the famous fly-dresser, James Ogden of Cheltenham, and samples of the materials employed for the dressing of each pattern are also included, all being set in sunk mounts. The flies are beautifully tied all being dressed to gut save the two specimen Mayflies which are tied on vertically-eyed Bartleet Limerick hooks,

which latter Hills states to have been dressed by James Ogden himself and likely to be the earliest examples of the floating fly extant. Some of the flies are stated to have been dressed by David Foster of Ashbourne.

The dressing of the specimen flies is in the true Derbyshire style, and many, if not all, the patterns could be effective to-day in the hands of any competent wet-fly fisherman. Such well-designed trout flies never grow old-fashioned or ineffective, and it is quite important that the patterns which have proved themselves over so many years of practical fly-fishing should not be forgotten or in any way overlooked by contemporary fly-fishermen.

The patterns given by Aldam are as follows:

1. *March Brown (Derbyshire)*, also called Partridge Rump, Cuckoo Creel and Old Man.
Whisks: None.
Hackle: Partridge feathers from between root of wings.
Wings: Large feathers from under Woodcock's wing.
Body: Hare's belly dyed mahogany, or orange silk and brown Squirrel's fur.
Hook: 2. Also
Wings: Outside Partridge Tail.
Legs: Wren's tail.
Body: Fur from the back of a fox's ear.
Silk: Medium orange.
 Or, Hackle dressing:
Wings & Legs: Rich red brown creeled feather from a Partridge's rump.
Body: Same as above.
Season: End of March to end of May.

2. *Spring or Dottrill Dun*
Wings: Brown dun hen from the back, or Dotterel quill feather.
Legs: Dark straw-coloured hackle.
Silk: Dark primrose.
Body: A little yellow carritted stuff* and blue rabbit fur well mixed.
Hook: No. 2.
Season: End of March to end of May.

*See quotation of directions on p. 130.

3. *Little Chap*
Hackle: Dark dun hen.
Silk: Lead colour.
Body: Copper coloured Peacock herl.
Hook: 0 or 1.

4. *Iron Blue or Watchett*
Wings & Legs: Jackdaw ruff feather, or Tom Tit tail.
Silk: Lead colour, or dark purple.
Body: Mole's fur.
Hook: 0 or 1.
Season: April to June, cold stormy days.
   or
Wings: Tom Tit tail feather.
Legs: Straw-coloured cock or hen hackle of small size.
Body: As above.

5. *Orange Brown* (Woodcock Fly, Downlooker or Ash Fly)
Wings & Legs: Feather from the bow of a Woodcock's wing.
Silk: Orange.
Body: Brown Squirrel fur.
Hook: 2 or 3.
Season: Late May to late June.
   or
Wings: Feather from the quill of a Woodcock's wing.
Legs: Small dark Furnace cock's hackle.
Body: As above.

6. *Green Tail* or *Granum*
Wings & Legs: Feather from under wing of a Woodcock.
Silk: Lead colour.
Body: Fur from a leveret's back well mixed.
Hook: 2.
   or
Wings: Feather from under wing of a Woodcock.
Legs: Point of Partridge rump feather.
Body: As above.
Season: Mid to late April.

7. *Black Gnat*
Wings & Legs: Feather from the breast or side of a hen Starling.
Silk: Lead coloured.
Body: Two laps of fine black Ostrich herl twisted with the silk.
Season: Late May to August.
　or
Wings: Feather from the quill of a hen Starling wing.
Legs: Small ruff feather from the hen Starling.
Body: As above.

8. *Tailey Tail* (Female Black Gnat)
Wings & Legs: Sooty black hen's feather, from the ruff.
Silk: Dark fawn or fleshy drab.
Body: Brown Turkey tail twisted with the silk.
Season: Late May to beginning of August.
　or
Wings: Feather from the quill of the Long Wing.
Legs: Small Starling neck hackle.
Body: As above.
Hook: 0 or 1.

9. *Green Drake*
Wings: Fine creeled Drake feather dyed yellow.
Legs: Black-brown cock's hackle.
Silk: Light primrose.
Body: Yellow carritted stuff and blue rabbit fur well mixed to a primrose colour.
Whisks: 3 long fibres from a black cock's shoulder hackle.
Hook: No. 6, long shanked.
Season: June.

10. *Dark Blue*, or *Orange Headed Dun*
Wings & Legs: Dark blue hen or chicken feather from the ruff or back.
Silk: Lead colour.
Body: Blue rabbit fur.
Hook: 2.
Season: Late April to late May.
　or

Wings: Blue or Merlin Hawk feather from the wing.
Legs: Small dark straw-coloured hackle.
Body: As above.
Head: Orange (optional.)

11. *Orange Dun,* or *Buff Dun*
Wings & Legs: Feather from a middle dun hen or chicken.
Silk: Faded orange.
Body: Brown Squirrel fur.
Hook: 1.
Season: Early June to end of season.
   or
Wings: Quill feather from a Starling wing.
Legs: Red cock's hackle.
Body: As above.

12. *Light Dun*
Wings & Legs: Feather from a light dun or chicken, or sea Swallow or Gull.
Silk: Light primrose colour.
Body: Yellow caritted stuff and blue rabbit fur well mixed to the colour of primrose.
Hook: No. 1.
Season: Beginning to end of July.
   or
Wings: Sea Gull wing feather.
Legs: Small straw-coloured hen or cock hackle.
Body: As above.

13. *Big Dun*
Wings & Legs: Light dun hen or chicken feather, or Sea Swallow or Gull.
Silk: Light primrose.
Body: The same as the Green Drake (See pattern No. 9.)
Hook: No. 6, long shanked.
Season: Beginning of May to late end of June.
   or
Wings: Feather from a Sea Gull.
Legs: Small dark straw-coloured hackle.
Body: As above.

Chalk-Stream May Flies and Spent Gnats

VARIANT DRY FLIES

TOP ROW: Baigent's Brown; Baigent's Black; Rusty Variant (Baigent). SECOND ROW: Dark Olive; Dark Spring Olive; Dark Variant (Baigent). THIRD ROW: Red Variant (Baigent); Tup's Indispensable Variant; March Brown (Baigent). BOTTOM ROW: Black Variant; Red Spinner; Dark Olive Spinner (Baigent)

14. *Crossing Brown*
Wings & Legs: Brown hen feather of a dark sandy colour.
Silk: Light Mahogany.
Body: Any fur of a mahogany colour.
Hook: No. 1.
   or
Wings: Darkest part of the quill feather of the Corncrake.
Legs: Small dark Furnace cock hackle.
Body: As above.
Season: July on.

15. *Sand Gnat*, or *Spider Flee*
Wings & Legs: Feather from a sandy dun hen, with black edges.
Silk: Lead coloured.
Body: Blue rabbit fur.
Season: Late April to late May.
   or
Wings: Quill feather of a Thrush.
Legs: Large black hen or cock hackle.
Body: As above.

16. *Black Ant*
Wings & Legs: Light dun hen or chicken feather.
Silk: Black.
Body: Black Ostrich herl, made thick at the heel.
Hook: 2 or 3.
   or
Wings: Quill feather of a Fieldfare's wing.
Legs: Black cock hackle.
Season: July to September.

17. *Large Red Ant*
Wings & Legs: Light dun hen or chicken feather.
Silk: Faded orange.
Body: Orange or chestnut coloured silk, made thick at the heel.
Season: July to September.
   or
Wings: The light part of the quill feather of a Fieldfare's wing.
Legs: Small ginger cock hackle.
Body: As above.

18. *Small Common Ant*
Wings & Legs: Dun hen or chicken feather.
Silk: Blood red.
Body: Copper Peacock herl, made thick at the heel.
Hook: 2.
Season: July to September.
 or
Wings: Starling quill feather.
Legs: Small red cock hackle.
Body: As above.

19. *Small Caterpillar*
Wings & Legs: Light dun hen or chicken feather.
Silk: Black.
Body: Black Ostrich herl, made small and fine.
Hook: 0 or 1.
Season: Latter part of May to end of June.
 or
Wings: Light part of Starling wing quill feather.
Legs: Small hackle from a Starling's ruff.
Body: As above.

20. *Large Black Caterpillar* (Hawthorn Fly)
Wings & Legs: Light dun hen or chicken feather from the back or ruff.
Silk: Black.
Body: Black Ostrich herl.
Hook: No. 3.
Season: Mid-May to mid-June.
 or
Wings: Light part of a Starling wing quill feather.
Legs: Starling hackle, from the ruff.
Body: As above.

21. *Bank Flee*
Wings & Legs: Landrail feather from the bow of the wing.
Silk: Faded orange.
Body: Red Squirrel fur.
Hook: No. 3.
 or

Wings: Quill feather of the Landrail's wing.
Legs: A long ginger cock hackle.
Body: As above.
Season: End of May to end of August.

22. *Little Sky Blue*
Wings & Legs: Feather from the breast or side of a hen Starling.
Silk: Sky Blue.
Body: Sky-blue silk.
Hook: o.
   or
Wings: Starling wing quill feather—the bluest part.
Legs: Fine black hen feather.
Season: Beginning of May to August.

23. *Stream Flee*
Wings & Legs: Feather from a Jack Hawk or brown Cuckoo from the bow of the wing.
Silk: Lead-coloured.
Body: Blue rabbit fur.
Hook: 2.
Season: Mid to late August.
   or
Wings: Feather from the quill of a Woodcock's wing.
Legs: Brown cock or hen hackle.

24. *Willow Flee* (Yellow Sally)
Wings & Legs: A white hen feather from the ruff and wing dyed yellow.
Silk: Yellow.
Body: Caritted stuff spun on silk.
Hook: No. 2.
Season: End of May to beginning of July.

25. *White Mout* or *Busterd* (Moth)
Wings & Legs: White Barn Owl: the cream coloured feather from the bow of the wing.
Silk: Buff coloured.
Body: White Ostrich herl.
Hook: No. 6.

May be winged with the quill feather of the White Barn Owl.
Season: Mid-June to mid-July.

26. *Brown Mout* (Moth)
Wings & Legs: Brown Wood Owl feather from bow of the wing, next to the quill feathers.
Silk: Faded orange.
Body: Herl from Brown Owl quill feather.
May be winged with Brown Owl quill feather.

Patterns listed in Appendix No. 1: Aldam's

1. *Indian Yellow* (Mid-May to September)
Hook: Kendal, 1 or 2.
Body: Silk (colour of new Russia Leather), slightly waxed with transparent wax, ribbed with bright yellow unwaxed silk.
Whisks: Two or three hairs from a rich buff Guinea Pig, or fibres from a Bittern's feather, or from the hackle of a buff Cochin China fowl.
Wings: Under covert feather from the wing of a young Grouse.
Legs: Rich buff or ginger hackle from a Cochin China hen.
Head: Deep orange tying-silk slightly waxed, or very fine floss.

2. *The Eden Fly* (Mid-May to October)
Hook: No. 0 or 1 Kendal Sneck bend.
Wings: Outside wing covert of the Sea Swallow, or lightest part of a Jay's wing quill feather.
Legs: Honey dun or light buff Cochin China hen's hackle.
Body: Pale buff or light straw-coloured tying-silk, slightly waxed with transparent wax.
Whisks: 2 or 3 fibres of buff Cochin China hen or cock, or a medium blue dun cock or hen hackle.

3. *Summer Dun*
Hook: 2 or 3 Kendal Sneck bend, long shank.
Wings: Lightest part of a young Starling's wing quill feather.
Body: Gold-coloured silk with buff Berlin wool dubbing, or fur from the buff part of a foreign Marten (Sable's gill.)
Legs: Rich buff Cochin China hackle.
Whisks: From the Bittern or buff Cochin China cock or hen.

4. *March Brown of Great Britain**
Hook: 4, 5 or 6 Kendal Sneck (No. 3 long-shank for low water).
Wings: The large under covert feather from a Woodcock's wing, or the secondary feather (quill) of the English Cock Pheasant.
Legs: Feather from the tail or one of the three secondary quill feathers nearest the body of a Jenny Wren; or a bright coloured feather from the back of a Partridge; or a rich, almost red, honey dun from the domestic cock or hen.
Body: Yellow silk and the red-brown fur at the back of a fox's ear, below the black tip; or the exact shade can be obtained from a Tasmanian Opossum; ribbed with gold thread or gold coloured silk.
Tail: 3 fibres of the two centre brown mottled feathers of the tail or from the upper tail coverts of a Partridge.

5. *Jenny Spinner*
Hook: No. 1 or 0 Kendal Sneck.
Wings & Legs: A Bantam Hen's hackle, very slightly stained with Judson's slate colour; or a pale grey feather from the butt of the wing or back of a Sea Swallow or small Roseate Tern.
Silk: Mulberry.
Body: Middle part fine white floss silk, or horsehair of transparent watery whiteness.
Tag: Two or three turns of fine Mulberry floss.
Tails: 3 fibres white cockerel's hackle.

* * *

The twenty-six patterns from the old Manuscript, stated to have been written about the beginning of the nineteenth century, indicate clearly a first preference for the hackle fly, the winged patterns being given as alternatives in most cases. These patterns, with the text itself, show how close was observation of natural insects forming the food of trout, and how accomplished the means of suggesting them with artificial materials. The "Old Man" who wrote the Manuscript was fully justified in using the word "Art" in his title. The patterns

*As distinct from the "Derbyshire March Brown."

are very good, and, when properly dressed in the Derbyshire style, are exceedingly attractive, possessing qualities which too often are sadly lacking in the present-day trout fly. The specimens which Aldam had dressed for his book—and very fine work they are—show how far the trout fly had evolved in the 18th. and 19th. centuries.

Something of the fascination of this old Manuscript, preserved by Aldam's enthusiasm and inspiration, may be conveyed by quotation of the "Old Man's" directions on:

"How to Make Yallow Caritted Stuff"

"Take the white part of Hare or Rabbitts belley—then take one table spoonful of Aquafortis and tow of water mixt them togeather—then by the acisstance of a ragg at the end of a short stick and a fark to keep your fingers from being bruned—lay the Hares belley upon a plate—and with acisstance of the fark hould it fast and wett it well down to the roots with the mop—then hold it before the foir with the fark untill it is gone Yallow—when Yallow enough wash it well in Could water to kill the Aquafortis—and when droy it is fit for use—this and a little blue Rabbitt well mixt will be made to any shade suitable for all the Dun flees that is required in the Art a Artyfichall flee making—It makes your flee much nater and comes more to nature then than stiff brisley Dubbing—You find nothing coace in nature—When you have made a Artyfichall flee as nate as hand can make It is a thousand times behind a natural one when dresst with the natest meatearills—When wee come to Examin thoes small beautyfull tender dellagate and nate water bred Duns that ought to be the Anglers coppiing—I can find no room for coace meatearills—the natest are very coace when compared."

Despite the quaintness of phraseology and orthography, the advice and observations are wholly sound and practical. Indeed, the literature of fly fishing would have been greatly the poorer had this contribution, with all its originality, been permitted to become lost or destroyed, as has undoubtedly been the case with similar old manuscripts and records. It is thanks to the vision of W. H. Aldam that the matter of this record of early patterns, as used on the streams of Derbyshire, has been

preserved. And in doing so, as has been observed, he produced possibly the most attractive of all the fishing books containing actual specimen flies.

The Quaint Treatise is a fitting work with which to complete any survey of the evolution of the wet fly up to the end of the nineteenth century. It marks the zenith of wet-fly fishing for trout and of the dressing of delicate and effective flies for the purpose. It is only to be regretted that so few copies of Aldam's work were published—a mere 100 copies—for there are many fly-fishermen to-day who have no idea of the style and form of the old-established and killing wet flies.

The Close of the Nineteenth Century: The Dry Fly

The nineteenth century—a century which produced so many outstanding contributions to fly-fishing literature, and which brought the art of trout-fly dressing to a high standard—was, in its closing years, to witness a further development of great importance in the evolution of the trout fly. This was a Golden Age of fly-fishing without doubt, and men who were giants of the Gentle Art pursued their recreation with the fly-rod with unequalled interest and enthusiasm.

Right up to the eighties, all the treatises and fly-fishing books had dealt with the wet or sunk fly—the traditional method of fishing for trout from the time of the *Treatyse* attributed to Dame Juliana Berners. Yet, in this same nineteenth century, fly-fishermen had noted that trout would respond well to a dry fly which, although designed for wet-fly fishing, would float until it became waterlogged. There can be no doubt that many observant fly-fishermen of skill had long been aware of this fact, but it is generally conceded that first mention of the floating fly and its deliberate drying by false casting was made by G. P. R. Pulman in his book *The Vade Mecum of Fly-Fishing for Trout*, third edition, 1851. His description of the presentation of a floating fly to a trout feeding at the surface accords closely to modern practice, and the principle of such a mode of fly-fishing is undoubtedly the same.

The interest in the natural insects which formed the food of trout had undoubtedly been sparked by angler-naturalists, such as Ronalds and Theakston, the masterpiece of the former dating as far back as 1836, so that it was inevitable that consideration of floating flies should increasingly occupy the thoughts of fly-fishermen. Time alone was required for the evolution of a fly which would not only float properly, but one which could be more easily changed when necessary. As is so often the case, progress had to await a technical improvement,

and this came with the invention of the eyed-hook by H. S. Hall, which made the modern dry fly a practical proposition.

The floating fly began to be used increasingly, particularly on the chalk streams of the South Country, during the latter part of the century, and fishing techniques and fly-dressing methods became more and more subjects of discussion in Clubs and Associations devoted to fly-fishing. Interest and enthusiasm were strong, but the movement still lacked the establishment of system in the use of the floating fly. The time was ripe at last for the emergence of an authority on the subject.

In 1886, there appeared a book entitled *Floating Flies and How to Dress Them* by F. M. Halford—a book for which the fly-fishing world had been waiting. This book—deemed by many to have been Halford's best work—did much to meet a need for guidance on the fascinating subject of the dry fly and its effective and proper use, and with his later works made a great impression, establishing the author as the leading figure in all that appertained to dry-fly fishing in the South Country. Dry-fly fishing at last had been defined and systematically established, and was a fitting development with which to crown the steady progress of the century.

F. M. HALFORD

F. M. Halford has been described as the historian of the Dry Fly: he was, in fact, the establisher of an acceptable system of dry-fly fishing on the chalk rivers of southern England and a leading crusader in the movement towards the serious study of angling entomology and the precise representation of natural insects constituting the food of trout. In this, as he himself acknowledges, he was guided and assisted by his friend, George Selwyn Marryat, widely regarded as the finest fly-fisherman of his day in England. A man of strong opinions, Halford was also a precisian as may be judged from his careful definition of dry-fly fishing itself:

"To define dry-fly fishing, I should describe it as presenting to the rising fish the best possible imitation of the insect on which he is feeding in its natural position. To analyse this further, it is necessary, firstly to find a fish feeding on the winged insect;

secondly, to present to him a good imitation of this insect, both as to size and colour; thirdly, to present it to him in its natural position or floating on the surface of the water with its wings up, or what we technically term, "cocked;" fourthly, to put the fly lightly on the water, so that it floats accurately over him without drag; and, fifthly, to take care that all these conditions have been fulfilled before the fish has seen the Angler or the reflection of his rod."

The invention of the eyed fly-hook, the guidance of Marryat, and Halford's own ideal of precise representation of natural insects, all contributed to the design of the modern dry fly and its artistic use as a new and fascinating method of taking individual trout from the gin-clear, steady-flowing rivers of the South. Inspired by Marryat in particular, he played a leading part in the evolution of a winged fly which floated better than the average fly of his time, and one which could not only be cast without any tendency to spin but would alight correctly and "cock" properly on the surface of the water. Bearing in mind that no aid to flotation of flies, such as paraffin oil, was in use, the achievement was considerable and important. Improved winging of flies intended to float by the use of slips of feather taken from the corresponding quills of the opposite wings of a bird in place of the old method of using slips taken from the same wing, and so eliminating the tendency of a fly to spin or twist during actual casting, the use of waterproof materials, such as quill for the making of bodies, the employment of first-class hackles and whisks, adoption of the eyed fly-hook, and the improvement of the oiled-silk casting line, were all utilized by Halford in his successful endeavour to establish dry-fly fishing. This accomplishment, together with his interest in the entomology of the riverside and his ideal concerning precise representation of insects, as set forth in his second work, *Dry-Fly Fishing in Theory and Practice*, 1889, established Halford as the greatest writer on fly-fishing of his time.

The case for the dry fly and its use, however, was later marred by dogma and over-statement, which led to controversy—often bitter controversy; but, unfortunate as this may have been in its short-term impact, such bigotry inspired a school of thought holding that there was still a place for the intelligent use of wet or sunk flies even on the sacred chalk rivers, and, in the long run, tolerance and reason replaced the original, rigid Dry-Fly

Code. The importance of Halford to fly-fishing, however, is undeniable, and his figure fittingly crowns four centuries of progress.

Although Halford's endeavours in the matter of precise representation have not stood the test of time, many of his patterns are still used in chalk-stream fishing with the dry fly, and are still sold by Tackle Houses. In his *Dry-Fly Entomology,* a hundred patterns were described, but later this number was reduced to thirty-three. As a matter of interest, however, the list which follows is taken from *Floating Flies,* since the selection is much more catholic, and still of service.

Note:

The numbers in the patterns which follow refer to Crawshaw's Special Dyes. These are as follows: No. i Green Olive; No. ii Medium Olive; No. iii Brown Olive; No. iv Green Drake; No. v Grannom Green; No. vi Slate; No. vii Iron Blue; No. viii Canary; No. ix Red Spinner.

1. *Rough Olive*
Wings: Dark Starling.
Body: Heron herl, dyed in No. ii, ribbed with fine gold wire.
Hackle and Whisk: Dyed in No. iii.
Hook: 0 or 00.

A very good pattern of the earliest spring olive dun, and for a variety may be winged with pale blue coot.

2. *India-Rubber Olive*
Wings: Medium Starling.
Body: A thin slip of india-rubber ribbed with fine gold wire.
Hackle and Whisk: Dyed in No. ii.
Hook: 0, 00, or 000.

This is one of Mr. H. S. Hall's patterns, and a very good dressing of the April tint of olive dun, the india-rubber body being particularly effective in appearance.

3. *Detached Olive*
Wings: Medium or light Starling.
Body: A thin slip of india-rubber, worked over an undyed double bristle.

Hackle and Whisk: Dyed in No. 11.
Hook: 0, 00, or 000.
Probably the best imitation of the natural olive extant, but very difficult and troublesome to dress.

4. *Dark Olive Quill*
Wings: Dark or medium Starling.
Body: Peacock quill dyed in No. 1.
Hackle and Whisk: Dyed in No. 111.
Hook: 0, 00, or 000.

5. *Medium Olive Quill*
Wings: Light Starling.
Peacock quill, dyed in No. VIII.
Hackle and Whisk: Dyed in No. 11.
Hook: 0, 00, or 000.

6. *Pale Olive Quill*
Wings: Palest Starling.
Body: Quill from young Starling wing or pale condor, dyed slightly in No. 11.
Hackle and Whisk: Very slightly dyed in No. 11.
Hook: 00 or 000.

7. *Pale Olive Dun*
Wings: Pale Starling.
Body: Pale yellowish olive floss silk, ribbed with fine white silk, or, better still, white hair from the Polar bear being the very best.
Hackle and Whisk: Dyed in No. 11.
Hook: 0, 00, or 000.

8. *Hare's Ear Quill*
Wings: Pale or medium Starling.
Body: Peacock quill, dyed in No. VIII.
Legs: Hare fleck (from outside shoulder of the hare).
Whisk: White or yellow cock's beard hackle, dyed in No. 11.
Hook: 0, 00, or 000.
A very good summer pattern of pale olive.

9. *Drake's Extractor*
Wings: Light Starling.
Body: Pale yellow olive floss silk, ribbed with fine gold wire.
Hackle: Carried down the entire length of the body, from shoulder to tail; a white cock's hackle, dyed in No. 1.
Whisk: Cock's beard hackle, dyed in No. 1.
Hook: o, oo, or ooo.
The invention of Mr. Drake, a celebrated Hampshire amateur.

10. *No. 1 Whitchurch*
Wings: Pale Starling.
Body: Primrose floss silk.
Hackle and Whisk: Pale sandy ginger.
Hook: o, oo, or ooo.
A favourite fly with the members of the Whitchurch Club, and a successful example of the pale olive or yellow dun.

11. *Flight's Fancy*
Wings: Palest Starling.
Body: Very pale yellow floss silk, ribbed with fine flat gold.
Hackle and Whisk: Pale buff Cochin cock hackle, or pale honey dun for a variety.
Hook: o, oo, or ooo.
Originated by and named after Mr. Flight of Winchester. Kills well throughout the hot weather, but is especially useful during the rise of May-Fly, when a pale delicate dun of this colour is generally on the water, and at times is taken even in preference to the May-Fly itself.

12. *Goose Dun*
Wings: Palest Starling.
Body: A single strand from plume of a grey goose pinion feather, slightly dyed in No. 11., and ribbed with fine gold wire.
Hackle and Whisk: Dyed lightly in No. 1.
Hook: oo or ooo.
This is Major Turle's rendering of the palest of olive duns.

13. *Detached Iron Blue*
Wings: Tom-tit tail.
Body: A thin slip of india-rubber, worked on a double bristle fully dyed in Crawshaw's "purple."
Hackle and Whisk: Dark honey dun.
Hook: oo.

14. *Iron Blue, A*
Wings: Tom-tit tail.
Body: Peacock quill dyed in No. vi, or a strip of the quill from one of the outside small feathers of a Coot wing, which will be found to be exactly the right shade.
Hackle and Whisk: Dark blue Andalusian.
Hook: oo.

15. *Iron Blue, B*
Wings: Tom-tit tail.
Body: Pale Mole fur, ribbed with yellow silk.
Hackle and Whisk: Honey dun.
Hook: oo.

16. *Iron Blue, C*
Wings: Tom-tit tail.
Body: Peacock quill dyed in No. 111.
Hackle and Whisk: Dyed in No. 111.
Hook: oo.

17. *Adjutant Blue*
Wings: Medium Starling, or pale Coot.
Body: A strand from the pinion or tail feather of an Adjutant.
Hackle and Whisk: Blue Andalusian.
Hook: oo or ooo.

If the strand of Adjutant is not procurable, a strip of quill from the pinion feather of an oldish Starling can be substituted although this is not so good an imitation as the Adjutant. This is the October tint of iron blue.

18. *Blue Quill*
Wings: Light Starling.
Body: Peacock quill undyed.
Hackle and Whisk: Pale blue dun.
Hook: o, oo, or ooo.

For a change, dress with very pale honey dun hackle—an old favourite with dry-fly fishermen. It is a winged example of the celebrated Devonshire "Blue Upright."

19. *Blue Dun*
Wings: Light Starling, or Snipe, for a change.
Body: Pale mole fur, or fur from a water-rat, spun on primrose silk.
Hackle and Whisk: Pale blue dun.
Hook: o, oo, or ooo.

20. *Autumn Dun*
Wings: Snipe.
Body: Heron herl undyed.
Hackle and Whisk: Palest blue bun.
Hook: oo or ooo.

This is the dressing of the pale blue dun, so frequently seen during the autumn.

21. *Golden Dun*
Wings: Pale Coot.
Body: Flat gold.
Hackle and Whisk: Dark blue Andalusian.
Hook: oo or ooo.

Very successful for "smutting" trout.

22. *Hare's Ear*
Wings: Pale Starling.
Body: Pale primrose silk.
Legs: The lightest fur from a hare's face spun on pale yellow tying-silk, and worked as a hackle.
Whisk: Four or five strands of a ginger cock's-beard hackle.
Hook: o, oo, or ooo.

Ogden's original pattern.

23. *Gold-Ribbed Hare's Ear*
Wings: Medium or pale Starling.
Body and Legs: The body is formed of dark fur from a hare's face, ribbed with fine flat gold, and the hare's fur picked out at the shoulder to form legs.
Whisk: Red cock's beard hackle.
Hook: o or oo.

This is probably the most killing pattern of the present day in the Test and other chalk streams; in fact, one of the most skilful and successful anglers in the county of Hants. scarcely ever uses any other dun, from the opening of the season in March until the closing of the river.

24. *Saltoun*
Wings: Palest Starling.
Body: Black silk, ribbed with silver wire.
Hackle and Whisk: Pale ginger cock.
Hook: oo or ooo.

A very useful summer fly, invented by and named after the late Lord Saltoun, a prominent member of the old Stockbridge Club.

25. *Red Quill*
Wings: Pale or medium Starling.
Body: Peacock quill dyed in No. 1x.
Hackle and Whisk: Red game hackle.
Hook: o, oo, or ooo.

The Red Quill is one of the sheet anchors of a dry-fly fisherman on a strange river, when in doubt.

26. *Red Spinner*
Wings: Honey dun cock-hackle points.
Body: Peacock or Adjutant quill dyed in No. 1x. and ribbed with fine gold wire.
Hackle: Black butted red game cock.
Whisk: From a pale cream-coloured Dorking cock hackle.
Hook: o, oo, or ooo.

Mr. Marryat's well-known pattern.

27. *Detached Red Spinner*
Wings: Honey dun cock-hackle points.
Body: Foundation of doubled bristle dyed in No. 1x; white horse-hair also dyed in No. 1x, worked over this foundation, and the body ribbed with crimson tying-silk.
Hackle: Red game cock.
Whisk: Pale cream colour.
Hook: o, oo, or ooo.

An improvement on No. 26.

28. *Claret Spinner*
Wings: Pale Starling.
Body: Claret floss silk ribbed with fine gold wire.
Hackle: Red game cock.
Whisk: Pale cream colour.
Hook: o, oo, or ooo.

Nos. 26 and 27 are evening patterns of the red spinner, but in the early morning, especially in hot weather, the claret spinner will frequently be found a more killing fly.

29. *Ginger Quill*
Wings: Pale Starling.
Body: Peacock quill dyed very lightly in No. ix.
Hackle and Whisk: Pale brown ginger.
Hook: o, oo, or ooo.

A very good dressing of the pale tints of dun so prevalent during the hot weather.

30. *Badger Quill*
Wings: Pale Starling.
Body: Black quill from Chaffinch tail.
Hackle: Badger cock (dark brown, nearly black centre, and cream-coloured points).
Whisk: Pale cream colour.
Hook: oo or ooo.

This is probably taken for the very dark, nearly black spinner, occasionally out in the evenings at the end of April and later in the season.

31. *Wickham*
Wings: Medium or light Starling.
Body: Flat gold ribbed with fine gold wire.
Hackle: Bright red Bantam cock carried from shoulder to tail.
Whisk: From bright red Bantam cock's beard hackle.
Hook: o, oo, or ooo.

32. *Pink Wickham*
Wings: Landrail.
Body:
Hackle and Whisk: } As in No. 31.
Hook:

A most successful pattern for "smutting" fish when dressed on very small hooks, oo or ooo.

33. *Cinnamon Quill*
Wings: Pale Starling.
Body: The root-ends of some strands of peacock herl when stripped are exactly this colour, but if such are not procurable, bleach an ordinary peacock eye in Dioxide of Hydrogen, and dye it slightly in No. ix.
Hackle and Whisk: Pale sandy ginger.
Hook o or oo.
This is one of the many brown-tinted autumn or winter duns, and for a variety can be dressed with pale Coot wings. It is essentially a grayling fly for August, September, and even October.

34. *Indian Yellow*
Wings: Inside grouse wing from a young bird or pale Coot.
Body: Floss silk about the colour of natural Russia leather, ribbed with bright lemon-coloured tying-silk.
Hackle and Whisk: Pale buff-coloured Cochin cock.
Head: Three or four turns of orange tying-silk.
Hook: o or oo.
Mr. Aldam's pattern, and an excellent one, especially for grayling.

35. *Little Marryat*
Wings: Palest Starling.
Body: Fur from flank of the Australian Opossum.
Hackle and Whisk: Pale buff Cochin cock.
Hook: oo or ooo.
Mr. Marryat's imitation of the pale watery dun prevalent in August, September, and October.

36. *Blue-Winged Olive*
Wings: Pale Coot.
Body: Peacock quill dyed in No. 11.
Hackle and Whisk: Dyed in No. 11.
Hook: o or oo.

This dun hatches chiefly in the evenings during the latter part of July, August, and occasionally even September.

Patterns Nos. 1 to 36 inclusive are upright winged duns.

37. *Hackle Red Spinner*
Hackle: Honey dun cock over three or four turns of black ostrich at shoulder.
Body: Peacock or Adjutant quill dyed in No. ix, ribbed with fine gold wire.
Whisk: Pale cream colour.
Hook: 0 or 00.

38. *Brown Badger*
Hackle: Badger cock.
Body: Peacock quill dyed in No. ix.
Whisk: Pale cream colour.
Hook: 0 or 00.

Nos. 37 and 38 are two of Mr. Marryat's patterns of red spinner.

39. *Detached Badger*
Hackle: Badger cock.
Body: White horsehair dyed in No. ix worked over a foundation of doubled bristle also dyed in No. ix, and the body ribbed with crimson tying-silk.
Whisk: Pale cream colour.
Hook: 0 or 00.

Without wishing to appear egotistical, I consider this the best imitation yet produced of the red spinner.

40. *Olive Badger*
Hackle: Badger cock.
Body: Peacock quill dyed in No. 11. with flat gold tag.
Whisk: Pale cream colour.
Hook: 0 or 00.

The dressing of the olive spinner.

41. *Jenny Spinner*
Hackle: Badger cock.

Body: Detached of white horsehair worked on undyed bristle, with four or five turns of crimson tying-silk at both ends.
Whisk: Pale cream colour.
Hook: oo or oo.

42. *Hackle Olive Quill*
Hackle: Pale silvery dun cock.
Body: Peacock quill dyed in No. VIII.
Whisk: White cock's-beard hackle dyed in No. 11.
Hook: o or oo.
  This is the olive quill dressed "buzz."

43. *Hackle Blue Quill*
Hackle: Pale honey dun cock.
Body: Undyed peacock quill.
Whisk: From honey dun cock's beard hackle.
Hook: o or oo.
  Similar to the Devonshire "Blue Upright."

44. *Grizzly Blue*
Hackle: Grizzled blue cock.
Body: Pale mole fur spun on pale yellow silk.
Hook: 1, o or oo.

45. *Hackle Hare's Ear*
Hackle: Pale blue dun cock.
Body: Dark fur from hare's face ribbed with fine flat gold.
Whisk: From red cock's beard hackle.
Hook : o or oo.
  The hackle tying of the "Gold-ribbed Hare's Ear."

46. *Hackle Iron Blue*
Hackle: Dark blue dun cock.
Body: Quill split from feather of old Starling or Coot wing.
Whisk: From dark blue dun cock's beard hackle.
Hook: oo.

47. *Needle Brown*
Hackle: Honey dun cock.
Body: Orange tying-silk.
Tag: Very pale primrose floss silk.
Hook: oo Long.

Mr. Marryat's imitation of the female "Needle Brown," the tag representing the eggs.

48. *Little Chap*
Hackle: Pale blue dun cock.
Body: Copper-coloured peacock herl.
Hook: 0 or 00.

49. *Yellow Bumble*
Hackle: Pale blue dun cock.
Body: Primrose floss silk ribbed with strand of peacock swordfeather.
Hook: 0 Long, or 00 Long.

50. *Orange Bumble*
Hackle: Honey dun cock.
Body: Orange floss silk ribbed with a strand of peacock swordfeather, and with fine flat gold.
Hook: 0 Long, or 00 Long.

51. *Claret Bumble*
Hackle: Medium blue dun cock.
Body: Claret floss silk ribbed with a strand of peacock swordfeather.
Hook: 0 Long, or 00 Long.

Nos. 49, 50 and 51 are invaluable patterns for hot weather, and good killers for grayling throughout the autumn—in fact, the "Orange Bumble" has proved so successful on the Test that many prominent anglers in that part of the country usually style it the *"Priceless Bumble"*.

52. *Furnace*
Hackle: Furnace or Coch-y-bonddhu (centre and extreme points black, and remainder of hackle blood red.)
Body: Orange floss silk ribbed with a strand of peacock swordfeather, and with fine flat gold.
Hook: 0 Long, or 00 Long.
A very favourite hot-weather pattern.

53. *Corkscrew*
Hackle: Brown ginger cock.
Body: The quill of a red-brown Partridge tail-feather from which the plume has been entirely cut away with scissors.
Hook: 1, o, or oo.
Before using the quill for the body, flatten it well by drawing it backwards and forwards between the thumb-nail and forefinger. In small streams or coloured water it is considered irresistible by Mr. Marryat, to whose inventive genius this pattern is due.

54. *Sanctuary*
Hackle: Coch-y-bonddhu.
Body: Dark hare's-ear ribbed with fine flat gold.
Hook: 2, 1, or o.
The invention of Dr. Sanctuary, of Salisbury.

55. *Green Insect*
Hackle: Pale blue dun.
Body: Two or three strands of peacock sword-feather twisted together.
Hook: o or oo.

56. *Red Tag*
Hackle: Blood red game cock.
Body: Copper-coloured peacock herl, two or three strands twisted together.
Tag: Ibis or scarlet wool.
Hook: o, or oo.

57. *Orange Tag*
Hackle: Blood red game cock.
Body: Two or three strands of peacock sword-feather twisted together and ribbed with fine flat gold.
Tag: Indian Crow or orange wool.
Hook: o, or oo.
A variety of No. 56.

58. *Half Stone*
Hackle: Honey dun cock.
Body: Lower half of primrose floss silk, upper half of pale mole fur.
Hook: 1 Long, or 0 Long.
  The hackle in this fly is carried down as far as the mole fur dubbing.

59. *Coch-y-bonddhu*
Hackle: Coch-y-bonddhu.
Body: Of two or three strands copper-coloured peacock herl twisted together.
Hook: 2, 1, 0, or 00.
  For a change, rib with flat gold.

60. *Hackle Red Ant*
Hackle: Honey dun.
Butt: Copper-coloured peacock herl.
Body: Orange tying-silk.
Hook: 0 or 00.

61. *Grannom Larva*
Wing: A very small piece of the point of a brown **Partridge** hackle.
Hackle: Rusty dun.
Body: Formed by working over the shank of the hook a foundation of pea-green floss silk, and ribbing it with a strand of peacock quill dyed in No. v.
Hook: 1.
  For many years the trout at Houghton have fed ravenously on the larva of the grannom, but neglected the fully developed fly, and, after many unsuccessful attempts, this pattern was at last produced by copying the grannom larva taken from the stomach of a fish in 1884.

62. *Grannom*
Wings: Palest hen Partridge wing.
Legs: Grey Ostrich herl dyed in No. v.
Body: Dark Heron herl undyed.
Hackle: Rusty dun game cock, or badger for a variety.
Hook: 3, 2, or 1.

63. *Alder*
Wings: Hen Pheasant tail.
Hackle: Rusty black cock.
Body: Copper-coloured peacock herl.
Hook: 2, 1, or 0.
 For a change, wing with Bustard. This fly is too well known and appreciated to need any comment.

64. *Welshman's Button*
Wings: Brown-pink feather from under the wing of a peacock.
Hackle: Rusty black cock.
Body: Copper-coloured peacock herl.
Hook: 3, 2, or 1.
 This fly is usually on the water during the same period as the May-Fly, but hatches earlier in the day, when the imitation is found most killing; and sometimes the fish take it in preference to the May-Fly, even during the heaviest of the rise.

65. *Cowdung*
Wings: Landrail.
Hackle: Ginger cock.
Body: Dubbing of crewel to tint.
Hook: 2 or 1.
 Occasionally very killing, especially on rough and blustery days.

66. *Red Ant*
Wings: Pale Starling.
Hackle: Red game cock.
Butt: Copper-coloured peacock herl.
Body: Orange tying-silk.
Hook: 0 or 00.
 One of the very best patterns for both trout and grayling during the daytime in the hottest weather, and one which is too often neglected by dry-fly fishermen.

67. *Black Ant*
Wings: Pale Starling.
Hackle: Cock Starling.
Butt: Black Ostrich.
Body: Black tying-silk.
Hook: 0 or 00.

It is, to our mind, very questionable whether this pattern is not taken by the fish for two black gnats in the act of sexual intercourse.

68. *Fisherman's Curse A*
Wings: Palest Starling.
Hackle: Cock Starling.
Body: Strand of cock golden pheasant tail.
Hook: ooo.
　Mr. Marryat's pattern.
　Nos. 61 to 68 inclusive are flat-winged flies.

69. *Fisherman s Curse B*
Hackle: Badger, over three turns of black Ostrich worked at shoulder.
Body: Black tying-silk with flat silver tag.
Hook: ooo.
　Sir Maurice Duff-Gordon's pattern.

70. *Black Gnat A (Male)*
Wings: Palest Starling.
Body: Black quill from Chaffinch tail-feather.
Hackle: Cock Starling worked in front of wings.
Hook: oo.

71. *Black Gnat B (Female)*
Wings: Starling tail; select the part of the feather with well-defined light brown tip.
Body: Black quill from Chaffinch tail-feather.
Hackle: Cock Starling worked in front of wings.
Hook: oo.
　The wings of the female black gnat are longer than those of the male.

72. *Black Gnat C*
Wings: One strip of prepared pike-scale cut to shape.
Body:
Hackle: } As in No. 71.
Hook:
　Mr. H. S. Hall's pattern.

73. *Silver Sedge*
Wings: Landrail.
Body: White floss silk ribbed with fine silver wire.
Hackle: Pale sandy ginger cock hackle, carried right down the body.
Hook: 0 to 3.

In hot weather, this pattern dressed on a 00 hook, kills very well during the afternoon, especially when the fish are feeding on the *"Fisherman's Curse."*

74. *Orange Sedge*
Wings: Landrail.
Hackle: Ginger cock, carried right down the body.
Body: Orange floss silk, ribbed with fine gold wire.
Hook: 0 to 3.

Or, for a variety, this can be dressed with a brown hare's ear body in place of the floss silk.

75. *Dark Sedge*
Wings: Cock Pheasant wing.
Hackle: Rusty coch-y-bonddhu carried right down the body.
Body: Dubbing of white crewel ribbed with gold wire.
Hook: 0 to 3, or even larger occasionally.

Usually known at Houghton as Mr. Hamborough's Sedge.

76. *Hammond's Adopted*
Wings: Woodcock wing.
Hackle: Brown-ginger cock carried right down the body.
Body: Dubbing of brown crewel to shade, ribbed with gold wire.
Hook: 2 to 4.

The late John Hammond's famous Winchester pattern.

77. *Artful Dodger*
Wings: Cock Pheasant wing.
Hackle: Blood-red cock carried right down the body.
Body: Dubbing of purple crewel to shade, ribbed with gold wire.
Hook: 2 to 4.

For a variety, dress with dark sage-green dubbing body. A good killer during the May-Fly season, both for day and evening.

78. *Coachman*
Wings: White Swan or any other white feather.
Hackle: Red cock.
Body: Copper-coloured peacock herl.
Hook: 1 to 4.
A good night pattern.

79. *Harlequin*
Wings: From Jay Wing.
Hackle: Black cock.
Body: Lower half orange floss silk, upper half blue floss silk, the whole body ribbed with gold wire.
Hook: 0 to 3.
An old-fashioned pattern, which might with advantage be used by the modern school of Anglers, especially for evening fishing.

80. *Governor*
Wings: Woodcock.
Hackle: Ginger cock.
Tag: Primrose floss silk.
Body: Copper-coloured peacock herl.
Hook: 0 to 3.

81. *Large Wickham*
Wings: Jay.
Hackle: Red game cock carried right down the body.
Body: Flat gold ribbed with gold wire.
Hook: 2 to 4.
Nos. 70 to 81 inclusive are flat winged flies.

Green Drakes

The following patterns of Green Drakes and Spent Gnats, should all be dressed on No. 2, 2 Long, 3 Long, 4, or 4 Long hooks.

A. Wings: Canadian Summer or Wood Duck.
Head: Bronze peacock herl.

Hackles: The first a hen Pheasant dyed in No. 11., and the second a good blue Andalusian cock.
Whisk: Four or five strands of Brown Mallard wing-feather.
Body: Detached, of white horsehair over wheaten straw or cigarette maize, worked on a doubled undyed bristle, and the body ribbed with waxed yellow tying-silk.

B. Wings: Canadian Summer or Wood Duck.
Head: Bronze peacock herl.
Shoulder Hackle: Grey hen dyed slightly in No. 11.
Ribbing Hackle: Pale ginger cock.
Body: Straw or maize ribbed with crimson tying-silk.
Whisk: Brown Mallard.

Or, for a variety, instead of carrying the ginger hackle down to the tail-end, turn it at shoulder close behind the grey hen hackle, and rib the body with fine flat gold and with the crimson tying-silk.

C. Wings: Canadian Summer or Wood Duck.
Head: Bronze peacock herl.
Shoulder Hackle: Hen Pheasant dyed in No. 11.
Ribbing Hackle: Blue Andalusian Cock.
Body: Straw or maize ribbed with pale tying-silk.
Whisk: Brown Mallard.

D. Wings: Rouen Drake, dyed in No. iv.
Head: Bronze peacock herl.
Shoulder Hackle: Grey Partridge, dyed in strong tea.
Ribbing Hackle: Pale ginger cock.
Body: Straw or maize ribbed with crimson tying-silk.
Whisk: Brown Mallard.

E. Wings: Rouen Drake dyed in No. iv.
Head: Bronze Peacock herl.
Hackles: The first a grey Partridge dyed in strong tea, and the second a pale ginger cock.
Body: Straw or maize ribbed with fine flat gold and crimson tying-silk.
Whisk: Brown Mallard.

In the Green Drake patterns D and E, the wings are dyed to

the colour of the late John Hammond's *"Champion."* Many fishermen prefer the wings of a greener tint, and certainly in the natural fly they are more decidedly blue green and less decidedly brown, than in the *"Champion."* If a small quantity of dye No. I be mixed with No. IV, this green shade will be obtained, or No. II is an intermediate tint between No. I and No. IV. As far as *killing* is concerned, I have found no pattern with dyed wings so uniformly successful as the *"Champion,"* dressed on a 2 hook, although my personal predilection is for the feathers from the undyed Canadian Summer Duck, a bird, which, unfortunately, is rapidly becoming extinct, owing to the great demand for the barred feather on the part of the Salmon fly-dressers.

F. Wings: Rouen Drake undyed.
Head: Bronze peacock herl.
Shoulder Hackle: Hen Pheasant dyed in No. 11.
Ribbing Hackle: Blue Andalusian Cock.
Body: Straw or maize ribbed with pale olive tying-silk.
Whisk: Brown Mallard.

An endless variety of green drakes can be made with the materials given for the above patterns, some ribbed with tinsel and both hackles worked close up behind the wings, and others with the cock hackles carried right down the body. Wings of Egyptian Goose are also very effective, and, for the shoulder hackles, florican, bittern, &c., can be used.

Spent Gnats or Black Drakes

A. Wings: Of four blue Andalusian cock hackles, set on flat, selecting those with well-defined ginger points.
Head: Bronze peacock herl.
Hackles: The first is a grey Partridge hackle, and the second a good badger (Dorking) cock hackle.
Body: Detached, of white horsehair on a foundation of an undyed doubled bristle; three or four turns of bronze peacock herl are worked on the bristle at the tail-end, under the horsehair, to form the dark ribs at the tail of the natural fly; the body is ribbed up at intervals with a single turn of pale olive tying-silk.
Whisk: Brown Mallard.

B. Wings: Four blue Andalusian hackles as above.
Head: Bronze peacock herl.
Shoulder Hackle: Grey Partridge.
Ribbing Hackle: Badger cock.
Body: White floss silk ribbed with an unstripped strand of peacock which is cinnamon-coloured at root and dark at point, the dark portion being worked at the tail-end.
Whisk: Brown Mallard.

C. Wings: Breast or saddle feathers from the Pintail.
Head: Bronze peacock herl.
Shoulder Hackle: Grey Partridge.
Ribbing Hackle: Badger cock.
Body: Of straw or maize ribbed with pale olive tying-silk, and with a strand of peacock herl, cinnamon-coloured at root.
Whisk: Brown Mallard.

Twentieth-Century Authors

THE twentieth century opened with the dry or floating fly riding high on the crest of popularity. Dry-fly fishing, as formulated by Halford and his adherents, was firmly established and accepted as the most effective method of taking trout; and at no time had there been greater interest in the entomology of those insects which formed the food of trout. On the chalk rivers of southern England, indeed, dry-fly fishing had come to be regarded as the sole sporting method—an attitude carried to such length that the use of the traditional wet fly was regarded as improper. The rigid "dry-fly code" was frequently carried to extravagant extremes, and there was even quibbling as to whether the oiling of a fly in order to improve flotation could be regarded as permissible. Absurd as such bigotry seemed to many impartial thinkers at the time, such fanaticism, viewed historically, served a useful purpose and, by its very extremism, led to its own defeat and made possible more enlightened and tolerant opinions and attitudes. The genius of the English for compromise was to show itself in this sphere of interest also.

Apart from the chalk streams, dry-fly fishing spread steadily to rivers of the type traditionally regarded as "wet-fly waters", gradually extending northwards over the Border to the streams of southern Scotland. On such rivers, however, the use of the floating fly was regarded as complementary to the traditional method of wet-fly fishing and in no sense challenging the latter. There was, therefore, little of the controversy and tendency to intolerance such as sometimes marred the fair name of the sport in the South.

This first decade of the new century could be regarded as a period of expansion and consolidation of the developments of the late nineteenth century. Considerable improvements of fishing gear and tackle—rods, reels, and oiled-silk lines, in particular, were achieved. The dry-fly rod of split-cane material

began to follow the trend towards lightness and shorter lengths, while retaining all the strength and "courage" demanded by the method of dry-fly fishing. The day of the heavy, long rod and inferior reel-lines was over.

As to the floating fly itself, the design and patterns devised by Halford and his friends were firmly established and accepted as being the epitome of "precise representation" of natural water-born insects, particularly the *Ephemeroptera* which flourished in the chalk rivers. There was, therefore, no generally recognized need to seek for improved floating flies, and fly-dressers concentrated on already established patterns, tied with the best materials available, to cater to the demands of increasingly discriminating fly-fishermen—and trout. First-quality Game Cock hackles—scarce even in the days when Halford wrote his first book—became still scarcer as demand increased.

Even at this early stage of the century, however, there were those who were not content to be borne along unthinkingly by the force of dogmatic opinion. There were individuals who, amid all the plaudits accorded the "dry-fly code," found it impossible to reconcile the exclusive use of the dry fly on chalk streams with the facts of what they observed in Nature. They could find little justification for the total rejection of the proper use of the wet fly in circumstances requiring it, and they felt strongly that the "dry-fly-only" school of thought wholly ignored the lessons and findings of the past. Such a one was George Edward Mackenzie Skues, whose fame spread far beyond southern England, and whose right to be regarded as the greatest authority on the subject of trout flies is beyond all dispute or question. Although a chalk-stream fisherman almost exclusively throughout his long life, Skues studied and considered the work of all the early authorities and possessed an encyclopaedic knowledge of trout-fly styles and dressings throughout the ages. Unlike the "dry-fly-only" school of his time, he had the wisdom to recognize and utilize the best of all the past had to offer in his own contributions to the art of fly dressing, and to appreciate that there was still a place in chalk-stream fishing for the wet fly.

In 1910, the first book by G. E. M. Skues, entitled *Minor Tactics of the Chalk Stream*, was published. This work, based on observation, a deep dislike of dogma, and a profound knowledge of the work and findings of the early authorities, presented the case for wet-fly fishing on chalk rivers so subtly and convincingly that it could not be, and never has been challenged. The book, in the face of very vocal opposition, rapidly

became a classic of chalk-stream fly-fishing, and was certainly the first great step towards the replacement of the blind dogma of dry-fly purism by a more informed and intelligent attitude. Such a work, in fact, was possible only from the pen of one who had fully informed himself of all that the past had to teach, and who had sifted what was of enduring value from the dross of dogma and plagiarism which so often posed as authority.

It was by virtue of such knowledge that Skues was able to select for his purpose the type of wet fly which he deemed to be most suitable and effective. Surprisingly enough, he turned not to the designs and styles of the North Country or to those of Wales or the West Country but to those favoured for the fishing of the Clyde and Tweed in Scotland, as described by David Webster in his book: *The Angler and the Loop Rod*, 1885. Utilizing the method by which such flies were dressed, Skues employed the following patterns which he found to be entirely adequate to cope with those occasions when trout were not a-feed on insects floating on the surface of the river:

1. *Greenwell's Glory*
Wings: Hen Blackbird.
Body: Yellow or primrose silk waxed with cobbler's wax and ribbed with fine gold wire.
Legs: Dark furnace hen.

As the season advanced, this pattern was varied and made with lighter Starling wings—dark, medium and light; and the hackle was similarly varied in shade to medium honey dun with the advancing season. Hook sizes: No. 1, 0, 00.

2. *Blue Dun*
Wings: Snipe.
Body: Water-rat spun on primrose or yellow tying silk.
Legs: Medium blue hen.
Hook: No. 1 or 0.

Skues varied the body of this standard pattern by using undyed heron's herl taken from the wing, and ribbing with fine gold or silver wire.

3. *Rough Olive*
Wings: Darkest Starling.

Body: Heron herl from a wing feather dyed brown-olive, and ribbed with fine gold wire.
Legs: Brown-olive hen hackle, with dark centre and yellowish-brown points.
Hook: No. 1.

4. *Iron Blue*
Wings: Tomtit's tail.
Body: Mole's fur spun on claret tying silk.
Legs: Honey-dun hen hackle with red points.
Hook: No. o or oo.

5. *Watery Dun*
Wings: Palest Starling.
Body: Hare's poll or buff opossum spun on primrose tying silk.
Legs: Ginger hen's hackle.
Hook: No. oo.

6. *Hare's Ear*
Wings: Dark or medium Starling.
Body: Hare's fur ribbed with fine gold wire.
Legs: Body-fibres picked out, or fibres placed between the strands of the silk and spun.
Hook: No. 1 or o.

7. *Black Gnat*
Wings: Palest Snipe rolled and reversed.
Body: Black tying-silk, with two turns of black Ostrich herl or knob of black silk at shoulder.
Legs: Black hen or cock Starling's crest, two turns at most.
Hook: No. oo.

All the foregoing patterns are standard or slightly modified standard patterns, and Skues employed them not with any view to challenging the floating fly but with the object of complementing or supplementing it on appropriate occasions and circumstances. This he did with marked success, so much so that the name of Skues, and his pen-name, "Seaforth & Soforth," became legendary in fly-fishing circles in southern England.

Minor Tactics became and remains one of the classics of chalk-stream fishing, and the restoration of the wet fly to its rightful, traditional place in such fishing was due very largely to this notable book. Never was a case presented so pleasantly and unanswerably, and the pendulum of fly-fishing opinion began to swing back from extremism to the more liberal and logical view which now obtains. It is from this point that development and experiment leading up to the design and representation of the various species of natural nymphs may be traced—a possibility deliberately ignored by the doctrinaire "dry-fly-only" school.

The important contributions by G. E. M. Skues to fly-fishing on the chalk streams were carried further by the publication in 1921 of his second classic work: *The Way of a Trout with a Fly*—a work considerably influencing contemporary thought concerning the proper use and representation of nymphs, and of serious endeavour to improve upon traditional wet-fly patterns. The book is a model of its kind, of great significance to the present-day fly-dresser, and of no less practical guidance and service to fly-fishermen of rough as well as chalk rivers. And not until 1939 did this distinguished author have published his third book, entitled: *Nymph Fishing for Chalk Stream Trout*, which records a full series of nymphal representations evolved from the study and observation of natural nymphs. These three works are essential to the modern fly-dresser and student of trout flies.

It will be appreciated, now that time has elapsed and allows of better perspective in the matter of judgment, how much Skues was influenced in his work by exhaustive study of fly-fishing literature from the *Treatyse* on, and, at the same time, by contemporary thought and opinion. Unconsciously, perhaps, the enduring lessons of the past stained and spread into his work, and afforded an insight into the true art of fly-dressing which he could not have otherwise obtained, while, in his own time, the increasing dogmatism and narrow-mindedness of the adherents of the dry fly school provided a valuable stimulus to produce new and corrective work in the face of formidable opposition and even indifference. It was work which demanded the abilities of a mind trained to reason and of a scholar with exceptional powers of observation, and such gifts enabled G. E. M. Skues to succeed where lesser men would undoubtedly have failed. "Seaforth and Soforth" exemplifies the value of research of the kind, it is hoped, that is offered by this present work.

The fact that fly-fishing, dry-fly fishing in particular, was concerned with but one or two Orders of river-flies—mainly the *Ephemeroptera* and Sedge flies— had not escaped attention in the first decade of the century. Evidence, as provided by autopsy, revealed how, even in chalk rivers, the forms of food ingested by trout were remarkably varied and that, in addition to nymphs, duns, spinners, shrimps, and other water-bred insects and crustaceans, a whole host of land-bred insects formed a considerable part of the diet of trout. This fact opened up yet another field of exploration in the matter of extending patterns to suggest such insects while providing at the same time a further unanswerable challenge to doctinaire narrow-mindedness concerning trout flies.

As the result of such investigation, Leonard West published privately, in 1912, a book entitled: *The Natural Trout Fly and Its Imitation*, dealing with description and identification and representation of various insects of interest to trout, including *Diptera, Perlidae* (Stone Flies), *Trichoptera* (Sedge Flies), Beetles (*Coleoptera*), *Hymenoptera*, *Araneida* (Spiders), as well as the *Ephemeroptera*. The work, illustrated with colour plates showing 102 insects with their representations, and similar plates of hackles and feathers used for dressing the flies, would have had still greater value had the author adhered to the correct entomological names of the various insects in place of employing his own nomenclature. Nevertheless, this book succeeded in bringing home to fly-fishermen and fly-dressers the need for an extension of fly-designs and patterns to cover insects forming an important part of the food of trout.

During the early years of the new century, the theory of precise representation, so-called, continued to govern the dressing of dry flies, and patterns had become largely stereotyped. Halford's "hundred best patterns," as described in his fourth work, in 1897, *Dry Fly Entomology*, continued to float in favour on the chalk streams, though in 1910, that number was reduced to thirty-three in *The Modern Development of the Dry Fly*, in which work the "exact imitation" theory was carried further. Yet, as is ever the case, there were individuals who were not entirely content to accept stereotyped trout flies, and such independent spirits were continually engaged in experiment and trial of fresh ideas, albeit these in essence amounted only to a variation of the established theme. Thus, floating flies of the variant type, dressed with long hackles of superb quality, were created by Dr. Baigent of Northallerton, and similar dry flies of this type were designed by Mr. Martin E. Mosely—a nephew

of the great F. M. Halford, and a distinguished entomologist. Another design was the "Fore and Aft" floater invented by a Kennet fly-fisherman, Mr. Horace Brown. These, with a few new patterns of floating flies by individual fly-fishers and fly-dressers, merely rippled the fast-stagnating pool of dry-fly development, a situation continuing right up to the outbreak of World War 1.

In 1914/15, Dr. J. C. Mottram published his interesting book: *Fly Fishing: Some New Arts and Mysteries* introducing some original ideas concerning trout-fly design and dressing which, but for the war, might well have made a greater impact in fly-fishing circles. Here, at least, was fresh and reasoned thought, and the outcome of practical trial and experiment. The fetters of dogma were being further loosened.

Dr. Mottram re-examined the whole question of trout-fly representation, and, with particular regard to the dry fly, considerations such as colour, transparency, form, weight, and movement. He reasoned that since the illumination of a fly when seen by a fish is against the sky, when all opaque objects look black, colour is not a quality the dry-fly tier need very seriously consider except under a few comparatively rare conditions. In this context, also, he opined that even if a floating fly were to match exactly in colour a natural insect, when both are moved to varying light-conditions, they may not match since the materials composing the natural and the artificial, being different, react differently to a change of lighting.

Transparency, it is pointed out, is a feature which must be noted by trout, since light illumining a floating insect is bound to reveal the opaque and transparent parts of the fly. Moreover, in passing through an insect's body, the white light of the sun becomes coloured, and it is suggested that it is this coloration which is of real importance in terms of trout-fly representation.

Form is a factor considered by Dr. Mottram to be the most important of all, since any living creature is instantly recognizable by its shape. The theory therefore is that since trout largely see natural insects as silhouettes against bright light, the fly-dresser must pay greatest attention to representing the silhouette of an insect and its outline against the sky. Movement, since the majority of flies on the water-surface keep quite still, need only be considered in exceptional cases. Weight, on the other hand, is a matter of first importance.

These considerations were ranked in order of importance as: Form, buoyancy, lightness, transparency, transparent colour,

reflected colour, and movement. Accordingly, since it was found to be impractical to incorporate all these qualities in any single representation, the author employed flies of different designs for different occasions. In brief, a coloured fly would be used in early morning and in the late evening since at such times the colour of a fly is seen by reflected light, casting it close in to shore or under overhanging trees so that a trout would see it against a dark background. The transparent fly, on the other hand, would be used on very bright days or against a sunset, since then transparency is of much importance. The buoyant fly would be used for water covered with scum, and on very calm days, as well as in rough water—in fact, in all circumstances under which it is difficult to keep a fly floating. Finally, the silhouette fly could be used at all times, since it was held that trout rarely see more than the floating flies' silhouettes.

Here, then, was a complete break-away from the rigid concepts of Halfordian dry-fly representation by a mind trained to research and accurate deduction from observed facts. The theories advanced contained much of real practical interest and value to the fly-dresser, and had it not been for the preoccupations and turmoil of a Great War, the pointers afforded might have been followed and developed with great advantage. Although half-a-century has elapsed since they were first advanced, such ideas are well worthy of careful re-examination to-day, and are by no means to be lightly discarded in the face of existing problems.

As examples of the new flies, Dr. Mottram gave the following patterns:

The Buoyant Olive Dun
Wings: Two grey hackle points.
Body: Turnings of the brown base of a peacock herl.
Thorax: Peacock herl.
Hackle: White cock—two turns only.
Whisks: Three Guineafowl hackle barbs.

"It will be seen that this fly is entirely made of feathers; it is so light and buoyant that it possesses the pretty property of bouncing off the water when thrown heavily on it. Mention here may be made of other buoyant types, namely, the long hackle, the fore and after, and the variant."

The Transparent Jenny Spinner
Wings: White cock hackle—four or five turns round the hook, afterwards cut, leaving only those fibres which project laterally; these will rest flat on the water and keep the fly afloat.
Body: A few turns of red-brown floss silk near the bend of the hook, the remainder of the hookshank up to the thorax being left bare.
Thorax: Red-brown floss silk.
Whisks: Three long white cock hackle barbs.

The Silhouette Olive Dun
Type 1. Wingless:
Body & Thorax: Hare's ear fur thickly wound on and afterwards cut to shape.
Legs: Two barbs from the primary wing of a hen Pheasant, tied cross-wise so as to suggest four legs.
Whisks: Three Guineafowl hackle barbs.
Type 2. Winged:
Wings: Grey hackle points.
Body & Thorax: Very fine olive floss silk carefully wound on to the hook so as to copy correctly the shape of these parts of the fly.
Hackle: White cock—two or three turns only.
"To prevent the silk body from becoming sodden, dip the fly after it has been made in a solution of solid paraffin in xylol (paraffin the size of a pea to ½ oz. xylol)."
"All the common natural flies can be dressed as silhouette flies, those of gnats, midges, and smuts being particularly deadly. They have also this to recommend them—they are easily and quickly made."

The Colour Olive Dun
"This fly is an imitation of the natural fly as it is seen by reflected light. This is exactly the type of fly that is always made . . ."

Dr. Mottram thought and wrote primarily as a dry-fly fisherman, and his opinion of wet flies and what he considered these to represent or suggest is not so reliable. He did, however, produce some interesting dressings, which may be cited:

The Alevin Fly

The transparent body is represented by using peacock herl for the opaque alimentary canal, and the rest of the body by golden pheasant topping, with small black beads for the eyes.

The Fry Fly

This fly is designed to suggest the quivering motion made by a little fish swimming against the current. "Small pieces of brown down from the Turkey and white down from the Seagull are tied one over the other up the shank of a long-shanked hook, the brown being used above and at the sides, the white below. When in this way the hook has been covered almost to the eye, a few turns of grey hackle are wound round; finally, in front of this, on a thick silk foundation, peacock herl is wound round. The hackle is cut away so as to extend only laterally . . ."

Midge Larva

Tail: Turkey down—a small piece.
Body: White silk ribbed with black floss silk, the thorax also of black floss silk.

This fly is tied on the tiniest hook obtainable, and is used with a greased cast.

The Smut

Body: A bead of black floss silk wound close to the eye of the hook, the remainder of the hookshank being left bare.
Hackle: Half a turn of the tip of a Starling's hackle. The smallest and lightest of hooks to be used.

The object of Dr. Mottram's book was to do something to speed up the lagging in the evolution of the trout fly, and to provide fly-fishers and fly-dressers with ideas which could be pursued and developed. Had the times been more favourable, his work would have received greater acclaim; but certainly Dr. J. C. Mottram is to be remembered for his independent contributions to fly-dressing, submitted modestly and without any taint of dogmatism.

In 1916, the private publication in Bradford of a book entitled: *Brook and River Trouting*, by the authors Harfield H.

Edmonds and Norman N. Lee, leavened the literature of fly-dressing which had tended to concentrate on dry-fly representation. Concerned purely with the wet flies of the North Country, this work aimed not only at providing a working list of patterns of a reasonable number in a field in which patterns were already excessively numerous, but also at reviving true and correct dressings of North-Country flies and describing the precise materials with which they were tied. Thirty-four wet-fly and two dry-fly dressings were given, together with admirable plates in colour showing the proper design of the flies and the exact materials with which they were made. Most of these North-Country flies had been described by Pritt, but the time was ripe for fresh exposition which would be of real value to the novice, although the book makes no attempt to describe the processes of fly-tying, and there is no question that the work succeeded admirably in all its objectives.

Brook and River Trouting is a work which was launched in the middle of a World War, and, had it not been for such circumstances, this notable book would certainly have had to be reprinted. It exemplifies the need to revive the best of traditional dressings regularly in order that fresh generations may appreciate these, and so that valuable traditional patterns may not be relegated to the limbo of forgotten things. Design is no less important than pattern, and there is a constant need to keep this factor of successful trout-fly dressing before newcomers to the art. The work of Messrs. Edmonds and Lee can well be regarded as a model in such respects.

The turmoil of war over, there appeared, in 1921, a little work of extreme interest to the angler-entomologist, so beautifully illustrated with hand-coloured plates of natural insects as to be worthy to rank with Ronalds' classic work. This new work, entitled: *The Dry-Fly Fisherman's Entomology,* was written by Martin E. Mosely, a nephew of F. M. Halford, an Entomologist by profession, and a fly-fisherman himself.

The book is written from the point of view of the entomologist rather than that of the fly-fisherman, and the scientific value of both text and illustrations is beyond question. It is always a delicate and difficult question to determine the degree of value of an authoritative work on entomology to the fly fisher and fly-dresser in the practical sense. Science is one thing, art another. It is possible to acquire perfect scientific and technical knowledge of insects and yet be unable to create killing representations of them. Nevertheless, the desirability of gleaning knowledge of every kind is undeniable, and it is a

decided asset to be able to identify instantly any insect upon which trout may be feeding on any occasion. *The Dry-Fly Fisherman's Entomology* may be regarded as the standard work on the subject of this century, and it is regrettable that only a single costly edition was published.

Martin E. Mosely's work is supplementary to the books of his uncle, F. M. Halford. Unlike Ronalds, he made no attempt to include trout-fly patterns representative of the superb illustrations of the work, and the inference is that the patterns of Halford sufficed.

The ground broken by the theories and investigations of Dr. J. C. Mottram concerning the representation of natural insects and their appearance in the eyes of the trout, was carried further by Mr. J. W. Dunne in his book, *Sunshine and the Dry Fly*, published in 1924. As did Dr. Mottram, Mr. Dunne came to appreciate that, from the trout's point of view, a natural insect floating on the surface of a river might have a very different appearance from that interpreted by the Halfordian school of so-called precise representation. Accordingly, he examined matters such as light, transmitted and reflected, the translucency of insects and their coloration under varying light-conditions, and the problems of representation of insects floating under and illumined by the sun. The ability with which he dealt with such questions was matched by the modest and pleasant approach to the whole subject, and this work is yet another pointer along the way of progress in the art of trout-fly dressing.

The author of this clever and interesting book obtained results in representing translucency of the fly-body, first, by painting the shank of the fly-hook with white paint in order to obtain diffuse reflection, and, second, by dressing the treated hook with artificial silk in place of natural silk. The result was an excellent translucent body when thick, colourless paraffin oil was applied and absorbed, with no shadow of the hookshank showing. This was the discovery which enabled Mr. Dunne to invent some thirty-three dry-fly patterns of insects as they were likely to appear to trout under conditions of bright light and sunshine. The approach was both original and ingenious.

Why did not these cellulite flies achieve greater popularity among the fly-fishermen of the chalk rivers? It is difficult to advance any reason or reasons beyond suggesting that the notorious barrier of conservatism, resistance to change, laziness, indifference, scepticism, and the apparent difficulty of dressing the flies with a new material may have been responsible— together with the undeniable fact that in even the most favoured

parts of these Isles the sun does not always condescend to shine. And when the light was not bright, the cellulite flies lost all their advantages and in appearance were, perhaps, even inferior to those of ordinary dry-fly patterns. The flaw seems to have been that the cellulite fly catered only to the condition of strong transmitted light, whereas what is required is a fly which, will respond to *all* light-conditions in the same way as does the natural insect. The means may have proved disappointing, but the ideas and theories of Mr. Dunne remain perfectly sound as a working hypothesis for fly-representation of the floating variety. For that reason, *Sunshine and the Dry Fly* merits careful consideration by the student of trout-fly evolution.

* * *

The first quarter of this turbulent century, which is ours, may be regarded as having achieved the following main advances:

1. A change of thought and attitude concerning the relationship of wet- and dry-fly fishing, and the beginning of a wiser and more liberal appreciation of the complementary nature of the two methods.
2. A broadening of the field of trout-fly representation.
3. The initiation of enquiry into the matter of representing flies in terms of what the trout, rather than the fly-fisher, might be supposed to see, and endeavour to improve representation accordingly.

The outstanding personality of this period was undoubtedly that of G. E. M. Skues. With the death of F. M. Halford in 1914, Skues was the last of the great figures of his day, and his part in bringing about an end to extremism on the chalk streams of the South, by the restoration first of the wet fly and then of the modern nymphal representation, cannot be over-estimated as a major accomplishment and contribution to the sport of fly-fishing. "Seaforth and Soforth" was not only an able tactician, but, in the matter of trout-fly representation, an undoubted master with an immense store of knowledge of and insight into his subject. That this is so is exemplified by his contributions to contemporary journals and magazines, which reveal not only his scholarly attributes but an expert appreciation of all that appertained to fly-fishing and fly-dressing. There were no aspects of the sport which he could not discuss, analyse, and judge fairly and accurately, and, in addition to his three classic

books, mentioned in the preceding pages, these abilities are fully revealed in his collection of diverse and highly informative articles, published in book-form under the title: *Sidelines, Sidelights and Reflections,* 1932. This volume, now regrettably scarce, contains much of interest to fly-dressing fishermen not only of the chalk streams but of all trout waters in these Isles. Yet another ingenious and strictly practical little work by G. E. M. Skues was published posthumously in 1950, aptly entitled: *Silk Fur and Feather.*

The seeds for future development were all sown during this period, and the change of attitude and the more liberal spirit shown by fly-fishermen began to be reflected in the literature of the sport. It was a period, also, during which there were many improvements in the gear and tackle of fly-fishing—shorter and lighter rods, better reels, and better oil-dressed silk lines in response to enlightened and steadily increasing demand. A new generation was rising in an age which was to become increasingly technical and scientific; but the secrets of the optics of trout remained to challenge and tantalize the dressers of trout flies.

Trout-fly patterns of all kinds were now being invented by an increasing number of fly-fishermen, many of whom were extremely artistic and skilled dressers, and already the number of patterns, wet and dry, was excessive. Of these, the majority proved to be as ephemeral as their prototypes, while only a few have endured and survived. The secret of optimum representation has still to be discovered.

* * *

Seven years after *Sunshine and the Dry Fly* was published, in 1931 a very noteworthy book: *The Flyfisher & the Trout's Point of View* by Col. E. W. Harding, commanded the respect and interest of thoughtful fly-fishermen and fly-dressers alike. Here was a work that investigated matters such as light, optics, and a whole maze of factors which affect the appearance of natural insects to the trout, with a method and care, not to mention brilliant thinking, rare in fly-fishing literature. Here was a book that carried yet a stage further the enquiries and theories of J. W. Dunne and Dr. J. C. Mottram concerning the appearance of the floating insect, and extending research into the trout's view of subaqueous insects. Well illustrated by the author himself, and with the text reinforced by mathematically accurate diagrams and drawings, this work merits rating as one of the outstanding contributions to fly-fishing literature of the century.

Col. Harding's book, which the author himself regards as merely touching the fringe of a vast and complex subject, by virtue of practical investigation provides many relevant pointers of great value to the fly-dresser of today, and, incidentally, reveals how sound were some of the principles and ideas of early authorities on fly-dressing. Much more would certainly have come from this gifted author had he been spared to complete his investigations, and his untimely death left so much unrecorded that might have been of first importance in practical application to the problems of the sport.

Col. Harding's book gives no original patterns, and he relies upon those of G. E. M. Skues for the most part.

The years which followed Col. Harding's work produced no further major developments, and it seemed to be a period of marking time and the testing of contemporary ideas—a lull which was to be shattered in 1939 by the outbreak of World War II. For the second time in under half a century the grim intervention of war interrupted the possibility of further progress.

The post-war years, while contributing very little to the evolution of the trout fly, have witnessed vast changes, social and economic, which have had a direct bearing on the whole sport of fly-fishing. Problems—serious problems—have arisen. With greater prosperity and the facilities for private transport, the popularity of fly-fishing has increased by leaps and bounds and shows no sign of moderating or abating. During the last two decades, an enormous number of books on the sport has poured forth from the presses, and the production of fishing tackle by commercial firms is now 'big business' in every sense of the term. The number of fly-fishermen in these Isles today is very great, and the resultant pressure on the limited available fisheries is severe. Prices for fishing waters have soared accordingly, and continue to soar as demand increases. Prices of trout flies increase also.

Such periods of rapid and violent change, with the whole trend towards mass-thinking, scarcely make for steady progress —in the evolution of the trout-fly, at least. The tempo of living creates impatience, and it is as though the past had no significance. This conceit—for conceit it certainly is—has resulted in retrogression in the art of fly-dressing, and the modern trout-fly of commerce reveals this regrettable trend. The commercial Houses are experiencing increasing difficulty in meeting the great demand for trout flies. There is a dearth of skilled fly-dressers available for employment, on the one hand, and an

acute shortage of some fly-dressing materials, on the other. Particularly is the latter situation true of the quality hackle from the Old English Game Cock, so long valued for the dressing of first-rate dry flies. Almost unobtainable in this country—and then only at very costly prices—it has become necessary to rely upon imported capes from inferior birds. Hence, it is inevitable that inferior trout flies have become the rule and not the exception, for it is impossible to produce a first-rate trout fly with second-rate materials. The danger is that fresh generations of fly-fishermen will come to regard the inferior fly as all that is necessary and will accept it as normal, even if the more discerning trout do not.

Yet, despite the present-day decline of fly-dressing, there is no justification for pessimistic assumption that this is other than a temporary set-back, and even as these lines are being typed a solution of the difficulty concerning materials is on the stocks. The trout fly will not only survive the times, but will assuredly continue its evolution as it has done for nigh on five-hundred years. In all that time, neither trout nor the delicate insects that so largely constitute the trout's diet, have changed. Only Man and his ideas are changing; and despite all the scientific advances and discoveries of recent years which have carried us to the very threshold of space itself, it is still good to know that the making of a trout-fly is something that cannot greatly change, and that the art of such creation is deeply rooted in the past.

Five centuries of trout-flies! The trout-fly that has survived all manner of turmoil and crisis and has remained evergreen in the minds of sportsmen throughout the ages! This is a proud heritage shared by no other nation, and a heritage which Englishmen worthy of their forefathers will, in their turn, pass down to their sons. The principles and discoveries of the past will almost certainly be combined with technical and scientific advances, so that there will be a renaissance in the art of trout-fly dressing in the not too distant future. The whole history of fly-fishing and fly-dressing has ever been progressive, and, if the lessons of history be applied to present problems, there is no need to doubt that out of existing difficulties and perplexities will come positive good. The future is bright.

PART TWO
Reference Lists of Trout-fly Patterns

AUTHORITIES

'ARUNDO' (John Beever)
AUSTIN, R. S.
BAINBRIDGE, GEO. C.
BLACKER, WM.
'CLERICUS' (Rev. Wm. Cartwright)
DICK, ST. JOHN
FRANCIS FRANCIS
'HALCYON' (Henry Wade)
HALL, H. S.
HOFLAND, T. C.
JACKSON, JOHN
MACKINTOSH, ALEXANDER
OGDEN, JAMES
PULMAN, G. P. R.
SALTER, ROBERT
SHIPLEY & FITZGIBBON
TAYLOR, SAMUEL
THEAKSTON, MICHAEL
TURTON, JOHN
CONTEMPORARY LIST

'ARUNDO'
(pseud. John Beever)
Practical Fly Fishing
1849

(Hooks: Hutchinson of Kendal, successor to Adlington)

The Spring Black. Hook No. 1.
Wings: From the quill of the Swift.
Body: Silk, the colour of Lundy Foote's snuff, with a bit of fine black Ostrich's herl laid on like a screw, to show the silk underneath.
Legs: Small hen's hackle, of a sooty black.
Season: End of March to middle of May.

This fly may often be seen in great numbers in the cold afternoons of spring, upon fresh horse dung.

The March Brown. Hook 2 or 3. (Dun Drake, Brown Drake, Turkey Fly).
Wings: From the tail of a hen Pheasant, or the quill of a Partridge.
Body: Silk, generally primrose, but sometimes chocolate.
Legs: Hackle dappled, or cuckoo-coloured (prevailing colours, light-blue dun and tawny yellow).
Season: April and part of May.

The Lesser March Brown. Hook 1 or 2.
Hackle: A feather taken from the back of the cock Partridge, in November or December, which is then beautifully speckled.
Body: Silk, mahogany colour; and a little coarse claret-coloured dubbing, of mohair.

The Granam or *Green-Tail.* Hook No. 2.
Hackle: From a feather which grows on the bone underneath

the Woodcock's wing, and is of a lead colour, barred with white.
Body: Silk, of a grass or ivy-green colour. About half the body should be made with fur from a hare's face, leaving the remainder of it bare to show the green silk.
Season: April, on warm days.

The Spring Dun. Hook 1, 2, or 3. (The Middle Dun, the Dun Cut, the Yellow Dun, the Dotterel Dun, the Honey Dun, the Brown Dun).
Wings: Feather from the wing of a young Starling, before it attains the adult plumage. It is a beautifully blended tint of blue, brown, and yellow.
Body: Mixed body of a primrose and dandelion-coloured silk.
Legs: Hen's hackle of the same colour as the wing feather.
Season: All season.

The Ruddy Fly. Hook No. 2.
Hackle: From a ruddy cock.
Body: Silk, bright red, between scarlet and crimson; black Ostrich's herl, rather full.
Season: Spring and summer.
    The Ruddy is a beetle, most useful as an afternoon or evening fly. Also called Marlo Buzz, the Furnace, Coch a Bondu.

The Cowdung Fly. Hook 2.
Wings: A yellowish brown feather from the bastard-wing of the female Woodcock.
Body: Silk, orange; dubbing, a mixture of orange and red mohair, with a few hairs from the hare's face.
Season: Cold, windy days.

The Dark-Blue Dun, or *Merlin.* Hook 2.
Wings: From the dark-blue part of the quill of the male Merlin Hawk.
Body: Silk, dark lead, with a little Mole's fur for dubbing, very sparingly introduced.
Legs: Hackle from the grey part of a Jackdaw's neck.
Season: Excellent throughout season on dark, cold, and stormy days.

The Black Caterpillars. Hook 1.
Wings: From a Starling's quill.
Body: Silk, dark lead colour; a turn or two of black Ostrich's herl under the wings.
Season: About the middle of May.

    The above is The Little Black Caterpillar: the Large Black Caterpillar is made in a similar way, on a 3 or 4 hook, and is an excellent fly for Lake or Tarn fishing.

The Black-Headed Red. Hook 1 or 2.
Hackle: Either a cock's hackle, of which about one-half is red and the other black; or with a deep red hackle, having a black stripe up the middle of it.
Body: Silk, dark orange, or red.
Season: Good all season, especially in clearing flood waters.
    This is a beetle or Lady-bird.

The Little Chap. Hook 0 or 1.
Hackle: A Pewit's topping, or a very small sooty-black hackle, of cock or hen.
Body: Silk, dark lead or very dark brown; Peacock's herl; short.
Season: Good April to October on sunny days.

    In July, orange silk is very good, made to show a turn or two of silk below the Peacock. A very dark-blue dun hackle may sometimes be substituted with advantage.

The Black Gnat. Hook 0 or 00.
Hackle: Feather from the bastard-wing of the Swift, or small hackle from a very dark brown (nearly black) hen's neck.
Body: Silk, the colour of Irish snuff; a very fine piece of black Ostrich's herl put on open like a screw to show the silk.
Season: May.

The Orange Dun. Hook 0, 1, 2.
1. *The Dark Orange Dun:*
Wings: From the Merlin Hawk's wing.
Body: Silk, deep orange; no dubbing.
Legs: Hackle from a dark-blue cock or hen's hackle.

2. *Orange Dun:*
Wings: From the Starling's quill.
Body: Silk, orange.
Legs: Hackle from dun cock or hen.

3. *Light Orange Dun:*
Wings: From a light-coloured Seagull or Sea Swallow, very light blue dun.
Body: Silk, tawny or faded orange.
Legs: Hackle, very light-blue dun.

   Season for the Orange Dun runs from mid-May to end of October.

The Grouse. Hook 1, 2, 3.
Hackle: A dark mottled feather from the back of the cock moorgame.
Body: Silk, orange; Peacock's herl of a copper colour.
Season: Middle of May to middle of July.

The Iron Blue. Hook 0.
Wings: Either Tomtit's tail, or Jackdaw's ruff. The Merlin's wing is best.
Body: Silk, dark lead colour; a little Mole's fur.
Season: May and June, on cold days.

The Green Woodcock. Hook 1, 2, 3.
Hackle: From a Woodcock's wing, a light-coloured feather of mixed brown, dun, and dirty yellow.
Body: Silk, ivy or apple-green: hare's ear (dark part).
Season: Middle of May to the middle of July. An evening fly.

The Silk Fly. Hook 2.
Hackle: Brilliant yellow breast feather of the North American Starling.
Body: Floss silk, of the same colour as hackle.

The Sand Gnat, or *Gravel Fly.* Hook 1.
Wings: From the brown part of the quill of a Thrush.
Body: Light-blue silk.
Legs: A dark sooty-dun hen's hackle.
Season: Early June.

The Big Dun. Hook 2, 3.
Hackle: From a Sea-Gull or Sea-swallow.
Body: Yellow camlet and pale blue Rabbit's fur mixed; silk primrose colour.
Season: End of May or beginning of June.

The Bracken Clock. Hook 2, 3.
Wings: From a Landrail's wing.
Body: Silk, red; Peacock's herl.
Legs: Hackle from a red cock.
Season: Middle of May to middle of June.

The Flat Yellow. Hook 1, 2.
Hackle: A white cock's or hen's hackle, dyed with the "Green Drake Dye."*
Body: Silk, bright yellow; a mixture of stained Hare's fur (yellow), which may be got at the hatters, and a little blue Rabbit's, or Water-rat's fur mixed.

The Stone Fly. Hook 3.
Hackle: Dark grizzly cock's.
Body: Silk, light brown; yellow mohair and Water-rat's fur mixed.
Season: May and June.

The Downlooker, or *Oak Fly.* Hook 2.
Hackle: Feather from the top of a Woodcock's wing.
Body: Silk, orange; fur from a Squirrel's cheek.
Season: May and June.

The Green Drake, or *Cadow.* Hook 2, 3.
Hackle: Light-grey feather from the side or breast of an old cock Partridge, in December or January, dyed in the "Green Drake Dye" to correct shade.
Body: Wool from the lower part of the abdomen of an old sheep; silk, rather a bright yellow.
Season: End of May or beginning of June.

*See recipe at the end of this list.

The Black Drake, or *Grey Drake.* Hook 2, 3.
Hackle: A dark grey feather from the side of the Teal Drake.
Body: Silk, light brown; white floss silk.
Season: End of May or beginning of June.

The Pale Blue, or *Willow Fly.* Hook 1.
Wings: From the Sea-swallow.
Body: Silk, pale straw or brimstone colour; dubbing, Water-rat's fur.
Legs: Very light pale-blue hen.
Season: September, October and November.

The Orange Fly. Hook 1.
Wings: From the bright buff part of a Thrush's quill.
Body: Silk, orange; a little fur from the cheek of a Squirrel.
Legs: A feather from a Wren's tail, used as a hackle, the long side of the feather being pulled off.
Season: May and June, in the afternoon and evening.

The Shamrock Fly. Hook 1, 2.
Hackle: Middle dun or blue cock's or hen's hackle.
Body: Silk, ivy green; dubbing, a little Hare's face.
Season: September, October and November.

The Black Ant.
Wings: The lightest part of a Starling's quill.
Body: Silk, dark brown; a strand of Peacock's herl, and one of black Ostrich's herl, laid on together.
Legs: Hackle from a black Cock.

The Red Ant. Hook 1.
Wings: Starling's quill.
Body: Silk, red; Peacock's herl.
Legs: Hackle from a red Cock.

Dye for the Green Drake

Take a large table-spoonful (heaped) of ground quercitron bark, and put it into a glazed mug, with a small tea-spoonful of pounded alum. The feathers to be dyed must first be well washed with soap and warm soft-water, and slowly dried. Pour

about half-a-pint of boiling water upon the mixture of bark and alum. Put the feathers in, one by one, and stir them well up with a bit of clean wood. Take out a feather or two—rinse them in cold clear water, and dry them. If the colour is not deep enough, add another spoonful of bark, and a little more hot water, till it is to your mind. The higher coloured ones will be best for the Silk Fly. Put in a few white cock's and hen's hackles at the same time, they will be useful for the Flat Yellow or the Silk Fly.

R. S. AUSTIN
N.D. (c. 1890)
Manuscript Book of Dry-fly Fishing on Exe and other North Devon Streams

1. *Blue Upright*
Body: Brown peacock's quill.
Hackle: Dark blue cock (occasionally rusty).
Whisks: Dark blue cock.
Hook: No. o to ooo sneck.
Tying silk: cream.
Season: Throughout season.

2. *Female Blue Upright*
As above pattern except:
Body: White rooted quill.
Whisks: None.
Season: Throughout season.

3. *Red Fly*
Body: Orange floss.
Ribbing: Peacock herl—strand from eye.
Hackle: Red—ribbed from head to tail.
Hook: No. o, sneck.
Tying silk: Brown.
Season: Throughout season.

4. *Half Stone*
As No. 1, except:
Body: Bright yellow floss silk.
Hook: No. oo or ooo sneck.
Tying silk: Cream.
Season: Throughout season.

5. *Honey Dun Half Stone*
Hackle: Honey Dun Cock.
Whisks: Honey Dun Cock.
Otherwise a Variant of No. 4.
Season: Throughout season.

6. *Dark Blue Quill Gnat*
Wings: Dark Starling.
Body: Brownish Peacock quill.
Hackle: Two turns of stiff dark blue cock—long fibres.
Tying-silk: Brown.
Hook: No. oo sneck.
Season: To mid-April; then No. 36.

7. *Dark Gold Twist*
Body: Hare's Flax, from back of Hare.
Ribbing: Gold twist.
Hackle: Medium blue cock.
Whisks: Same colours as hackle.
Tying-silk: Cream.
Hook: Nos. o and oo.
Season: Good when March Brown hatching.

8. *Light Gold Twist*
As in No. 7, except:
Body: Fawn coloured Seal's fur.

9. *The Silver Twist*
As No. 7, except:
Body: Roots of fox's fur (pale dun).
Ribbing: Silver Twist.

10. *Heron's Blue Body*
Body: Heron's wing fibres.
Hackle: Medium blue cock.
Whisks: Medium blue cock.
Tying-silk: Cream.
Hook: Nos. oo and ooo.

11. *Dark Blue Dun*
Body: Water Rat.
Tying-silk: Yellow.
Tag: Turn of gold tinsel.
Hackle: Darkish blue cock.
Whisks: Darkish blue cock.
Hook: No. oo.

12. *Dark Olive Dun*
As No. 11, except:
Body: Water-rat and fur from Hare's back dyed yellow, in equal portions; or Peacock's quill dyed olive.

13. *Light Olive Dun*
Body: Pale fawn-coloured Opossum.
Tying-silk: Pearsall's green.
Hackle: Medium blue cock.
Whisks: Medium blue cock.
Hook: No. oo.
Season: Mild weather in Spring, in very clear water.

14. *Pukshall Dun* (Wet or Dry)
Body: Finch-yellow floss silk.
Tying-silk: Yellow.
Wings: Dark Starling.
Hackle: Medium Olive.
Whisks: Medium Olive.
Hook: No. o or oo.

15. *Hare's Flax Upright*
Body: Peacock quill (eye feather) stripped.
Tying-silk: Cream.
Wings: Woodcock—light part of the outside of wing—dressed reversed.

Legs: Hare's flax.
Whisks: Honey dun cock.
Hook: No. o to ooo.

16. *March Brown*
Body: Dark Hare's Ear and a little Brown Bear mixed.
Ribbing: Yellow silk.
Wings: Partridge Tail, dressed reverse style.
Hackle: Brown Partridge.
Tying-silk: Cream.
Hook: No. 1.
    Later the fly is lighter and brighter and body more orange:
Body: Amber-coloured fur from behind ear of a Spaniel.
Ribbing: Gold Twist.
Whisks: Honey dun.
Hackle: Honey dun cock.
Tying-silk: Bright Orange.
Wings: Partridge Tail, or hen Pheasant, dressed reverse.
Hook: No. 1 or No. o Sneck bend.

17. *Female March Brown*
Not described.

18. *Little Iron Blue*
Body: Water-rat with a little claret mohair.
Tying-silk: Mulberry.
Hackle: Dark dun cock.
Wings: Coot, or dyed grey Goose, dressed upright.
    Later:
Tying-silk: Red.
Wings: Tomtit tail.
Hackle: Honey dun cock.
Hook: No. ooo Sneck.
Ribbing: Occasionally—yellow silk.

19. *Badger*
Body: Mulberry silk.
Tag: Red tinsel.
Hackle: Badger cock.
Hook: No. oo or ooo Sneck.
Good in stickles with no apparent rise.

20. *Hare's Flax* (Rough dressing)
Body: Lightish Hare's Ear.
Ribbing: Gold twist.
Legs: Hare's flax.
Wings: Woodcock, dressed reverse style.
Hook: No. o Kirby.
Tying-silk: Cream.

21. *Grannom* (Rough dressing)
As above, with addition of:
Tag: Two or three turns of greenish-yellow mohair.
Omit Gold twist.
Hook: No. o or oo Kirby.

22. *Alder*
Body: Peacock herl slightly tinged Magenta.
Hackle: Black cock.
Wings: Pheasant tail (mottled); reversed and turned back to 45 degrees.
Tying-silk: Red.
Hook: No. o Kirby.

23. *Black Gnat*
Body: Purple silk.
Ribbing: Metallic-hued central tail-feather of a Magpie.
Hackle: Dark cock.
Wings: House Sparrow wing, upright and divided; or young Blackbird quill.
Hook: No. ooo Kirby.
Season: End of April.

24. *Yellow Quill*
Body: Pale watery yellow quill.
Hackle: Medium blue.
Hook: No. oo or ooo Sneck.
Tying-silk: Cream.
Season: End of April.

25. *Yellow Dun*
Body: Light fur from Hare's back dyed yellow. Yellow tying-silk.
Ribbing: Fine Gold twist.
Hackle: Light blue cock.
Whisks: Light blue cock.
Hook: No. oo sneck.
Season: April.

26. *Pale Evening Dun*
Body: Very light fawn Opossum.
Hackle: Lightish medium blue cock.
Whisks: Lightish medium blue cock.
Tying-silk: Cream.
Hook: No. ooo sneck.
Season: Throughout summer to end of season, in warm weather and low water.

27. *Claret Spinner* (Sparse Dressing)
Body: Claret tying-silk.
Wings: Dark Starling—two slips, not reversed.
Hackle: Red cock.
Whisks: Red cock.
Hook: No. oo.
Season: From April on.

28. *Red Spinner* (Tup's Indispensable)
Body: White ram's testicle fur and lemon spaniel's fur in equal parts, with a little hare's poll fur and enough red mohair to give pinkish tinge or shade. Applied sparsely.
Hackle: Yellow spangled lightish blue cock.
Whisks: Yellow spangled lightish blue cock.
Hook: No. oo sneck.
Season: Throughout summer evenings.

29. *Jenny Spinner*
Body: White horsehair.
Tying-silk: Crimson at head and tail.
Hackle: Silvery blue cock.
Whisks: Silvery blue cock.
Hook: No. ooo Sneck.
Season: Mid April.

30. *Red Tag* (Wet or Dry)
Body: Peacock herl slightly dyed in magenta.
Tag: Red floss.
Tying-silk: Claret.
Hackle: Furnace.
Hook: No. oo Kirby.

31. *Dirty Dun*
Body: Half light dun fox, half light Opossum.
Ribbing: Silver twist.
Hackle: Light blue cock.
Whisks: Light blue cock.
Tying-silk: Cream.
Hook: No. oo Sneck.
Season: May to end of season, afternoons.

32. *Rusty Dun*
Body: Rust coloured fur, half pink Opossum, half Hare's poll.
Tying-silk: Cream.
Hackle: Light blue cock.
Whisks: Light blue cock.
Wings: Darkish Starling.
Hook: No. oo Sneck.
Season: End of May and through summer.

33. *Pale Dun*
Body: Cream coloured Peacock quill.
Hackle: Very light blue cock.
Whisks: Very light blue cock.
Wings: Hen Blackbird.
Tying-silk: Cream.
Hook: No. oo Sneck.
Season: May and June.

34. *Orange Drake* (Spent Fly)
Body: Wool (half orange, half brown) and a little orange floss silk.
Hackle: Honey dun cock.
Whisks: Honey dun cock.
Wings: Light Starling, dressed upright.

Hook: No. ooo.
Tying-silk: Orange.
Season: Mid June in evenings.

35. *Grey Gnat*
Wings: Cock Partridge breast.
Body: Olive coloured Hare's Ear fur.
Hackle: Medium blue cock.
Hook: No. ooo Kirby.
Tying-silk: Olive.
Season: Throughout season.

36. *Grey Quill Gnat*
Body: Light Peacock quill.
Hackle: Two turns long-fibred silver blue cock.
Wings: Light Starling.
Tying-silk: Cream.
Hook: No. ooo Kirby.

37. *Dark Olive Silver Horns*
Body: Peacock quill dyed olive.
Wings: Cock Blackbird, longish.
Tying-silk: Dark olive.
Hackle: Light blue dun cock.
Horns: Two fibres very light dun cock's hackle.
Hook: No. ooo Sneck.
Season: June, after rain.

38. *Light Brown* (Sparse Dressing)
Body: Half light coloured dun Opossum fur, and half fawn Hare's ear fur.
Hackle: Light blue cock.
Whisks: Light blue cock.
Tying-silk: Cream.
Wings: Underside Woodcock's wing: dressed upright.
Hook: No. ooo.
Season: End of June; evening or dull day.

39. *Autumn Brown*
Wings: Partridge rump feather.

Body: Squirrel's back fur.
Hackle: Rusty blue cock.
Tying-silk: Brown.
Hook: No. oo or ooo Kirby.
Season: July.

40. *Medium Summer Dun* (Very sparsely dressed)
Wings: Dark Starling quill feather.
Body: Fawn coloured Opossum fur.
Hackle: Light blue cock.
Whisks: Light blue cock.
Hook: No. oo Sneck.
Tying-silk: Primrose.

41. *Light Summer Dun* (Very sparsely dressed)
Wings: Underside Starling.
Body: Cream or golden coloured Seal's fur and white Ram's testicle wool mixed.
Hackle: As in No. 40.
Whisks: As in No. 40.
Tying-silk: White.
Hook: No. ooo Sneck.

42. *Yellow Summer Dun* (Very sparsely dressed)
Wings: Dark Starling.
Body: Half yellow Spaniel fur from behind ear, and half yellow Seal's fur.
Hackle: Light red cock.
Whisks: Light red cock.
Tying-silk: Yellow.
Hook: No. oo.

43. *Pale Summer Dun* (Sparsely dressed)
Wings: Sea-swallow.
Body: Blue Rabbit's fur, pale Fox, and a little yellow Seal's fur.
Hackle: Silver blue cock.
Whisks: Silver blue cock.
Tying-silk: White.
Hook: No. oo Sneck.

44. *Dark Silver Horns*
Body: Black fur, tip of Hare's ear.
Tying-silk: Slate.
Wings: Cock Blackbird with brown Partridge inside.
Hackle: Rusty blue cock.
Horns: Two fibres silver-blue cock.
Hook: No. oo or ooo Sneck.
Season: End of season.

45. *Red Midge*
Body: Magenta Peacock herl.
Hackle: Light Furnace.
Whisks: Light Furnace.
Tying-silk: Claret.
Hook: No. ooo Kirby.
Sparsely dressed on Gut.

46. *Brown Midge*
Body: Brown tying-silk.
Hackle: Two or three turns rusty blue cock.
Hook: No. oo Sneck.

47. *White Midge*
Body: Two or three turns silver Pheasant's tail-fibre.
Hackle: Silvery blue cock.
Tying-silk: White.
Hook: No. ooo Kirby.

48. *Golden Midge*
Body: Rich yellow-gold Seal's fur.
Hackle: Bright Honey cock.
Tying-silk: Orange.
Hook: No. ooo Kirby.

49. *Green Midge*
As No. 47, except:
Body: Pale sea-green Cockatoo, or dyed Swan.

50. *Dark Midge*
Body: White-tipped strand Turkey tail feather.

Hackle: Dark blue cock.
Tying-silk: Flesh coloured.
Hook: No. ooo Kirby.

51. *House Fly*
Body: Mottled Turkey tail with two strands fawn-coloured worsted underneath.
Wings: Lark or Hen Blackbird.
Hackle: Plover's topping.
Tying-silk: Mulberry.
Hook: No. oo Kirby.
Season: End of season, where drains fall into river or on mudbanks.

GEO. C. BAINBRIDGE
The Fly-Fisher's Guide
1816

1. Wings: Fieldfare back or Hen Blackbird back.
Body: Black Water-Spaniel fur or Rabbit, with a small proportion of claret coloured camlet.
Legs: Dusty black hackle.
Season: March.

2. *Black Gnat*
Wings: Pale Starling.
Body: Black Ostrich, thick and rather short.
  or Hacklewise:
Hackle: Pale dun
Body: As above.
Season: April.

3. *March Brown* or *Dun Drake*
Wings: Partridge tail, dark mottled.
Body: Hare's ear fur with small portion of yellow worsted.
Legs: Grizzled hackle.

Whisks: Two fibres of Partridge tail.
  or Hacklewise:
Hackle: Brown Partridge.
Body: As above.

4. *Hazle Fly* (May and June)
Wings: Sandy Throstle, or light-red Partridge tail.
Body: Black and purple and herl twisted.
Legs: Blueish hackle, tolerably full for underwing and legs.

5. *Great Dark Dun* (4 wings)
Wings: Wild Mallard wing with brownish tinge.
Legs: Dark grizzled hackle.
Season: February.

6. *Stonefly*
Wings: Mottled hen Pheasant or Peahen.
Body: Dark brown fur—bearskin or Hare's ear mixed with yellow camlet or mohair; yellowest near tail.
Legs: Grizzled hackle of good length under wings.
Whisks; (Optional) 2 hairs from a black cat's beard.

7. *Mealy Brown* or *Fern Fly* (4 wings)
Wings: Throstle or Fieldfare yellowish, or common hen. Split.
Body: Dusky orange (light-brown fur from Fox's breast).
Legs: Pale dun hackle.

8. *Blue Dun*
Hackle: Pale blue dun cock.
Body: Water-rat with small proportion lemon coloured mohair.

9. Un-named
Wings: Starling, split.
Body: Mole or black Greyhound.
Hackle: Reddish ginger.

10. *Orange Fly* (4 wings)
Wings: Blue feather from Mallard teal.
Head: Dark Hare's ear.
Body: Gold mohair, orange camlet, and a little brown fur.
Legs: Small blue cock's hackle.

Frederic Maurice Halford: the third outstanding figure in fly-fishing history

The Old Master: George Edward Mackenzie Skues. The fourth outstanding figure in the history of English fly-fishing

11. *Cowdung Fly*
Wings: Landrail, flat.
Body: Yellow camlet or mohair with a little brown bear's fur (full).
Legs: Ginger hackle.

12. *Yellow Dun* (April, May, September)
Wings: Snipe.
Body: Marten's fur, or yellow yarn unravelled mixed with a little pale ash coloured Fox-cub fur from near tail.
Legs: Pale dun.

13. *The Cream Coloured Fly* (May till August)
Wings: Yeasty hen.
Body: Dark blue fur.
Hackle: Pale ginger.
 or Hacklewise:
Wings & Legs: Cream hen.
Body: As above.

14. *Harry Longlegs*
Wings: Dark mottled Partridge.
Body: Brown Bear's fur and mole mixed.
Legs: Brown cock's hackle of good length.

15. *Little Iron Blue*
Wings: Cormorant wing or Tomtit tail.
Body: Pale blue fur on purple silk.
Legs: Picked-out fur.

16. *Gravel* or *Spider Fly*
Wings: Goatsucker or Woodcock.
Body: Lead coloured silk with Ostrich herl at shoulder.
Hackle: 2 turns of a small dark, grizzled hackle.

17. *Grannom* or *Greentail*
Wings: Partridge wing, or hen Pheasant wing.
Body: Dark Hare's ear with a little blue fur.
Tag: Green Peacock herl, or bright green wax.
Legs: Yellow grizzled hackle.
 or Hacklewise:

18. Legs & Wings: Under Woodcock wing.
Body: As above, and Tag.

19. *Hawthorn Fly*
Wings: Palest Snipe or Mallard.
Body: Black Ostrich herl.
Legs: Black hackle.

20. *Summer Dun*
Wings: Wood Pigeon.
Body: Mole fur, ribbed with ash coloured silk.
Legs: Ash coloured hackle.

21. *Black Harl Fly*
Wings: Pale Starling.
Body: Ostrich herl, dressed thin.

22. *Orl Fly* (4 wings, flat)
Wings: Brown hen.
Body: Peacock herl with no green.
Legs: Grizzled hackle.
   or Hacklewise:
Wings & Legs: Grizzled hackle.
Body: As above. Alternative body: Brown Spaniel fur mixed with dark red or claret mohair and ribbed with orange silk.

23. *Little Yellow May* or *Willow Fly*
Wings: Mallard dyed yellow.
Body: Marten's neck, or yellow worsted with a little Hare's ear. Yellow on belly.
   or Hacklewise:
Wings & Legs: White cock's hackle dyed yellow.
Body: As above.

24. Un-named (Hacklewise)
Wings & Legs: Green Woodpecker's back or dusky green Parrot.
Body: Dark brown fur ribbed with orange silk.

25. Un-named (June, July, August)
Wings: Brown Grouse feather.
Body: Dark blue fur with black Sheep's wool.
Legs: Dark cock's hackle.

26. *Brown Dun*
Wings: Fieldfare.
Body: Otter's fur mixed with lemon mohair.

27. *Green Drake*
Wings: Dyed Mallard.
Body: Hog's down and light Bear's hair with yellow mohair, or yellow silk warped with pale floss.
Head: Peacock herl.
Legs: Bittern's hackle.
Whisks: Long hairs of Sable or Fitchet.

28. *Blue Blow* (Very small)
Wings: Thistledown, or bluish-white hackle.
Body: Very dark blue fur, or Pewit's topping.

29. *Black Midge*
Wings & Legs: Blue cock's hackle.
Body: Brownish-black silk.

30. *Grey Drake*
Wings: Mottled Mallard or Teal.
Body: Cream crewel on flesh-coloured silk.
Hackle: Dark grizzled cock, down body.
Head: Peacock herl.
Whisks: Sable or Fitchet.

31. *Peacock Fly*
Wings: Starling (flat).
Body: Dark peacock herl, mulberry silk.
Legs: Grizzled hackle.

32. *Cinnamon Fly*
Wings: Pale red-brown cinnamon hen (full).
Body: Dark brown fur.
Legs: Ginger hackle.

33. *Sandfly*
Wings: Sandy Landrail.
Body: Sandy Hare's neck with a little orange mohair.
Legs: Ginger hackle.
or Hacklewise:

34. Wings & Legs: Under Throstle wing.
Body: As above.

35. *Great Red Spinner*
Wings: Starling.
Body: Seal's fur or hog-down dyed red and mixed with brown mohair.
Legs: Red hackle.
"or it may be dressed like Marlow Buzz":
Wings & Legs: Coch-y-bonddhu hackle.
Body: Peacock herl.

36. *Pale Evening Dun*
Wings: Mallard dyed very pale yellow.
Body: Marten's yellow fur with a little mouse.

37. *Blue Gnat*
Wings: Snipe (very small). Or:-
Wings & Legs: Blue dun hackle.
Body: Dark Mole wrapped with bright purple silk.

38. *Oakfly, Downlooker,* or *Canon Fly*
Wings: Yellowish brown hen.
Body: Head, Hare's ear; Thorax, Dun fur; Middle, Orange and yellow; Tail, Brownish dun.
or
Wings & Legs: Bittern hackle.
Body: As above.

39. *Great Black Ant*
Wings: Snipe or Tomtit tail or thistledown.
Body: Black Ostrich herl, thick at tail and under butt of wings.
Legs: Reddish brown hackle.

40. *Great Red Ant*
Wings: Light Starling.
Body: Gold mohair or copper Peacock herl.
Legs: Ginger cock.

41. *Small Black Ant*
As No. 39.

42. *Yellow Sally* (4 wings, flat)
Wings: Dyed (yellow) feather or hackle.
Body: Yellow Marten's fur, crewel, or mohair.

W. BLACKER
The Art of Angling and Complete System of Fly-Making and Dyeing of Colours
1843

1. *Wren Tail* (Standard)
Wings: Partridge, grey tail feather.
Body: Amber mohair.
Tag: Gold.
Legs: Wren tail.
Whisks: 2 fibres of Drake feather.
Hook: f.

2. *Grouse Hackle* (May & June)
Wings & Legs: Grouse hackle.
Body: Gold or orange silk.
Tag: Gold.
Hook: ff.

3. *Ant Fly* (August)
Wings: Starling wing.
Body: Cinnamon brown mohair.
Legs: Small red hackle.
Hook: fe.

4. *Sooty Olive Fly* (July)
Wing: (a) Woodcock.
      (b) Starling.
Body: Dark olive mohair.
Tag: Gold.
Hook: f.

5. *Soldier Palmer Fly* (Standard)
Legs: 2 Black-red hackles at shoulder.
Body: Peacock herl.
Tag: Gold.
Hook: ff.

6. *Red Palmer Fly* (May to July)
Legs: 2 Red hackles—tail to head.
Body: Red or orange mohair.
Ribbing: Gold twist or tinsel.
Hook: ff.

7. *Golden Palmer* (July)
Legs: 2 Red hackles.
Body: Yellow silk.
Ribbing: Tinsel.
Hook: fff.

8. *Grey Palmer* (April)
Legs: 2 Grey hackles.
Body: Peacock herl.
Ribbing: Gold or silver twist.
Hook: fff.

9. *Black Palmer* (May)
Legs: 2 Black hackles.
Body: Black mohair or silk.
Tag: Gold.
Hook: fff.

10. *Little Castle Fly* (1st June)
Wings: Thrush or yellow feather.
Body: Yellow silk.
Tag: Gold.

Whisks: 2 fibres Mallard dyed yellow.
Legs: Yellow hackle at shoulder.
Hook: fe.

11. *The Grey Housewife*
Wings: Hen Pheasant or grey Drake.
Body: Light brown mohair mixed with Hare's ear.
Legs: Partridge neck, or a grey cock's hackle.
Whisks: 2 fibres Mallard.
Hook: ff.

12. *Stone Fly* (April & May)
Wings: Brown Mallard, or hen Pheasant tail.
Body: Brown and yellow mohair mixed.
Legs: Black-red hackle, close at head.
Whisks: 2 fibres Mallard.
Hook: fff.

13. *Cowdung Fly* (July)
Wings: Landrail.
Body: Lemon mohair.
Legs: Cinnamon hackle.
Hook: f.

14. *Black Gnat* (June)
Wings: Starling.
Body: Black Ostrich herl.
Tag: Gold.
Legs: Small black hackle.
Hook: fe.

15. *Little Soldier Fly* (Standard)
Wings: Starling and Partridge tail.
Body: Mixed gold mohair and floss.
Legs: Small black-red hackle.
Hook: fe.

16. *Hare's Ear Fly* (March, April)
Wings: (a) Starling; (b) Bunting; (c) Woodcock.
Body: Hare's ear fur and a little yellow mohair mixed.
Hook: f.

17. *Blue Blow Fly* (June)
Wings: Tomtit's tail.
Body: Mole or Water-rat's fur mixed with yellow mohair.
Legs: Dun hackle.
Whisks: Mouse's whiskers.
Hook: Midge.

18. *Green Drake* ⎫
              ⎬ Usual dressings.
19. *Grey Drake* ⎭

20. *Hawthorn Fly* (May)
Wings: Starling or Jay.
Body: Black mohair.
Legs: Black hackle at shoulder.
Hook: ff.

21. *Black Ant* (July)
Wings: Waterhen or Woodcock.
Body: Black mohair.
Legs: Black hackle.
Hook: f.

22. *The Little Gosling* (July)
Wings: (a) Starling; (b) Bunting.
Body: Yellow-green mohair.
Legs: Red or cinnamon hackle.
Hook: fe.

23. *Evening Moth*
Wings: Owl.
Body: Cream mohair (full).
Legs: Same colour.
Hook: C.

24. *The Bee* (Standard)
Wings: Hen Pheasant or Partridge wing.
Body: Yellow tail, then brown, then black.
Legs: Black-red hackle.
Hook: fff.

25. *Brown Bear* (End of March)
Wings: Woodcock.
Body: Cinnamon brown mohair.
Legs: Cinnamon hackle.
Whisks: 2 fibres Mallard.
Hook: ff.

26. *Faren Fly* (July)
Wings: (a) Starling; (b) Partridge tail.
Body: Peacock herl.
Tag: Yellow tag.
Legs: Red hackle at shoulder.
Hook: fe.

27. *The Blue Midge* (June)
Wings: (a) Starling; (b) Lark.
Body: Ash-coloured fur (Fox-face, or American Squirrel).
Legs: Pick-out dubbing.
Whisks: 2 fibres of a grizzle hackle.
Hook: Midge.

28. *The Emerald Fly*
Wings: (a) Starling; (b) Bunting.
Body: Emerald-green silk or mohair.
Legs: Black-red hackle at shoulder.
Whisks: 2 fibres grizzle hackle.
Hook: Midge.

29. *Whirling Dun* (June & July)
Wings: Starling.
Body: Water-rat's fur.
Ribbing: Yellow silk.
Legs: Dun hackle.
Whisks: 2 fibres dun hackle.
Hook: f.

30. *Pismire*
Wings: None.
Body: Brown mohair.
Legs: Small red hackle from tail to head.
Hook: fe.

31. *Whirling Brown*
Wings: Woodcock wing.
Body: Cinnamon brown mohair.
Legs: Red or Cinnamon hackle.
Hook: f.

32. *Fire Fly*
Wings: Partridge grey and red feathers mixed.
Body: Copper Peacock herl.
Ribbing: Gold twist (optional)
Tag: Gold.
Legs: (a) Small red hackle at shoulder; (b) black-red hackle.
Hook: No. 9 or 10.

33. (No name)
Wing: Snipe.
Body: Dark Hare's ear, Water-rat's fur, yellow mohair, in equal parts.
Legs: Pick-out dubbing.
Hook: fe-ff or 9 to 12.

33 a. *Light Hare's Ear*
Wings: Partridge wing or tail.
Body: Light Hare's ear.
Legs: Partridge hackle.
Whisks: 2 fibres Mallard, or hen Pheasant or grey Partridge.

34. *Five Flies for the Axe, Devon:*
1. *Wren Tail* (Hacklewise)
Wings & Legs: Wren tail feather, or small red feather from a cock Grouse's head.
Body: Yellow silk.
Ribbing: Gold twist (Optional)
Hook: Midge.

2. *Iron Blue*
Wings: Water-rail.
Body: (Very thin) Light dun fur warped on pale yellow silk.
Legs: Brown-red cock's hackle.
Whisks: Brown-red cock's hackle.
Hook: f or No. 12.

3. *Yellow Dun or Upright*
Wings: Thrush or Landrail.
Body: Pale yellow silk a little waxed.
Hackle: Yellow grizzle.
Whisks: Yellow grizzle.
Hook: No. 12 or 13.

4. *Alder Fly*
Wings: Redstart's tail, or red Partridge.
Body: Chestnut silk.
Legs: Hackle from ear of Raven or Crow (blue-black).
Hook: No. 12 or 13.

5. *Partridge or Grouse Hackle*
Wings & Legs: (a) Brown Partridge hackle; (b) Grouse hackle.
Body: Brown fur.
Ribbing: Fine silver twist.
Hook: No. 12 or 13.

35. (No name).
(1) Wing: Brown Mallard—very short.
Body: Dark Hare's ear mixed with brown mohair (taper).
Legs: Dubbing picked out.

(2) Wings: Starling.
Body: (a) Hare's ear mixed with olive mohair; (b) golden olive, sooty and green mohair and Hare's ear mixed.

(3) Wings: (a) Mallard; (b) Woodcock.
Body: Hare's ear.

(4) Wings: Starling.
Body: Hare's fur and orange mohair.
Hooks for above four patterns: 9 to 13.

(5) Wings: Grey Partridge.
Body: Peacock herl.
Tag: Gold or yellow silk.
Legs: (a) 2 Black hackles either at shoulder or from tail to shoulder; (b) 2 Black-red hackles either at shoulder or from tail to shoulder.

(6)   Wings: Starling or Woodcock.
      Body: Cinnamon brown.
      Tag: Gold.
      Legs: Small brown-red hackle at shoulder.
      Whisks: 2 fibres Mallard.

(6a.) Black hackle over brown body.
(6b.) Cinnamon hackle over yellow body.
(6c.) Same body with black hackle and Teal wings.

36. Three Flies for the Doon & Stincher, Ayr, Scotland:
(1)   Wings: Starling.
      Body: Yellow tying-silk.
      Legs: Red hackle.

(2)   Same as (1) with a Black hackle.

(3)   Wings: (a) Starling; (b) Bunting; (c) Stormy Petrel.
      Body: Dark Hare's ear.

37. *Golden Plover Hackle* (Evenings August & Autumn)
Wings & Legs: Golden Plover hackle (back) at shoulder.
Body: Gold tinsel wrapped over with thin-cut india rubber.
Hook: No. 8.

38. *Light Grouse Hackle*
Dressed in same way as 37.

39. *Needle Fly*
Wings: Hen Pheasant mixed with brown Mallard.
Body: Light dun mixed with dark Hare's ear and a few hairs of yellow mohair. (Taper long and thin).
Ribbing: Gold—optional for evening.
Legs: Large brown-red cock saddle at shoulder.
Hook: No. 6 or 7.

40. *Partridge Hackle*
Wings & Legs: Partridge back.
Body: Hare's ear fur mixed with yellow mohair.
Ribbing: Yellow silk (Optional).
Hook: No. 8.

41. *Four Dun Palmers*
(1) Wings & Legs: Light dun hackle at shoulder.
    Body: Light Hare's ear mixed with a little yellow mohair.
    Ribbing: Yellow silk.
    Hook: No. 10.

(2) Wings & Legs: Yellow dun hackle at shoulder.
    Body: Yellow dun ribbed with light green silk.
    Hook: No. 12.

(3) Wings & Legs: Dark dun or grizzle hackle at shoulder.
    Body: Dun mohair, or Water-rat fur.
    Ribbing: Yellow silk.
    Hook: No. 12.

(4) Wings & Legs: Dun hackle at shoulder.
    Body: Silver tinsel.
    Hook: No. 5, 6, 7 for night.

42. *Four Celebrated Evening Flies for Thames at Weybridge:*
(1) Wings: Hen Pheasant tail.
    Body: Fiery brown mohair.
    Ribbing: Gold tinsel.
    Tag: Tuft mohair or topping.
    Legs: Brown hackle.

(2) Wings: Brown Mallard.
    Body: Brown and yellow mohair mixed.
    Hackle and tinsel as above.
    Hook: No. 5 or 6.

(3) Wings: (As in No. 1).
    Body: Copper Peacock herl (Full).
    Ribbing: Flat gold.
    Hackle: As in (1) and (2).

(4) Wings: Two Toppings and two neck feathers of Golden Pheasant sprigged each side with tail feather of Golden Pheasant, yellow-green parrot, sword feather of Peacock, yellow and blue Macaw feelers, Argus Pheasant, and Bustard feather—2 fibres of each. Let the toppings extend two-eighths of an inch longer than the other sprigging.

Body: Very gaudy bright yellow-green silk or mohair.
Ribbing: Gold twist or flat silver tinsel.
Whisks: Golden Pheasant topping (long).
Legs: Bright yellow-green hackle from tail up.
Hook: No. 9.

(Note: It may be made with the Golden Plover back feather for hackle—a good killer on Tweed.)

'CLERICUS'
Rambles and Recollections of a Fly-Fisher
1854

March

1. *February Red*
Wings: Dark Drake (flat).
Body: Red Sheepskin Mat or dark Red Squirrel.
Legs: Red hackle.
Hook: No. 9.

2. *Large Dark Blue*
Wings: Starling, not too light, upright.
Body: Mole and Mouse fur, slightly tinged with yellow.
Legs: Dark blue hackle.
Whisks: 2 strands dark blue hackle.
Hook: No. 9.

3. *Cockwing Blue*
Wings: Starling.
Body: Squirrel's blue fur mixed with yellow, either floss-silk or mohair.
Legs: Lightish blue hen's hackle.
Whisks: 2 strands blue cock's hackle.
Hook: No. 10.

4. *March Brown*
Wings: Woodcock or Pheasant or Partridge tail, upright.
Body: Brown Sable fur or Hare's ear.
Ribbing: Yellow silk.
Legs: Partridge back.
Whisks: 2 strands of hen Pheasant's or Partridge's tail.
Hook: No. 8.

5. *Small Red Spinner*
Wings: Starling.
Body: Reddish brown silk.
Ribbing: Fine gold thread.
Legs: Red hen's hackle.
Whisks: 2 strands red cock's hackle.
Hook: No. 10.

6. *Red Palmer*
Hackle: Red.
Body: Peacock herl.
Ribbing: Gold twist (optional).
Hook: No. 8 or 9.

April

7. Most of the previous flies.

8. *Sand Fly*
Wings: Landrail, flat and very full.
Body: Sandy fur from Hare's neck.
Legs: Ginger hackle.
Hook: No. 9.

9. *Great Red Spinner*
Wings: Starling, upright.
Body: Reddish-brown silk.
Ribbing: Gold thread.
   or
Body: Peacock herl stripped.
Ribbing: Fine yellow silk.
Legs: Red hackle.
Whisks: 2 strands red cock's hackle.
Hook: No. 9.

10. *Stone Fly*
Wings: 2 small grizzled cock's hackles, flat and close, and longer than the body.
or
Wings: Dark mottled hen Pheasant, or Woodcock well shaded.
Body: Brown Sable fur well mixed with yellow towards the tail especially.
Legs: Grizzled cock's hackle.
Whisks: 2 strands from a Partridge tail.
Horns: 2 short Rabbit whiskers.
Hook: No. 6.

11. *Gravel Bed* or *Spider*
Wings: Woodcock wing.
Body: Lead coloured silk.
Legs: Black hackle, long in fibre, two turns.
Hook: No. 10.

12. *Grannam* or *Green Tail*
Wings: Partridge or hen Pheasant wing.
Body: Dark Hare's ear.
Silk: Brown.
Tag: Green silk.
Legs: Pale ginger hen hackle.
or Buzz:
Hackle: Partridge neck.
Body: As above.
Hook: No. 9.

13. *Yellow Dun*
Wings: Light Starling or Snipe. Upright.
Body: Yellow silk well waxed, or a very light blue fur ribbed with yellow silk.
Legs: Very fine light blue hen hackle.
Whisks: 2 strands light blue cock's hackle.
Hook: No. 10.
or Buzz:
Hackle: Light blue hen, with body as above.

May

14. Many of the preceding flies.

15. *Iron Blue*
Wings: Tomtit tail, or hen Blackbird. Upright.
Body: Mole's fur with a little yellow floss, or a paler fur ribbed with purple silk.
Legs: Small yellowish dun hackle.
Whisks: 2 strands yellowish dun hackle.
Hook: No. 11.

16. *Black Gnat*
Wings: Starling, flat, short and full.
Body: Black Ostrich herl (short and thick).
Legs: Fine black hackle.
 or Buzz:
Hackle: Light dun hackle over same body.
Hook: No. 11.

17. *Downhill*
Wings: Woodcock wing, flat.
Body: Orange silk tied with ash coloured silk, showing most towards tail and under wing.
Legs: Furnace hackle.
Hook: No. 9.

18. *Fern Fly—Soldier & Sailor*
Wings: Soldier: Red hen or darkest Starling—flat. Sailor: Heron wing.
Body: Orange silk.
Legs: Red hackle.
 or Buzz:
Hackle: Furnace, over same body.
Hook: No. 9.

19. *Alder*
Wings: Woodcock wing or mottled cock Pheasant.
Body: Peacock herl, or copper coloured silk, or mulberry silk.
Legs: Blue hackle, almost black.
 or Buzz:

Hackle: Black or blue hackle over Peacock herl body.
Hook: No. 9.

20. *Black Palmer*
Hackle: Black or blood-red.
Body: Black Ostrich herl.
Ribbing: Silver twist.
Hook: No. 8 or 9.

June

21. *Green Drake*
Wings: Drake's feather stained yellow. Upright and full.
Body: Yellow silk waxed a little.
Legs: Grey Partridge stained yellowish.
Whisks: 3 long strands black hackle, or anything you can get.
  or Buzz:
Hackle: Drake's feather stained yellow over same body.
Hook: No. 6 or 7.

22. *Grey Drake*
Wings: Drake's grey feather. Upright and full.
Body: French white silk, or white Ostrich herl.
Ribbing: Dark brown silk.
Legs: Grizzled cock's hackle.
Whisks: 3 long strands black cock's hackle.
Hook: No. 6 or 7.

23. *Marlow Buzz* or *Coch-y-bonddhu*
Hackle: Coch-y-bonddhu.
Body: Peacock herl, or Peacock herl and Ostrich herl mixed.
Ribbing: Gold twist.
Hook: No. 9 or 10.

24. *White Moth*
Wings: White feather. Flat and full.
Body: White Ostrich herl.
Legs: White hackle.
Hook: No. 7.

July

25. *Sky Blue*
Wings: Light Starling stained pale yellow. Upright.
Body: Pale blue fur mixed with yellow mohair.
Legs: Pale dun hackle.
Whisks: 2 strands pale blue hackle.
Hook: No. 10.

26. *Wren Tail*
Wings & Legs: Wren tail.
Body: Light brown Sable fur.
Ribbing: Fine gold thread.
Hook: No. 11.

27. *July Dun*
Wings: Dark Starling. Upright.
Body: Mole's fur mixed with yellow mohair and spun on yellow silk.
Legs: Dark blue hackle.
Whisks: 3 strands dark blue hackle.
Hook: No. 10.

28. *Partridge Hackle*
Wings & Legs: Partridge back.
Body: Light brown Sable.
Ribbing: Gold thread.
Hook: No. 9.

August

29. *Red Ant*
Wings: Starling—flat.
Body: Peacock herl stripped below wings to near tail.
Legs: Red hackle.
Hook: No. 10.

30. *August Dun*
Wings: Brown hen. Upright.
Body: Brown silk ribbed with yellow tying-silk.
Legs: Grizzled hackle, brownish, or red hackle stained brown.
Whisks: 2 strands grizzled hackle.
Hook: No. 10.

31. *Orange Fly*
Wings: Dark Starling. Upright.
Body: Orange silk tied with dark silk.
Legs: Furnace hackle.
Hook: No. 10.

32. *Cinnamon Fly*
Wings: Dark Landrail, flat and full.
Body: Fawn silk.
Legs: Ginger hackle.
Hook: No. 9.

September

33. *Whirling Blue*
Wings: Starling wing. Upright.
Body: Squirrel's red-brown fur mixed with yellow mohair, spun on yellow silk.
Legs: Red hackle.
Whisks: 2 strands red hackle.
Hook: No. 10.

34. *Willow Fly*
Wings: Pale brown hen wing, or later, Starling.
Body: Mole's fur ribbed with yellow silk or fine gold thread.
Legs: Dark grizzled hackle.
Hook: No. 10.
  Equally good Buzz.

35. *Pale Blue*
Wings: Sea Swallow.
Body: Finest pale blue fur mixed with yellow mohair and tied with pale yellow silk.
Legs: Palest blue hackle.
Hook: No. 10.
(*Note:* In all the foregoing, silk bodies mean not floss but silk unravelled.)

ST. JOHN DICK
Flies and Fly-Fishing
1873

1. *Blue Dun* (Spring pattern)
Wings: Dark Starling.
Body: Greenish-olive crewel and Hare's ear.
Ribbing: Olive silk very slightly waxed.
Legs: Dark blue dun hen.
Whisks: 2 strands dark blue dun hen.
Hook: No. 9, 10 or 11.

2. *Blue Dun* (Autumn pattern)
Wings: Rather lighter Starling.
Body: Dark olive silk.
Ribbing: Yellow silk very lightly waxed.
Legs: Dark blue dun hen's hackle.
Hook: No. 10 or 11.

3. *Blue Dun* (Buzz)
Hackle: Blue dun hen.
Body: Greenish olive crewel and Hare's ear, without rib, dressed rather fat.
Hook: No. 10 or 11.

4. *February Red*
Wings: Light mottled hen Pheasant wing.
Body: Brick-red Pig's wool (rough).
Legs: Red cock hackle.
Hook: No. 8.
(Often winged with a speckled black and white feather.)

5. *Cowdung Fly*
Wings: Light Landrail.
Body: Yellowish-orange mohair (fat and rough).
Legs: Light ginger hackle.
Hook: No. 8 or 9.

6. *March Brown*
Wings: Dark mottled hen Pheasant wing.
Body: Hare's ear.
Ribbing: Yellow silk, distinct.
Legs: Partridge hackle (dark).
Whisks: 3 strands of any brown mottled feather.
Hook: No. 8 or 9.
   (For large March Browns, wing with hen Turkey wing feather. Best feather is the wing of hen Capercailzie.)

7. *Grannam or Green Tail*
Wings: Light grey hen Pheasant wing.
Body: Lightish Hare's face fur.
Tag: Grass-green worsted—2 or 3 turns.
Hook: No. 10 or 11.

8. *Spider Fly or Gravel Bed*
Wings: Mottled lightest part of Woodcock (underneath part of wing).
Body: Lead-coloured floss silk.
Legs: Black hackle, long in fibre and sparsely wound on.
Hook: No. 10 or 11.

9. *Iron Blue*
Wings: Slip of Moorhen wing.
Body: Mole's fur.
Ribbing: Dark yellow silk slightly waxed.
Legs: Dark blue dun hackle.
Hook: No. 10, 11 or 12.
   or Buzz pattern:
Wings & Legs: Opaque looking blue lead-coloured hackle.
Body: Mole's fur.
Ribbing: Dark yellow silk slightly waxed.
Hook: No. 12 or 13.

10. *Stone Fly* (Buzz)
Hackle: Transparent looking grizzled dun hackle, with very long fibres; 3 or 4 turns wound very lightly close to the head. Fibres should be one-third longer than the hook.
Head: Several extra turns of tying-silk.

Body: Hare's ear and yellowish Pig's wool mixed, yellow predominating at tail.
Ribbing: Coarse yellow cotton thread, wound sparely but distinctly.

11. *Yellow Dun*
Wings: Light hen Starling wing (glossy).
Body: Light yellow mohair slightly greenish.
Legs: Lightish yellow dun hackle.
Whisks: Lightish yellow dun hackle.
Hook: Nos. 9 or 10.
 or Buzz:
Wings & Legs: Opaque buff-coloured hackle, rather full.
Body: Light yellow mohair with a greenish tinge, dressed fat.
Hook: No. 10, 11, 12.

12. *Brown Spinner*
Wings: Light glossy hen Starling wing.
Body: (a) Dirty claret silk; (b) dyed gut.
Legs: Dull reddish-brown hackle.
Whisks: 3 long strands dull reddish-brown hackle.
Hook: No. 10.

13. *Hardy Brown*
Wings: Dark Woodcock.
Body: Dark claret floss.
Legs: Red hackle.
Hook: No. 10.

14. *Wren Tail*
Wings & Legs: Wren-tail (spare).
Body: Hare's face.
Ribbing: Yellow silk.
Hook: No. 11 or 12.

15. *Oak Fly or Down-looker*
Wings: Ruddy brown hen wing.
Body: Reddish-orange worsted.
Ribbing: Light brown silk, frequent turns.
Legs: Orange and black, rather long in fibre.
Hook: No. 8 or 9.
 or Buzz:

Wings & Legs: Woodcock feather, long in fibre and rather thick.
Body: Dark brown and orange mohair mixed—thicker at head than tail.
Hook: No. 8 or 9.

16. *Orl* or *Alder Fly* (Buzz pattern)
Wings & Legs: Light smoky transparent grizzled hackle of a dun shade—rather full.
Body: Rich claret worsted.
Ribbing: Dark bronze Peacock herl.
Hook: No. 8 or 9, or 6 or 7 during Mayfly season.
   or Winged:
Wings: Dark mottled Pheasant's wing.
Body: Rich claret worsted over a dark bronze Peacock herl.
Ribbing: Silver wire.
Legs: Coch-y-bonddhu hackle.

17. *Grey Spinner*
Wings: Woodcock wing.
Body: Dark brown worsted.
Ribbing: Thin gold wire, distinct.
Legs: Yellowish-red hackle.
Whisks: 4 long strands yellowish-red hackle.

18. *Sand Fly*
Wings: Reddish Landrail.
Body: Sandy fur, rough.
Legs: Ginger hen's hackle.
Hook: No. 9 or 10.

19. *Hawthorn Fly*
Wings: Dark grey Starling.
Body: Black Ostrich herl, tied full.
Legs: Very long-fibred black hackle, sparely dressed.
Hook: No. 8.

20. *Black Gnat*
Wings & Legs: Black hackle (spare).
Body: Black Ostrich herl, tied in at tail with 3 or 4 turns of dark grey silk.

21. *Yellow Sally*
Wings & Legs: Long-fibred pale yellow hackle.
Body: Light lemon crewel.
Hook: No. 9, 10.
   or:
Wings & Legs: Dotterel.
Body: Bright lemon floss, thicker at head.
Hook: No. 10, 11 and 12.

22. *Orange Palmer*
Hackle: Yellow and black or yellow and red (Coch-y-bonddhu) rather full and short in fibre.
Body: Bright orange worsted—very tight.
Ribbing: Gold wire or gold tinsel.
Hook: No. 6 to 12.

23. *Red Spinner*
Wings: Most transparent glossy light smokey-grey feather obtainable.
Body: Reddish-brown crewel—tight.
Ribbing: Gold wire, distinct.
Legs: Light red hackle.
Hook: No. 10.

24. *Coch-y-bonddhu*
Hackle: Coch-y-bonddhu.
Body: Bronze Peacock herl, very fat.
Ribbing: Gold wire, or
Tag: Gold tinsel—optional.
Hook: No. 10 to 13.

25. *Female Yellow Dun*
Wings: Very light, shiny pale blue feather.
Body: Light buff mohair.
Legs: Very light, almost white hackle.
Whisks: 4 long strands of same.
Hook: No. 8.

26. *Fern Fly*
Wings: Brown mottled hen Pheasant wing.

Legs: Light yellowish-red hackle.
Body: Light orange floss, three-quarters of the hook; 3 or 4 turns of bronze Peacock herl.
Hook: No. 9 or 10.

26 (a).
Wings: Moorhen, tied long.
Legs: Glossy black hackle, long and fine in fibre.
Body: Light orange floss (tight).
Hook: No. 9 or 10.

27. *Caddis Fly*
Wings: Buff, creamy feather (full).
Body: Buff, creamy fur or crewel.
Legs: Very light, delicate red hackle, long in fibre—2 turns close to head.
Whisks: 2 thick strands of wing feather.

28. *Blue Bottle*
Wings: Any dark grey feather.
Body: Dark blue floss.
Ribbing: Black Ostrich herl, even and distinct.
Legs: Black hackle, long in fibre, dressed sparely.
Hook: No. 9 or 10.

29. *Large Red Spinner*
Wings: Most transparent glossy light smoky-grey feather obtainable.
Body: Crimson worsted—tight.
Ribbing: Gold tinsel, distinct.
Legs: Bright red cock's hackle.
Whisks: 4 long strands bright red cock's hackle.

30. *Sky Blue*
Wings: Very delicate light glossy blue feather.
Body: Delicate tinged blue fur.
Ribbing: Fine pale blue silk.
Legs: Pale buff hackle, 2 turns.
Hook: No. 11 or 12.

31. *Brown Owl*
Wings: Full slip of Brown Owl's wing.
Body: Yellowish-brown pig's wool, dressed very fat and rough.
Legs: Sandy hackle, rather full.
Hook: No. 8 or 9.

32. *Red Ant*
Wings: Light hen Starling.
Body: 2 or 3 turns of bronze Peacock herl (fat) and orange floss silk.
Legs: Light red hackle.
Hook: Nos. 10 to 12.

33. *White Moth*
Wings: Full long slip of any white feather.
Body: White worsted, very fat and tapered.
Tag: Touch of shellac varnish.
Legs: Long-fibred white hackle.
Hook: No. 5, 6, 7.

33(a). *Small White Moth*
Wings: Short full slip of any white feather.
Body: White worsted, with 3 or 4 turns of black floss silk.
Legs: Fine long-fibred black hackle.
Hook: No. 9.

34. *Brown Moth*
Wings: Any very light buff feather.
Body: Gingery-brown pig's wool.
Legs: Long-fibred yellowish-red hackle.
Hook: No. 7.

35. *Claret Spinner*
Wings: Light grey smoky feather.
Body: Crimson worsted, neat and tight.
Ribbing: Gold wire.
Legs: Any transparent hackle dyed crimson.
Whisks: 4 long strands of same.
Hook: No. 9 or 10.

36. *Silver Dun.* 1st pattern:
Wings & Legs: Light bluish-grey hackle—2 turns.
Body: Light grey crewel ribbed with silver wire.
Hook: No. 11 or 12.
    2nd pattern:
Ribbing: Silver tinsel instead of wire.
    Rest of dressing as in 1st. pattern.
    3rd. pattern:
Wings & Legs: Transparent grizzled grey hackle.
Body: Silver tinsel.

37. *Mulberry Dun.* 1st. pattern:
Wings & Legs: Light grey opaque hackle.
Body: Mulberry mohair.
Hook: No. 12 or 13.
    2nd. pattern:
Wings & Legs: Darker hackle (bushy).
Body: Mulberry mohair, dressed very fat.

38. *Black Palmer*
Wings & Legs: Fine black hackle.
Body: Black Ostrich herl tightly wrapped.
Ribbing: Silver wire or tinsel.
Hook: No. 11, occasionally 10.

39. *August Dun*
Wings: Dark mottled brown hen.
Body: Hare's face—very thin and spare.
Ribbing: Dull dark claret silk.
Legs: Grizzled black and sandy (coch-y-bonddhu) hackle.
Hook: No. 9 or 10, occasionally 11.

40. *September Dun*
Wings: Light glossy buff feather.
Body: Creamy buff worsted (tight)—picked out.
Ribbing: Fine silk of same colour.
Legs: Light buff hackle.
Whisks: 3 very long strands light buff hackle.
Hook: No. 11 or 12.
    The Buzz pattern is dressed with a fine buff hackle sparely applied.

41. *Green Insect*
Wings & Legs: Very light smoky-grey hackle.
Body: Brightest green Peacock herl.
Hook: No. 11 to 14.

42. *Blue Gnat*
Wings & Legs: Light bluish hackle.
Body: Lightest part of mouse.
Hook: No. 12.

43. *Mid Blue*
Wings: Medium blue-grey feather, dressed very upright.
Body: Gut flattened and dyed a dirty olive-green, wrapped neat and tight.
Whisks: 2 strands blue dun.
Legs: Blue dun hackle.
Hook: No. 10 or 11.

44. *Cinnamon*
Wings: Reddish Landrail.
Body: Cinnamon mohair.
Legs: Reddish yellow hackle.
Hook: No. 9 or 10; and for lakes, 6 or 7.

45. *Whirling Dun*
Wings: Medium hen Starling.
Body: Light foxy red fur.
Ribbing: Imperceptible, of same colour.
Legs: Ginger hackle.
Whisks: 4 long strands ginger hackle.

46. *Willow Fly* (Female)
Wings & Legs: Grizzled hackle with a reddish tinge.
Body: Mouse fur; at tail to halfway up the hook flattened gut lightly dyed greenish-olive.
Hook: No. 10.

47. *Willow Fly* (Male)
Wings & Legs: Dark dun cock.
Body: Gut dyed dark—very tight and even.
Hook: Nos. 10 to 14.

FRANCIS FRANCIS
A Book on Angling
1867

1. *February Red (Perlidae)*
Wings: Peahen's back.
Body: Two turns of dirty claret-red mohair at the tail, with a strand or two of Hare's ear and claret mohair for the rest of the body.
Legs: Dark grizzled blue cock's hackle.
Hook: No. 9 or 10.

2. *Blue Dun* (Also termed Early Dark Dun, Hare's Ear, Cock Tail: in Lancs., Cumberland etc. the Blue Bloa; in Yorks., the Blue Drake; in Devon, Hare's Pluck, Hare's Fleck & Blue Upright.)
Wings: Starling.
Body: Grizzled fibres from a Hare's ear warped in with yellow or olive silk. Or: Two or three strands of the long breast feather of a Heron, ribbed with fine straw-coloured silk, to make a light fly; or: Heron's wing for a darker fly, or a strip of quill.
Legs: A blue dun hackle (sometimes dyed yellow).
Hook: No. 9 or 10 or smaller.
and, the *imago:*

3. *Red Spinner* (The Red-tailed Spinner of Jackson, or Orange Drake of Theakston.)
Wings: Starling; or, better, dark shiny tips of a blue cock's hackle, grizzled or freckled with a golden tinge at the points.
Body: Red-brown quill, ringed with fine gold wire; varying from dark to light red.
Legs: Red hackle.

4. *Olive Dun* (A variety of Blue Dun)
Wings: Starling, dipped in onion dye.

Body: Peacock's eye feather quill dyed yellow or olive.
Hooks: Nos. 9 to 12.
Legs: Yellow or olive hackle.

5. *March Brown* (Cob Fly of Wales; Brown Drake of Yorkshire)
Wings: Blurred or mottled cock Pheasant preferably. Or:
(a) Partridge tail; (b) mottled Woodcock; (c) speckled game hen's rump.
Body: Dark brown Hare's ear or face fur, ribbed with tawny yellow silk or straw-coloured silk.
Legs: Partridge back.
Tail: Two strands of same.
  For the female pattern:
Legs: Partridge breast feather.
Tail: Two strands of same.
Body: Introduce fine shreds of olive fur.

6. *Great Red Spinner* (*Imago* of March Brown)
Wings: Glossy golden Thrush wing.
Body: Red Squirrel's fur, ribbed with gold twist.
Legs: Amber-red cock's hackle.
Whisk: Two long strands of same.

7. *Black Hackle*
Hackle: Black cock.
Body: Peacock and black Ostrich herl.

8. *Peacock Fly* (A small beetle)
Wings: Dark Starling.
Body: Bronze Peacock herl.
Silk: Mulberry.
Hackle: A hackle stained dark purple, appearing black but held to the light having a dark tortoiseshell hue.

April

9. *Yellow Dun* (Yellow-legged Bloa of Jackson)
Wings: Young pale Starling.
Body: Quill, or in the lightest shades of floss silk.
Legs: Delicate honey dun hen's hackle (smoke-blue centre with golden tips), or a light buff Cochin hackle.
Whisk: Two small strands buff Cochin hackle.

10. *Brown Spinner* (*vide* Red Spinner pattern)
Wings: A shade lighter than for Red Spinner.
Body: Lighter or browner silk.
Hackle: Lighter red cock.
   This is the spinner of the Yellow Dun.

11. *Little Iron Blue Dun* (Or Watchet of the North)
Body: Mole's fur spun on silk of a lighter shade.
Hackle: Two turns ginger hen.
Whisk: Two strands of blue hackle.
Shoulder: Half a turn of Squirrel's fur or burnt sienna silk.
   And a smaller sort of dun:
Ribbing the body with fine straw-coloured silk.

12. *Jenny Spinner* (Little White Spinner of Jackson; Pearl Drake of Theakston; Evening Bloa of Wade)
Wings: Tips of two very pale blue cock's hackle. Or dress buzz.
Legs: Light silvery dun hackle, or a small grey feather at the end of the wing or from the back of a Sea Swallow or Roseate Tern, or a fine-fibred white Bantam hen very slightly stained with Judson's slate dye.

13. *Black Gnat* (Male)
Wings: Pale Starling (low and flat).
Body: (Short) Black Ostrich herl.
Legs: A very small black hackle, if any.
   The female is the Tail-y-Tail.

14. *Black Gnat* (Female)
Same dressing as for No. 13, but on a hook three sizes larger.

15. *Hawthorn Fly* (Diptera, Crane Fly)
Same dressing as No. 14 with a dark lead-blue hackle.

16. *Gravel Bed* or *Spider Fly* (Diptera)
Wings: Two fine slips of Woodcock, dressed flat.
Body: Fine, dark slate or lead-coloured floss silk.
Legs: (Almost as long as the hook) Two turns of a black cock's hackle.
Hook: No. 10.

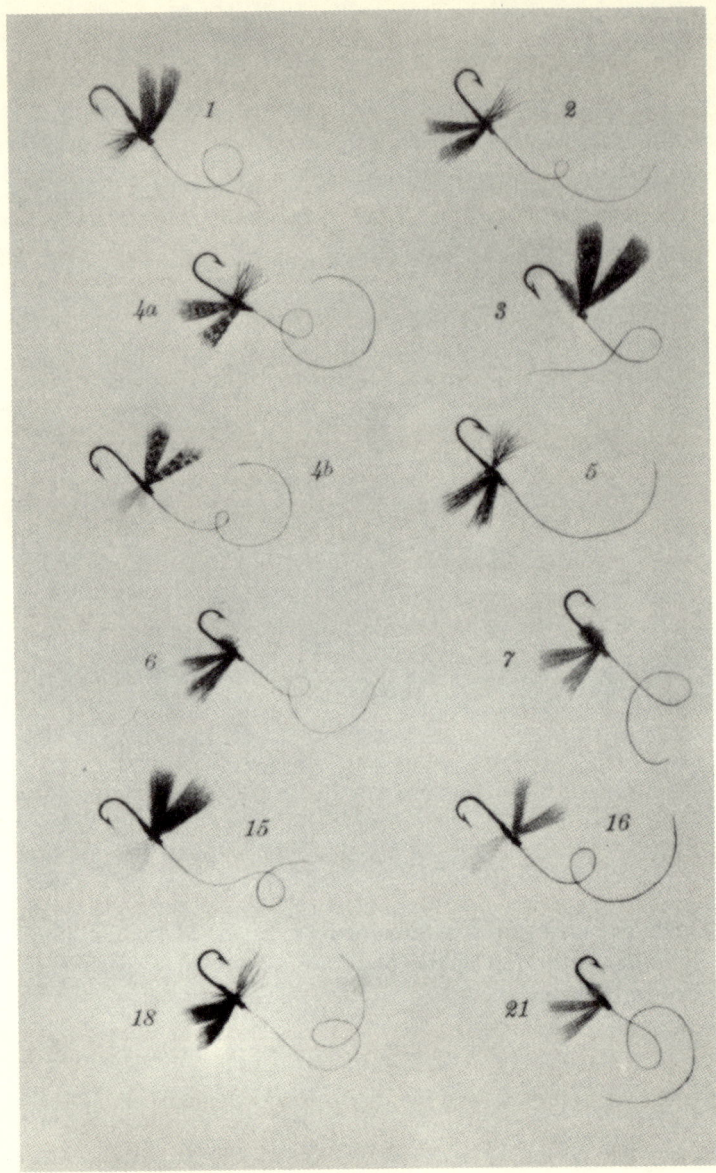

THE SCOTTISH FLY-DESIGN THAT CAME SOUTH

The wet-fly design adopted by G. E. M. Skues for the restoration of wet-fly fishing in the chalk streams. From David Webster's *Angler and the Loop-Rod*

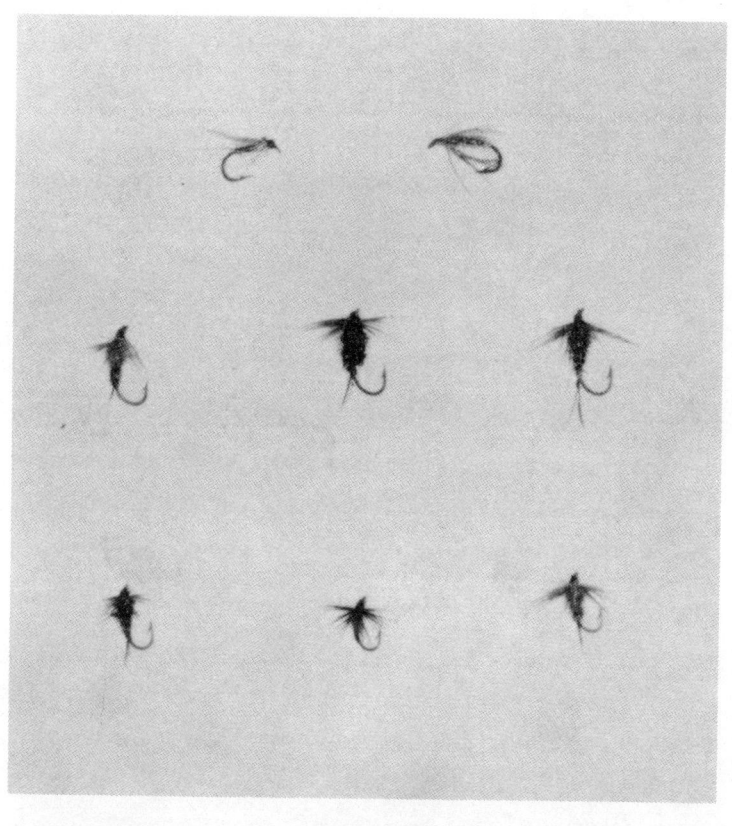

Chalk-stream nymphs as designed by G. E. M. Skues. The two flies at the top of the plate are actual early specimens dressed by Skues

17. *Sand Fly (Phryganidae)*
Wings: Two scraps of Starling, with two larger slips of Landrail's reddish wing feather over the Starling.
Body: Reddish fur from a Hare's poll mixed with buff fur to a sandy tinge.
Legs: Buff Cochin hen hackle.
Hook: No. 10.

18. *Cowdung* or *Lion Fly*
Wings: Light Landrail, dressed close and flat.
Body: Tawny orange crewel, with a few sprigs of Squirrel's fur worked into the body (as it is a hairy fly). Full and fat.
Legs: Yellowish-red hackle (Cochin China cock or darker red).
Hook: No. 8 or 9.

19. *Needle Brown (Perlidae)*
Wings: Starling's feather for the underwings, and two fine slips of hen Blackbird for the upperwings.
Body: Yellowish quill from a Thrush's wing.
Hook: No. 11 or 12.

20. *Palmer*
Body: Peacock herl (full).
Hackle: Blood-red cock carried down the body.
Hook: Nos. 8, 9, 10.

21. *Grannom*
Dress in two shades:
Light:—
Wings: Very light sandy hen Pheasant.
Body: Brown fur from a Hare's ear.
Hackle: Cochin China.
Dark:—
Wings: Same as above but of a darker tint.
Body: As above mixed with Mole's fur.
Hackle: A darker red.
Hook: Nos. 9 to 12.

22. *Sedge Fly*
Wings: (Full) Starling under, Landrail upper.

Body: Light buff crewel.
Hackle: (Tail to head) Pale red.
Ribbing: Fine gold wire run over the hackle the reverse way.
Hook: No. 8 and 9.

23. *Quill Gnat*
Wings: Bright Starling.
Body: A strip of Starling quill.
Legs: A dark blue dun cock's hackle. A red hackle is used for the June and July dressing.
Hook: Nos. 10 and 11.

May

24. *Stonefly*
Wings: Hen Pheasant.
Body: (Large & full) Mixed Hare's ear and Water-rat's fur with a few strands of yellow mohair worked in—the tail part brighter yellow and ribbed distinctly with yellow silk.
Legs: A grizzled dark blue dun cock's hackle.
Whisks: Two strands of brown Mallard's feather.
Horns and Feelers: Two Rabbit's whiskers.
　To be worked on the water. The female is much larger than the male.
Hook: No. 6 or 7.

25. *Oak Fly* (Downhill or Downlooker)
Wings: Woodcock or hen Pheasant.
Body: Orange floss.
Legs: Coch-y-bonddhu hackle tied in at the tail and worked to the shoulder. Snip off hackle short all the way up the body leaving rings of short black stubs.
Hook: No. 9 or 10.

26. *Little Blue* (Sky Blue, the Eden Fly of Aldam)
Wings: Small slip of outside wing of a Roseate Tern, or of common Tern, or of Sea Swallow.
Body: Straw-coloured silk.
Legs: Two turns of a small honey dun hackle.
Hook: Very small.

27. *Alder* or *Orl Fly*
Wings: Brown speckled feather from the rump of a brown game hen.
Body: Peacock herl, dressed full.
Legs: A dark grizzled blue dun or rusty black cock's hackle.
Hook: Nos. 6 to 10.

28. *Pale Evening Dun*
Wings: Pale Starling, lightly dyed in onion dye.
Body: Dirty yellowish-buff mohair, ribbed with light lemon silk.
Legs: Honey dun hackle.
Hook: No. 10 or 11.

June

29. *Coch-y-bonddhu* (Shorn Fly; Hazel Fly; Marlow Buzz; Fern Web; Bracken Clock etc.)
Body: Dark copper Peacock herl and black Ostrich herl, dressed fat.
Hackle: Dark red with a black streak in the centre.

30. *Welshman's Button* (A beetle)
Wings: Corncrake.
Body: Black Ostrich herl.
Legs: A black hackle.

31. *Fern Fly* (A winged beetle)
Two kinds: Orange wing-case; blue wing-case.
Wings: Hen Pheasant or Dark Starling.
Body: Orange-yellow or orange crewel.
Legs: A red hackle.
Hook: No. 9 or 10.

32. *Yellow Sally*
Wings: Light transparent feather stained palest watery yellow.
Body: Pale yellow crewel, ribbed with tawny brown silk.
Legs: A pale lemon hackle.
Hook: No. 10.

33. *Barm Fly (Phryganidae)*
Wings: Dark speckled cock Pheasant.
Body: Light creamy-brown fur.
Legs: A red hackle.
Hook: No. 7 or 8.

34. *Foetid Brown* (Mushroom Fly)
Wings: (Upright & full) Starling under wing, Corncrake over it.
Body: (Full) Mixed Hare's ear and Water-rat's fur.
Legs: Pick out body-dressing, or use a grizzled blue dun hackle.
Hook: No. 9 or 10.

35. *Caperer*
Wings: Marbled part of hen Pheasant's wing.
Body: Rusty-red mohair.
Tag: Two turns gold twist.
Legs: A red cock's hackle, not too dark.
Hook: No. 8 or 9, or larger.

July

36. *Red Ant*
Wings: Light shining Starling.
Body: Peacock herl tied in at the waist with copper-coloured silk.
Legs: A red cock's hackle.
Hook: No. 8, 9 or 10.

37. *Black Ant*
Wings: Dark Starling.
Body: Black Ostrich herl and Peacock herl mixed and tied at waist with black silk.
Legs: A black cock's hackle.

38. *Housefly*
Wings: (Flat) Dark Starling.
Body: (Fat) Two or three strands of rusty dark bluish feather from a Heron's back wound on like herl. Tie in at each side at the tail two fine shreds of buff-coloured silk, and carry along the sides when finishing off.
Legs: Rusty black cock's hackle.
Hook: No. 9.

39. *Hammond's Adopted* (Akin to the Foetid Brown)
Wings: Hen Pheasant.
Body: Dark Hare's ear and Mole's fur mixed.
Legs: Grizzled blue dun hackle.
 or:
Hammond's Dressing:
Wings: Pheasant or Woodcock.
Body: Medium ruddy brown crewel.
Legs: Rusty brown hackle, dressed head to tail.

40. *Wrentail*
Wings & Legs: (Hacklewise) Tail of a Tomtit or Wren or Golden Plover hackle.
Body: Yellow silk.
Hook: No. 11 or 12.

41. *White Moth*
Wings: White Goose, or underwing of a Grey Owl.
Body: White crewel, or Ostrich herl.
Legs: White hen's hackle. Or a light ginger hackle.
Hook: No. 5 or 6.

42. *Brown Moth*
Wings: Speckled Brown Owl.
Body: Yellowish-brown crewel.
Legs: Light brown hackle.

43. *Green Midge* (Hacklewise)
Wings & Legs: A very fine, soft, pale silvery blue hen's hackle.
Body: Applegreen floss.

44. *Blue Midge*
Wings & Legs: As above.
Body: Pale slate floss.

45. *Ashy Dun*
Wings: Light Starling.
Body: Silver-grey silk, the colour of ash bark.
Hackle: Pale blue dun.

46. *July Dun*
A shade lighter and one size larger than the Iron Blue pattern, *q.v.*

47. *Black Silverhorns* (Trichoptera)
Wings: Fine-grained, shiny black feather dressed close.
Body: Dark lead-coloured silk, ribbed with yellow silk.
Legs: Short dark slate hackle, sparely applied.
Horns: Two strands of bright speckled Drake's feather.
Hook: No. 9 or 10.

48. *Brown Silverhorns*
Wings: Under: Dark Starling; Over: Landrail.
Body: Rusty black Ostrich herl spun on brown silk, and dressed short. Buff stripes along body.
Legs: Dark grizzled dun hackle.

August

49. *August Dun* (Ronald's dressing)
Wings: Brown hen.
Body: Light brown floss silk, ribbed with yellow silk.
Legs: A red hackle stained brown.
Whisks: Two Rabbit's whiskers.
Hook: No. 9 or 10.

50. *Cinnamon (Phryganidae)*
Wings: Reddish cinnamon feather, or yellowish hen, Landrail or Owl.
Body: Dark barm-coloured silk.
Legs: Light or dirty brown hen's hackle with a darkish centre.

51. *Whirling Dun* (Ronald's dressing)
Wings: Darkest Starling.
Body: Squirrel's red-brown fur mixed with yellow mohair and tied with yellow silk, well waxed.
Legs & Whisks: A ginger hackle.
Hook: Nos. 10 and 11.

September

52. *Willow Fly* (Old Besom of Devonshire)
Wings & Legs: (Hacklewise) Dark dun copper-tinged cock's hackle.
Body: Mole's fur spun on yellow silk.
Hook: Nos. 10 and 11.

General Flies

1. *Francis Fly*
Wings: Two hackle-points of a grizzled blue dun *cock's* hackle set well up.
Body: Copper Peacock herl, ribbed distinctly with copper-red silk.
Hackle: Medium blue dun.
Hook: Nos. 7 to 12.

2. *Wickham's Fancy*
Wings: Light or dark Starling.
Body: Gold tinsel.
Legs: A red hackle carried from head to tail.
Hook: Nos. 8 to 11.

3. *Coachman*
Wings: Any small white feather.
Body: Peacock herl.
Legs: A red cock's hackle.
Hook: Nos. 8 to 11.

4. *Hofland's Fancy*
Wings: Hen Pheasant or Woodcock.
Body: Dark brown-red silk.
Legs: A red cock's hackle.
Whisk: Two strands of same.
Hook: No. 10 or 11.

5. *Governor*
Wings: Hen Pheasant.
Body: Peacock herl (full).
Tag: Orange floss or gold twist.
Hook: Nos. 7 to 11.

6. *Mackerel Governor*
Same as above, but with a grey Drake wing.

7. *Greenwell's Glory* (Not the original dressing)
Wing: Woodcock.
Body: Dark olive silk, thickly ribbed with very fine gold wire.
Legs: A small dark coch-y-bonddhu hackle.
Hook: No. 12 or 13.

8. *Edmead*
Wing: Grey Drake.
Remainder of dressing as for Red Spinner pattern, *q.v.*

9. *Grouse Hackle*
Hackle: Hen Grouse.
Body: Yellow silk.
Tag: One turn gold tinsel.
Hook: No. 11 or 12.

10. *Partridge Hackle*
Hackle: Grey Partridge.
Body: Lemon silk.
Tag: One turn gold tinsel.

11. *Soldier Palmer*
Wings & Legs: (Hacklewise) A bright red cock's hackle wound on from head to tail.
Body: Bright red crewel, ribbed with gold thread.
Hook: Nos. 9 to 11.

'HALCYON'
(Henry Wade)
Rod Fishing with Fly, Minnow and Worm
1861

1. *Prime Dun*
Wings: Starling.
Head: Ash-coloured silk.
Body: Ash-coloured silk.
Legs: Dark red or black cock's hackle.
Hook: No. 3 Limerick.
Season: February and March.

2. *Ash Dun* or *Fox*
Wings: Starling.
Head: Ash-coloured silk.
Body: Fox cub fur.
Ribbing: Straw-coloured silk.
Legs: Ash-coloured hackle.
Whisks: Two strands Squirrel's tail.
Hook: No. 2 Limerick.
Season: February and March.

3. *Palmer Fly*
Body: Black hog's wool.
Ribbing: (a) Dark red silk;
(b) Peacock herl.
Hackle: Red cock over all.
Season: All.

3a. Sometimes add a red tail tuft.

4. *Golden Hackle*
Body: Black Spaniel's ear and dark yellow silk.
Ribbing: Gold twist.
Hackle: Black, dark red, red, or tinged, over all.
Season: All.

5. *Black Wing Hackle*
Wings: Starling.
Body: Black water-dog's fur.
Legs: Black hackle.
Season: February and March.

6. *March Brown, Dun Drake,* or *Cob Fly*
Wings: Indian Bustard, Partridge tail, hen Pheasant, or Woodcock.
Body: Brown foal's hair—on orange floss silk.
Legs: Grey feather from Partridge breast.
Ribbing: Copper-coloured silk or gold twist.
Legs: Dark red or pale amber cock's hackle.
Whisks: Two strands of Partridge tail feather, or two hairs from a Squirrel's tail.

Hook: No. 3 Limerick.
Season: March and July.
The male is a chocolate brown, female a green-brown.

7. *Pheasant*
Wings: Strong marked feather from cock Pheasant's breast.
Body: Orange floss.
Head & Tail: With or without gold tinsel (discretionary).
Hook: No. 3 Limerick.

8. *Dark Bloa, No. 1*
Wings: Blackbird.
Body: Black fur and claret camlet.
Legs: Dusky black cock's hackle.
Hook: Limerick 1 or 2.
Season: Nearly all season.

9. *Small Stone Fly*
Wings: Redwing or Thrush quill feather, dressed flat.
Body: Dark claret silk.
Legs: Dark red or black hackle.
   or, hacklewise:
Wings & Legs: Snipe—outside wing feather.
Body: As before.
Season: Good throughout the year from April. Darker body early in the season and lighter in summer; darker again later.

10. *The Pale Green*
Wings: Very pale Starling, Stint, or Dotterel.
Body: Pale green silk.
Legs: Ash-coloured cock hackle.
Season: May, June and July.

11. *The Spring Bloa*
Head: Peacock herl.
Wings: Light Woodcock.
Body: Copper silk.
Legs: Chocolate or dark red cock's hackle.
Season: March and April.

12. *The Light Spring Bloa*
Head: Magpie.
Wings: Woodcock, under wing.
Body: Yellow silk.
Legs: Red cock's hackle.
Season: March and April.

13. *Partridge Tail*
Head: Peacock herl.
Wings: Mottled grey feather from Partridge tail.
Body: Orange silk, or dubbing from a Fox's ear, ribbed with orange silk.
Legs: Red cock's hackle.
Whisks: Two strands Squirrel's tail.
Season: February and March.

14. *Dark Grouse*
Head: Peacock herl.
Wings: Dark mottled Grouse feather.
Body: Orange silk.
Hook: No. 1 or 2 Limerick.
Season: All.

15. *Light Grouse*
Head: Peacock herl.
Wings: Light mottled Grouse feather.
Body: Orange silk.
Hook: No. 1 or 2 Limerick.
Season: All.

16. *Snipe Bloa*
Head: Magpie.
Wings: Snipe.
Body: Yellow silk.
Legs: Pale red or yellow cock's hackle.
Hook: No. 1 or 2 Limerick.
Season: All.

17. *Spanish Needle*
Head: Peacock herl.

Wings: Brown Owl.
Body: Brown silk.
Hook: No. 1 Limerick.
Season: May.

18. *Pheasant Brown*
Head: Peacock herl.
Wings: Cock Pheasant's breast feather.
Body: Brown silk.
Legs: Small mottled feather from a Grouse neck.
Hook: No. 2 or 3 Limerick.
Season: All.

19. *Sandfly*
Head: Peacock herl.
Wings: Inside Woodcock.
Body: Fibres from a Heron's quill.
Legs: Red cock's hackle.
   or:
Head: Peacock herl (optional).
Wings: Corncrake (ruddy feather).
Body: Rib with two strands from a cock Pheasant's tail.
Legs: Claret coloured hackle.
Season: April and September.

20. *Spider Fly*
Head: Peacock herl.
Wings: Outside Woodcock.
Body: Lead-coloured silk.
Legs: Black cock's hackle.
Hook: No. 1 Limerick.
Season: April to Mid-May.

21. *Green Body*
Head: Peacock herl.
Wings: Jay.
Body: Pale green silk.
Legs: Red cock's hackle.
Hook: No. 1 Limerick.
Season: July.

22. *Hare's Lug*
Wings: Light Woodcock.
Body: Hare's ear fur dressed with yellow silk. In the height of the season, wrap green floss thick at the tip—it is then called the Greentail.
Hook: No. 2 Limerick.
Season: All season without the green floss.

23. *Yellow Legs*
Wings: Lightest Golden Plover or Dotterel.
Body: Bright yellow silk.
Legs: Yellow cock's hackle.
Hook: No. 1 or 2 Limerick.
Season: April to July.

24. *Watchett*
Head: Magpie.
Wings: Jackdaw.
Body: Water-rat fur.
Hook: No. 1 Limerick.
Season: May.

25. *Stone Midge*
Head: Peacock herl.
Wings: Pewit.
Body: Two or three strands Heron's quill.
Hook: No. 0 Limerick.
Season: June and July.

26. *Knotted Midge*
Head: Magpie.
Wings: Pewit.
Body: Black fur from a Hare's scut.
Hook: No. 0 Limerick.
Season: June and July.

27. *Yellow Watchett*
Wings: Cormorant.
Body: Hare's ear.
Ribbing: Yellow silk.
Hook: No. 1 or 2 Limerick.
Season: May.

28. *Stone Dun* or *Bloa*
Head: Peacock.
Wings: Jack Snipe or Judcock.
Body: Ribbed with yellow and brown silk.
Legs: Red cock's hackle.
Hook: No. 1 or 2 Limerick.
Season: May and June.

29. *Yellow Dun* or *Bloa, No. 1*
Wings: Woodpecker.
Body: Yellow wool.
Legs: Body picked out.
Hook: No. 1 or 2 Limerick.
Season: June.

30. *Ant Fly*
Head: Peacock herl.
Wings: Light Starling.
Body: Peacock herl—thick at the tail—dressed with orange silk.
Legs: Wren.
Hook: No. 1, 2 or 3 Limerick.
Season: June and July.

31. *Dotterel*
Head: Brown silk.
Wings: Dotterel.
Body: Yellow and brown silk ribbed alternately.
Legs: Light red or golden cock's hackle.
Hook: No. 1, 2 or 3.
Season: April and May.

32. *Green-bodied Moth*
Head: Peacock herl.
Wings: Young Cuckoo, or Nightjar.
Body: Green silk.
Legs: Red cock's hackle.
Hook: No. 2 or 3 Limerick.
Season: June.

33. *Dark Bloa*, No. 2
Wings: Swift.
Body: Copper-coloured silk.
Legs: Wren.
Hook: No. 1 Limerick.
Season: All.

34. *Dark Midge*
Wings: Blackbird (short).
Body & Head: Black Ostrich herl.
Hook: No. 0 Limerick.
Season: June and July.

35. *The Sky-Blue Bloa*
Head: Peacock herl.
Wings: Blackcap.
Body: Sky-blue floss.
Legs: Partridge, grey neck hackle.
Hook: No. 0 Limerick.
Season: June and July.

36. *Dark Bloa and Copper*
Wings: Blackbird or Swift.
Body: Copper-coloured silk.
Legs: Dark grizzle or copper-coloured hackle.
Hook: No. 0 or 1 Limerick.

36a. *Dark Snipe* (hacklewise)
Wings & Legs: Snipe, dark outside feather.
Body: Copper-coloured silk.
Season: All.

37. *Dark Bloa and Purple,* or *Dark Snipe and Purple*
As No. 36 except body which is of purple silk.
Season: All.

38. *Light Bloa*
Wings: Snipe or blue Fieldfare.
Body: Light yellow silk.
Legs: Pale red grizzled hackle.
　or, hacklewise:

Wings & Legs: Small light coloured Dotterel, or Golden Plover.
Body: Light yellow silk.
Hook: No. 1 or 2 Limerick.
Season: All.

39. *Bloa and Orange,* No. 1
Wings: Starling.
Body: Orange floss.
Legs: Red cock's hackle.
Whisks: Two strands Squirrel's tail.
Hook: No. 2 Limerick.
Season: Midsummer.

40. *Bloa and Yellow*
Wings: Snipe or Starling.
Body: Yellow silk.
Legs: Yellow cock's hackle.
   or, hacklewise:
Wings & Legs: Inside shoulder feather of Snipe or Starling.
Body: Yellow silk.
Hook: Nos. 0, 1 or 2 Limerick.
Whisks: (optional) Two strands of fur from a Squirrel's tail.
Season: All season.

41. *Bloa and Orange,* No. 2
Wings: Palest Jay.
Body: Orange silk.
Legs: Golden hackle.
Season: All.

42. *Woodcock and Orange*
Wings: Woodcock.
Body: Orange floss.
Legs: Red cock's hackle.
Whisks: Two strands to match.
Hook: No. 2 Limerick.
   If the water is clear and low, add a Head of gold tinsel and make the fly smaller.
Season: All.

43. *Woodcock and Yellow*
Wings: Light Woodcock.
Body: Yellow floss.
  Remainder of dressing as in No. 42.
Season: All season.

44. *Blue Bloa*
Wings: Hen Blackbird.
Body: Mole's fur.
Legs: Blue cock's hackle, or pick out dubbing.
Hook: No. 2 Limerick.
Season: April and May.

45. *Little Blue Bloa*, No. 1
Head: Gold tinsel.
Wings: Hen Blackbird, upright and divided.
  Remainder of dressing as in No. 44.
Hook: No. 0 Limerick.
Season: Midsummer.

46. *Red Dun*
Head: Gold tinsel (for clear waters).
Wings: Corncrake.
Body: Deep orange silk (floss or waxed).
Ribbing: Gold tinsel.
Legs: Blood-red cock's hackle.
Hook: No. 1 or 2 Limerick; or for low waters, No. 0.
Season: April & May.
  May be dressed hacklewise, the Wings and Legs being represented with a feather from the outside of a Corncrake's wing. Rest of the dressing as above.

47. *The Light Dun*
Wings: Corncrake (light).
Body: Yellow silk (floss or waxed).
  Rest of dressing as in No. 46 only lighter.
  or hacklewise:
Wings & Legs: Daker hen's wing.
  Remainder of dressing as before.
Season: Spring and Autumn.

48. Golden Plover
Head: Gold tinsel.
Wings: Golden mottled feather of a Plover.
Body: Gold-coloured silk.
Legs: Gold-coloured cock's hackle.
Hook: No. 2 Limerick.
  or hacklewise:
Wings & Legs: Small golden mottled feather from outside of a Plover's wing.
  Rest of dressing as before.
Season: April, May, and June.

49. Plover and Yellow
As for No. 48, substituting yellow silk for orange.
  or, hacklewise: As last.
Season: April, May and June.

50. Moorpout and Orange
Wings: Small bloa feather from inside of Moorpout's wing.
Body: Orange floss, or waxed silk.
Legs: Pale red grizzled cock's hackle.
Whisks: Two strands Squirrel tail.
Hook: No. 1 Limerick.
Season: April, May and June.
  May be dressed hacklewise with the same feather.

51. Moorpout and Yellow
Same as No. 50, using yellow in place of orange silk.
  Hacklewise as above also.
Hook: No. 1 Limerick.
Season: April, May and June.

52. Black Jack
Wings: Jackdaw, or cock Blackbird, or Swift.
Body: Black silk, made thin.
Legs: Black cock's hackle.

53. *Salmon Jack*
Wings: Jackdaw's quill.
Body: Salmon floss, thinly wrapped.
Legs: Bright red cock's hackle.
Hook: No. 1 Limerick.
Season: Midsummer.

54. *Creeper*
Wings: Grey mottled feather with black bands in it from the large Creeper.
Body: Pale orange floss.
Legs: Pale red cock's hackle.
Hook: No. 1 Limerick.
Season: May.

55. *Fiery Clock*
Wings: Corncrake with a strand or two of Blackbird under and projecting.
Body: Bright scarlet worsted (pretty full).
Ribbing: Black silk.
Legs: Red or black cock's hackle.
Hook: No. 2 or 3 Limerick.
Season: Midsummer.

56. *The Clock*, No. 1 (Hackle Fly)
Wings & Legs: Inside Corncrake (pale).
Body: Copper Peacock herl, dressed with orange or copper-coloured silk.
Tag: Of the same silk.
Hook: No. 1 or 2 Limerick.
 or:
56a. *The Clock*, No. 2
Wings: Two pale red cock's hackles tied back to back and cut square at the points.
Body: Copper Peacock herl.
Ribbing: Crimson or pure copper-coloured silk, to show well at tip.
Legs: Longish ash-coloured or grizzle cock's hackle.
Season: All season.

57. *The Dark Soldier*
Wings: Snipe or Fieldfare.
Body: Dark crimson silk, well waxed.
Legs: Black or grizzle cock's hackle.
Hook: No. 0 Limerick.
Season: May and June.
   or, hacklewise:
Wings & Legs: Outside feather of Snipe's wing.
   Remainder of dressing as above.

58. *The Mussel Shell*
Wings: Bright blue feather from the outside of a Jay's wing.
Body: Black water Spaniel's fur mixed with claret coloured camlet.
Legs: Dusky black or claret coloured hackle.
Hook: Nos. 1 and 2 Limerick for February and March: No. 0 for the rest of the summer.

59. *The Fern Owl*
Wings: Fern Owl or Nightjar.
Body: Brown Bear's fur mixed with purple worsted (short and thick).
Legs: Dusky red cock's hackle.
Hook: No. 0 Limerick.
Season: April and May.

60. *The Red Hackle*
Wings & Legs: Red cock's hackle.
Body: Orange silk (or deep yellow at the latter end of the season).
Hook: No. 2 Limerick.
Season: All season.

61. *Red Palmer*
Body: Peacock herl.
Ribbing: Gold twist or tinsel.
Fur: Red cock's hackle over all to tail.
Silk: Orange.
Hook: No. 2 or 3 Limerick.
Season: May and June.

62. *Black Palmer*
Body: Black Ostrich herl.
Ribbing: Silver twist.
Fur: Black cock's hackle over all to tail.
Silk: Black.
Hook: No. 2 or 3 Limerick.
Season: May and June.

63. *Grizzled Palmer*
Body: Peacock herl.
Ribbing: Gold or silver tinsel.
Fur: Grizzled cock's hackle over all to tail.
Silk: Crimson, well waxed.
Hook: No. 2 or 3 Limerick.
Season: April and May.

64. *Ash Palmer*
Head: Gold tinsel.
Body: Ash-coloured fur or worsted, mixed with a little bright gold-coloured worsted.
Silk: Yellow.
Fur: Ash-coloured cock's hackle over all to tail.
Tip: Gold tinsel.
Hook: No. 2 or 3 Limerick.
Season: June and July.

65. *Black Hackle*
Wings & Legs: Black hackle.
Body: Yellow silk.
Hook: No. 1 Limerick.
Season: All season.

66. *Water Spider*
Wings & Legs: Two turns of a long-fibred black cock's hackle.
Body: Peacock herl.
Hook: No. 1 Limerick.
Season: All season.

67. *Little Blue Bloa,* No. 2
Wings: Blue Pigeon.
Body: Water-rat's or Mole's fur.

Hook: No. 1 Limerick.
Season: May (cold, black days).

68. *Large Red Ant*
Wings: Young Starling.
Body: Three or four turns of Peacock herl at the tip.
Silk: Copper coloured or orange.
Legs: Red cock's hackle.
  or (better):
Wings: Thrush, or Redwing's wing.
Legs: Red cock's hackle.
Silk: Orange.
Body: Near the tip or butt, three or four turns of two or three strands from the long feather of a cock Pheasant's tail.
Hook: No. 2 Limerick.
Season: June (11 a.m. to 6 p.m.)

69. *Black Ant*
Wings: Starling, Snipe, or Fieldfare.
Body: Black silk with two or three turns of black Ostrich herl at the tip.
Legs: Black cock's hackle.
Hook: No. 2 Limerick.
Season: June.

70. *Sea Swallow*
Head: Black Ostrich herl.
Wings & Legs: White hackle from Sea Swallow's wing.
Body: White silk.
Whisks: Two strands of feather for wing.
Hook: No. 1 Limerick.
Season: June and July.

71. *Red Spinner*
Wings: Brown Owl, or dingy copper-coloured Mallard, or young Cuckoo.
Body: Dark crimson or dingy copper-coloured silk.
Ribbing: Gold tinsel.
Legs: Dingy red cock's hackle.
Whisks: Two hairs from a bear's skin.
  or:

Wings: Inside Jay (of warm tinge).
Body: Orange silk ribbed with yellow, and two or three strands Golden Pheasant's topping.
Legs: Small Golden Pheasant's hackle.
Whisks: Two hairs from a bear's skin.
Hook: No. 2, 1 or 0 Limerick.
Season: April to July.

72. *Black Rabbit*
Wings: Blackbird.
Body: Black Rabbit's fur mixed with claret-coloured worsted just to tinge.
Legs: Dusky black hackle.
Hook: No. 2 Limerick.
Season: March.
   or, hacklewise:
Wings & Legs: Large feather from Fieldfare's back.
   Remainder of dressing as above.

73. *Brechan Clock*
Wings: Daker hen, or Corncrake, or Snipe.
Body: Hare's ear fur mixed with lilac worsted.
Ribbing: (Optional) Gold tinsel, or better, silver.
Hook: No. 1 Limerick.
Season: May, June and July.

74. *Hazle Fly* or *Marlow Buzz*
Wings: Inside Thrush, or Redwing (sandy coloured).
Body: Black Ostrich herl and purple Peacock herl (thick and dumpy).
Legs: Bluish cock's hackle, full under the wing.
Hook: No. 1 Limerick.
Season: May.

75. *Earliest Great Dark Dun*
Wings: Brownish Mallard.
Body: Mole's fur mixed with brown worsted.
Legs: Dark grizzled cock's hackle.
Hook: No. 2 or 3 Limerick.
Season: All season.
   Will take salmon.

76. *Fern Fly* or *Mealy Brown* No. 1
Wings: Yellowish tinged Thrush's wing.
Body: Dusky orange fur, or light yellowish brown of a Fox's breast.
Hook: No. 1 or 2 Limerick.
Season: May.

77. *Little Blue Bloa*, No. 3
Wings: Jack Snipe, or blue or black cap (Dressed erect).
Body: Blue fur of Water-rat, or Mole's fur mixed with lemon-coloured worsted.
Hook: No. 0 Limerick.
 or, hacklewise:
Wings & Legs: Ash-coloured cock's hackle.
Season: March.

78. *Red-Legged Blue Bloa*
Wings: Starling, or inside Moorpout.
Body: Mole's fur.
Legs: Picked-out fur, or gingery-red cock's hackle.
Hook: No. 0 Limerick.
Season: May and June.

79. *Lilac Bloa*
Wings: Corncrake.
Body: Lilac silk.
Legs: Red cock's hackle.
Hook: No. 0 Limerick.
Season: May.

80. *Crooked Back Dick* (Hackle Fly)
Wings & Legs: Inside Moorpout bloa feather (short fibres).
Body: Scarlet worsted thick round shoulders, black worsted for the remainder of the body, which is dumpy.
Hook: No. 3 Limerick.
Season: September and October.

81. *Dotterel and Yellow* (Hackle Fly)
Wings & Legs: Inside of a Dotterel's wing.
Body: Yellow silk, shaded according to season.

82. *Dotterel and Orange*
83. *Dotterel and Copper*
84. *Dotterel and Purple*
85. *Dotterel and Claret*
86. *Dotterel and Brown* or *Chocolate*
87. *Dotterel and Slate*
88. *Dotterel and Pale Green*
89. *Dotterel and Sky Blue*
90. *Dotterel and Scarlet*
91. *Dotterel and Olive*

All as above, with or without Peacock or black Ostrich herl for heads. Silk may be floss or waxed.

92. *Orange Fly*
Wings: Blue feather of a Teal drake.
Head: Dark Hare's ear fur.
Body: Gold-coloured mohair mixed with orange camlet and a little brown fur.
Legs: Slatey-blue cock's hackle.
Season: May.

93. *Cowdung Fly*
Wings: Landrail or Corncrake—flat.
Body: (Full) Yellow camlet or mohair mixed with a little brown bear's fur, giving a dusky lemon tinge.
Legs: Ginger cock's hackle.
Hook: No. 2 Limerick.
Season: All season.

94. *Yellow Dun* or *Bloa*, No. 2
Wings: Snipe (under part), dressed upright.
Body: Marten's fur or yellow worsted mixed with pale ash-coloured fur.
Legs: Pale slate cock's hackle.
Hook: No. 1 or 2 Limerick.
Season: April and May, and again September.

95. *Yeasty Dun* or *Bloa*
Wings: Yeast-coloured hen's feather, dressed upright.
Body: Dark blue Mole's fur.
Legs: Pale ginger hackle.
    May also be made hacklewise.
Hook: No. 2 Limerick.
Season: June.

96. *Harry Long Legs*
Wings: Dark mottled Partridge, or Woodcock, upright.
Body: Brown Bear's fur mixed with dark Mole, made long and taper.
Ribbing: (Optional) Brown or yellow silk.
Legs: Brown cock's hackle of length, but not thick.
Hook: No. 3 Limerick.
Season: Midsummer.

97. *Little Iron Blue*
Wings: Cormorant (upright), or Tomtit.
Body: Pale blue fur spun on purple silk.
Legs: Pick out body-fur.
Hook: No. 0 Limerick.
Season: May.
    Dress very fine.

98. *Gravel Fly*
Wings: Nightjar, or Woodcock.
Body: Lead-coloured silk for lower and middle, shoulders of black Ostrich herl.
Legs: Two turns of a small grizzled hackle.
Hook: No. 1 Limerick.
Season: April and May—lasts about three weeks.

99. *Grannam* or *Greentail*
Wings: (Flat) Hen Pheasant, or clouded Partridge.
Body: Dark Hare's ear with a little blue fur mixed.
Tail: Green herl of Peacock's eye feather, or green wax, or even a bit of grass.
Legs: Yellow grizzle or pale ginger hackle.
    or, hacklewise:

Wings & Legs: Woodcock.
Body: As above.
Hook: No. 2 Limerick.
Season: April.

100. *Hawthorn Fly*
Wings: (a) Palest Snipe; (b) Mallard; (c) horn shavings; (d) apple core; (e) Goose quill.
Body: Black Ostrich herl.
Legs: Black hackle.
Hook: No. 2 or 3 Limerick.
Season: March, April and May.

101. *Summer Dun*
Wings: Wood-pigeon.
Body: Mole's fur (thick).
Ribbing: Ash-coloured silk.
Legs: Ash-coloured hackle.
Hook: No. 1 or 2 Limerick, short.
Season: June and July.

102. *Black Herl Fly*
Wings: Pale Starling.
Body: Black Ostrich herl (close and thick).
Legs: Black hackle.
Hook: No. 1 or 2 Limerick.
Season: June and July.

103. *Brown Caddis* or *Orl Fly*
Wings: (Flat) (a) Brown hen; (b) Brown Woodcock.
Body: (Large and full to tail) Peacock herl, or brown Spaniel's fur mixed with dark red or claret mohair, ribbed with orange silk.
Hook: No. 3 Limerick.
Season: End of May, June and July.

104. *Little Yellow May,* or *Willow Fly*
Wings: Mallard, dyed yellow.
Body: (Tapering) Yellow worsted unravelled and mixed with a small quantity of Hare's ear fur.
Legs: Pick out body-dubbing.

Whisks: Two light-coloured fibres from Squirrel's tail.
  or, hacklewise:
Wings & Legs: Any small white feather dyed yellow.
Body: As above.
  or, winged:
Wings: Fieldfare, dyed yellow.
Body: Plain yellow silk.
Legs: Light ginger hackle.
  or, winged:
Wings: Pale Dotterel.
Body: Yellow Monkey's fur spun on lemon-coloured silk.
Hook: No. 0 or 1 Limerick.
Season: May and June.

105. *Dusky Green Parrot*
Wings: Inside Starling.
Body: Dark brown fur.
Ribbing: Orange silk.
Legs: Greenish hackle from a Woodpecker's back.
Season: June to September (warm evenings before sunset).

106. *Large Brown Grouse*
Wings: Mottled brown Grouse.
Body: Dark blue fur mixed with black Sheep's wool.
Legs: Dark cock's hackle.
Hook: No. 2 or 3 Limerick.
Season: June, July and August.

107. *Fieldfare* or *Brown Dun*
Wings: Blue-tailed Fieldfare (upright).
Body: (a) Otter's fur; or (b) Cat's black fur mixed with lemon-coloured mohair.
Legs: Ginger hackle.
Hook: No. 1 Limerick.
Season: April, May, June and July.

108. *Little Blue Midge*
Wings: (a) Thrush down; (b) Bluish-white hackle; (c) Pale bloa feather from inside Jack Snipe's wing; (d) Tomtit's tail; (e) Smallest light blue bloa feather from inside Moorpout's wing.

Body: Dark blue fur mixed with gold-coloured mohair.
Whisks: Two Monkey hairs (optional).
  or, hacklewise:
Wings & Legs: Pewit's topping.
  Remainder as in the above dressing.
Season: June, July and August.

109. *Little Coppered Blue*
Wings: As in pattern No. 108.
Body: Blue Mole's fur mixed with copper-coloured mohair.
Whisks: Two Monkey hairs.
Hook: Smallest.
Season: All summer.

110. *Small Black Midge and Ant* (Hackle Fly)
Wings & Legs: Blue cock's hackle.
Body: Brownish-black silk.
  also:
Wings & Legs: Very small feather from inside of a Jack Snipe wing.
Body: Two or three turns black Ostrich herl near tail.
  also:
Wings & Legs: Thistledown.
Body: As above.
Hook: No. o Limerick, short.
Season: June, July and August.

111. *Peacock Fly*
Wings: Starling (flat).
Body: Dark Peacock herl. Dress with mulberry silk.
Legs: Grizzled or claret hackle.
Season: All season on gloomy days.

112. *Cinnamon Fly*
Wings: Pale reddish-brown hen (full).
Body: (Slim) Dark-brown fur or silk only.
Legs: Ginger hackle.
Hook: No. 2 Limerick.
Season: August and September.

113. *Sand Fly* 2, or *Grouse Brown*
Wings: Sandy Landrail.
Body: Bright sandy fur from a Hare's neck mixed with a very little orange mohair.
Legs: Ginger hackle.
Hook: No. 2 Limerick. All season.
or:
Wings: Grouse.
Body: Black and blue fur.
Legs: Dark hackle.

114. *Fern Fly* or *Soldier* (Four wings)
Wings: (Upper) Red Corncrake; (Lower) Blue bloa feather from inside Moorpout's wing.
Body: Seal's fur or Hog's down dyed red and mixed with brown mohair, or orange floss only.
Legs: Pale red hackle.
Hook: No. 3 Limerick.
Season: May and June.

The Snail: reverse upper and lower wings.

115. *Pale Evening Dun*
Wings: Mallard breast dyed a very pale yellow.
Body: Marten's yellow fur with a little Mouse fur mixed.
Legs: Pale ginger cock's hackle.
Hook: No. 1 Limerick.

116. *Late Blue Gnat*
Wings: Snipe.
Body: Dark Mole's fur, tied with bright purple silk.
Legs: Dark bluish hackle.
Hook: No. 0 Limerick.
Season: September and October.

117. *Yellow Sally*
Wings: (a) White feather dyed yellow, or (b) a very pale Dotterel feather, undyed. Dressed flat.
Body: Yellow Marten's fur, mohair, or crewel, or yellow silk (rather full).
Season: May.

118. *Golden Wren* (Hackle Fly)
Wings & Legs: Wren tail.
Body: Sable fur with a little gold mohair, or brown silk with two turns of gold at the tail.
Hook: No. 0 Limerick.
Season: May and June.

Pattern No. 119 omitted.

120. *Smoky Dun Hackle*
Wings: Smoky dun cock's hackle.
Body: (a) Lead-coloured mohair, tapered; (b) Lead-coloured silk.
Hook: No. 1 or 2 Limerick.
Season: April.

121. *Golden Partridge*
Wings: (a) Speckled Partridge tail; (b) outside Woodcock wing, (c) Corncrake.
Body: Sable fur and gold mohair, darkest at the shoulders and tapering to the tail on orange or copper silk.
Ribbing: Thin gold tinsel.
Whisks: Two hairs Squirrel tail.
Legs: A dark chestnut cock's hackle.
Hook: Nos. 1, 2 or 3, all season.

122. *Hare's Ear*
Wings: Light Starling.
Body: Hare's ear fur, darkest at shoulder.
Legs: (Optional) Red cock's hackle.
Hook: No. 2 Limerick.
Season: All season.
  For deep streams:
Wing: Landrail.
Legs: Red cock's hackle.
  Remainder of dressing as above.
  Dress small for summer.

123. *The Light Red*
Wings: Starling.

Body: Red floss or mohair.
Legs: Red cock's hackle.
Hook: No. 0 or 1 Limerick.
Season: July.

124. *Dark Claret* (four wings)
Wings: (Upper) Starling; (Under) Partridge speckled tail feather.
Body: Dark claret mohair or worsted mixed with Hare's ear fur.
Hook: No. 2 or 3 Limerick.
Season: February, March and April.

125. *The Dark* or *Bloa Fox*
Wings: Starling.
Body: Fur from the Fox next to the skin mixed with black Rabbit scut and a little pale straw-coloured mohair.
Legs: (Optional) Ash-coloured cock's hackle.
Whisks: Ash-coloured hairs from a Squirrel's tail.

126. *Dun Fox*
Wings: Starling.
Body: Brass-coloured mohair.
Ribbing: Gold tinsel.
Legs: ⎫
Whisks: ⎬ As in pattern 125.
Season: April and May.

127. *Light Fox*
Wings: Starling.
Body: Light camel's hair and the lightest possible straw-coloured mohair; or, for clear streams, silk of the required colour.
Whisks: As in pattern No. 126.
Season: May.

128. *Brown Fly, Dun Drake,* or *Brown Caughlan*
Wings: Partridge, speckled tail feather.
Body: Light brown bear's fur mixed with high-coloured yellow mohair and Hare's face fur.

Legs: Partridge, grey neck hackle.
Whisks: Two strands dark grey Mallard's feather.
Hook: No. 3 Limerick.
Season: All season.

129. *Green Caterpillar*
Body: One or more strands of green Peacock herl.
Ribbing: (a) narrow gold tinsel; (b) narrow silver tinsel.
Hackle: (a) Red cock; (b) Black cock. The hackle must be even and run over all from end to end.
Hook: No. 3 Limerick.
Season: June and July.

130. *Black Caterpillar*
Body: Brown Peacock herl.
Hackle: Black cock, as last.
Ribbing: (Optional) Silver tinsel.
Season: June and July.

131. *Lochaber* (Hackle Fly)
Wings & Legs: Grouse mottled hackle of shining brown or dusky colour.
Body: Orange or yellow floss, rather full at shoulder.
Hook: No. 1 Limerick.
Season: July, August and September.

132. *The Green Bank Fly*
Wings: Young Starling.
Body: Mellow green mohair with yellow in it.
Legs: Fine pale red hackle.
Season: May, June and July (warm days).
    Dress with green silk; body fine and tapering.

133. *Owl*
Wings: Yellow Owl.
Body: Deepish cream camel's hair and gold-coloured mohair.
Legs: Pick out body-dubbing.
Hook: No. 2 Limerick.
Season: May, June and July (warm mornings and evenings).

134. *Red Spinner*, No. 3
Wings: Greyish Drake feather tinged with reddish-yellow.
Body: Gold twist with a red hackle over it.
Hook: No. 1 or 2 Limerick.
Season: July.
  Dress with orange silk.

135. *Little Pale Blue Fly*
Wings: Lightest blue feather of Sea Swallow (not too full).
Body: Bluest part of Fox fur mixed with a very little mohair; or pale blue silk, ribbed with yellow silk.
Ribbing: Straw-coloured silk.
Whisks: Two hairs from a (light) Squirrel's tail.
Hook: No. 0 or 1 Limerick.
Season: August to end of season.

136. *Dark Mackerel Fly*
Wings: Light grey Mallard.
Body: Orange silk.
Legs: Light red cock's hackle.
Hook: No. 1 or 2 Limerick.
Season: June.

137. *Peacock Fly*, No. 2
Wings: Hen Pheasant.
Body: Peacock herl.
Legs: Bluish cock's hackle.
  Dress with Pomona green silk.
Season: June.

Pattern 138 omitted.

139. *The Winter Brown*
Wings: Hen Pheasant.
Body: Fox-coloured fur from a Hare's poll.
Ribbing: Gold twist (or for a dropper without).
Legs: Furnace, or honey-coloured hackle.
Whisks: Hairs from Squirrel's tail.
Hook: Nos. 0 to 3 Limerick.
Season: February and March.

140. *Dark Claret*
Wings: Landrail.
Body: Deep claret silk.
Legs: Dark red claret-coloured cock's hackle.
Hook: No. 1 or 2 Limerick.
Season: March.

141. *Spider Fly*, No. 2 (Hackle Fly)
Wings & Legs: Woodcock.
Body: Lead-coloured silk.
Hook: No. 1 or 2 Limerick.
Season: May.

142. *Dark Dun*
Wings: Under Waterhen's wing.
Body: Water-rat's fur on yellow silk.
Legs: Blue cock's hackle.
Hook: No. 1 Limerick.
Season: May.

Pattern No. 143 omitted.

144. *Little Whirling Blue*
Wings: Starling.
Body: Hare's fur from back of neck with a little yellow mohair. Dress with primrose silk.
Legs: Blue dun hackle.
Hook: No. 0 Limerick.
Season: July and August.

145. *Little Pale Blue*
Wings: Young Starling.
Body: A very minute portion of Water-rat fur mixed with a little fine yellow Marten's fur. Dress delicately with fine pale yellow silk.
Legs: Very pale blue hackle.
Hook: No. 0 Limerick.

146. *The Chantrey*
Wings: Brown hen Partridge, or Pheasant tail.

Body: Copper Peacock herl.
Ribbing: Gold twist or tinsel.
Legs: Black cock's hackle.
Hook: No. 4, or smaller.
Season: All season.

147. *Hofland's Fancy*
Wings: Woodcock.
Body: Reddish-brown silk.
Legs: Red cock's hackle.
Whisks: Two or three strands red cock's hackle.
Hook: No. 4 Limerick.
Season: May.

148. *March Brown*, No. 2
Wings: Partridge—mottled tail feather.
Body: Hare's ear fur.
Ribbing: Olive silk.
Legs: Grey hackle from a Partridge's neck.
Whisks: Two or three strands grey Partridge feather.
Hook: No. 2 or 3 Limerick.
Season: March and April.

149. *High Tees Cocktail*
Wings: Inside Teal wing.
Body: Light blue fur from Rabbit or Mole spun on silk of the same colour. Full at shoulder, tapered to tail.
Legs: Dark blue cock's hackle.
Whisks: Two fibres white or grizzle cock's hackle.
Hook: No. 0.
Season: June and July.
 A body of very fine India rubber over blue silk can be used for variety.

150. *Coachman*
Wings: Landrail.
Body: Copper Peacock herl.
Legs: Red hackle.
Hook: No. 1, 2 or 3 Limerick.
Season: All season.

151. *Hare's Ear Dun*
Wings: Starling, or under Teal's wing.
Body: Hare's ear fur.
Legs: Picked out of body.
Whisks: Two or three fibres of wing feather.
Hook: Nos. 1 and 3 Limerick.
Season: All season.
 Dress with lead coloured silk for spring and autumn, and pale primrose as the season advances.

152. *Edmondson's Welsh Fly*
Wings: Woodcock wing, or hen Grouse tail.
Body: Dull orange mohair.
Legs: Partridge back.
Hook: No. 2 Limerick.
Whisks: Two strands Partridge breast feather.
Season: All season.

153. *Kingdom*
Wings: Woodcock wing.
Body: Pale yellow floss.
Ribbing: Crimson floss.
Hook: No. 1 or 2 Limerick.
Season: May and June.

154. *Brown Shiner*
Wings & Legs: Fine bright mottled Grouse feather.
Body: Peacock herl (spare).
Hook: No. 1 or 2 Limerick.
Season: April or May.

155. *Great Red Spinner*
Wings: Thrush with a golden cast (not too full).
Body: Red and brown mohair or Hog's wool mixed.
Ribbing: Gold twist.
Legs: A bright red cock's hackle.
Whisks: Three strands gold-red hackle.
Hook: No. 3 Limerick.
Season: June and July.

156. *Brachan Clock*, No. 2
Wings: Cock Pheasant breast.
Body: Peacock herl (full and tied with purple silk).
Legs: Red or dark cock's hackle.
Hook: No. 1 or 2 Limerick; No. 4 or 5 for lakes or ponds.
Season: All season.

157. *Alder Fly*, No. 1
Wings: Brown speckled Mallard's back.
Body: Peacock herl (tied with dark brown silk).
Legs: Coch-y-bonddhu, or a red cock's hackle.
Hook: No. 2 or 3 Limerick.
Season: May and June.
   No. 2:
Wings: Palest Jay.
Body: Canary-coloured worsted (dressed thick and dumpy).
Ribbing: Black silk.
Legs: Canary-coloured feather from a Parrot, or a cock's hackle dyed that colour.
Hook: No. 3 Limerick.
Season: June and July.

158. *Dee Fancy*
Wings & Legs: Pale bloa feather.
Body: Dull yellow mohair, tied with deep yellow silk.
Hook: No. 3 or 4 Limerick.
Season: June.
   Or vary by using:
Wings & Legs: Darker than above.
Body: Peacock herl.

159. *Soldier Palmer*
Wings & Legs: Bright red cock's hackle.
Body: Bright red mohair or worsted.
Ribbing: Gold twist.
Hook: No. 1 Limerick.
Season: All season.

160. *The Governor*
Wings: Hen Pheasant's wing.

Body: Copper Peacock herl.
Tag: Scarlet floss or twist.
Legs: Red-ginger cock.
Hook: No. 1 or 2.
Season: April and May.

161. *The Loch Awe*
Wings: Pheasant's tail.
Body: Orange mohair.
Legs: Red cock's hackle.
Hook: Limerick No.2; Nos. 4 and 5 for lakes.
Season: May to July.

162. *The Dark Loch Awe*
Wings: Water hen.
Body: Copper Peacock herl.
Legs: Black cock's hackle.
Hook: No. 2 Limerick; or 4 or 5 for lakes.
Season: May to July.

163. *Welsh Coch-y-Bonddhu*
Wings & Legs: Coch-y-bonddhu hackle.
Body: Peacock herl.
Hook: No. 0 Limerick—to No. 3 or 4 for large streams.
Season: All season.

164. *Yellow Sally* No. 3
Wings: White feather dyed yellow.
Body: Pale yellow fur or mohair.
Ribbing: Fawn-coloured silk.
Legs: Ginger hackle.
Hook: No. 2 Limerick.
Season: May and June.

165. *Aunt Sally*
Wings & Legs: Starling neck feather with light edge.
Body: Blue Mole's fur with a little lavender worsted mixed.
Hook: No. 0 Limerick.
Season: May.

166. *The Black Trooper*
Wings: Blackbird (full).
Body: Black silk.
Legs: Black cock's hackle.
Hook: No. 1, 2 or 3 Limerick.
Season: April.

167. *Golden Sooty Dun* or *Bloa*
Wings: Starling.
Body: Dark wool of a black Lamb, weather-beaten, and mixed with a little bright yellow Marten's fur (full under the wings).
Legs: Body-dubbing picked out.
Hook: No. 1 or 2 Limerick.
Season: June to September.

168. *Purple Hackle*
Wings & Legs: Blood-red cock's hackle.
Body: Spaniel's fur and purple mohair on dark red silk.
Hook: No. 1 or 2 Limerick.
Season: June.

169. *Badger Fly*
Wings: Inside hen Pheasant's wing.
Body: Badger fur on red silk.
Legs: Red hackle, or dubbing picked out.
Hook: No. 2 Limerick.
Season: March to July.

170. *Wasp Fly*
Wings: Grey Mallard.
Body: Dark Brown Bear's fur and black Rabbit mixed with a little yellow mohair.
Ribbing: Yellow silk.
Legs: Body-dubbing picked out.
Hook: No. 1 or 2 Limerick.
Season: July.

171. *Grey-Legged Bloa*
Wings: Jay.

'HALCYON'

Body: Pale sky-blue floss.
Ribbing: Yellow silk (thinly).
Legs: Small grey Partridge hackle.
Hook: No. 2 or 3 Limerick.
Season: May.

172. *Shell Fly*
Wings: Starling.
Body: Yellow Hog's wool mixed with Hare's ear fur, darkest under the wings, dressed on lead-coloured silk.
Hook: No. 1 or 2 Limerick.
Legs: Body-dubbing picked out.
Season: April.

173. *Little Green Peacock*
Wings & Legs: Dusky red hackle.
Body: Greenish Peacock herl, tied with green silk.
Tag: Gold or silver.
Hook: Limerick No. 1.
Season: May and June.
 or, for a dark day:
Body: Water-rat's fur, ribbed with silver twist.

174. *The Orange Beck Fly*
Wings & Legs: Red or black cock's hackle.
Body: Raw orange silk.
Ribbing: (Optional) Gold twist.
Hook: No. 1 Limerick.
Season: April, May, June and July.

175. *Black and Yellow*
Wings & Legs: Black cock's hackle.
Body: Pale yellow silk.
Hook: No. 1 Limerick.
Season: All season.

176. *Knotted Grey Gnat*
Wings: Partridge's grey neck feather.
Body: Dark Hare's ear on grey silk.
Hook: No. 0 Limerick.

177. *Heron Dun or Bloa*
Wings: Heron or Coot.
Body: Ash-coloured silk.
Legs: Ash-coloured hackle.
Hook: No. 2 Limerick.
Season: April and September.

178. *Orange Tawny*
Wings: Dark Starling or Snipe.
Body: Dark-brown fur on deep orange silk.
Legs: Black cock's hackle.
Hook: No. 2 Limerick.
Season: August.

179. *Knop Fly*
Wings & Legs: Partridge, grey neck feather.
Body: Black silk.
Hook: No. 1 or 2 Limerick.
Season: May.

180. *Fern Bud*
Wings: Fieldfare.
Body: Greenish Peacock herl, dressed with sad green silk (short and dumpy).
Legs: Dusky hackle.
Hook: No. 0 Limerick.
Season: May.

181. *The Huzzard*
Wings: Pale feather dyed yellow (longer than the body, and dressed flat).
Body: Yellow silk.
Ribbing: Gold twist.
Legs: Yellow hackle.
Hook: No. 1 Limerick.
Season: May.

182. *Death Drake*
Wings: Mallard (copper).
Body: Black Ostrich herl and Peacock herl.

Ribbing: Silver twist.
Legs: Black cock's hackle.
Hook: No. 2 Limerick.

183. *Pewit*
Wings: Partridge tail—red feather.
Body: Peacock herl and Lapwing's crest-feather twisted with red silk.
Legs: Dusky red hackle.
Hook: No. 1 or 2 Limerick.
Season: May.

184. *Thorn Fly*, No. 1
Wings: Grey Mallard, or Jay.
Body: Black wool.
Legs: Black hackle.
Hook: No. 2 or 3 Limerick.
Season: May.
  or, No. 2:
Legs: Blood-red cock's hackle.
Remainder of dressing as above.
Season: September

185. *Whitterish*
Wings: Seamew, or Sea Swallow.
Body: White floss.
Legs: White hackle.
Head: Dark Peacock herl.
Whisks: White or black.
Hook: No. 2 Limerick.
Season: June.

186. *Dark Brown Tag Tail*
Wings: Mallard, or outside Woodcock.
Body: Copper-coloured silk.
Tag: Bright orange, or gold twist.
Legs: Dark red cock.
Hook: No. 2 Limerick.
Season: July.

187. *Willow Cricket*
Wings: Starling (longer than the body).
Body: Green Peacock herl.
Legs: Grizzled hackle.
Hook: No. 0 Limerick.
Season: July.

188. *Buss Brown*
Wings & Legs: Outside Woodcock, hacklewise.
Body: Light brown fur on orange silk.
Head: Black herl.
Hook: No. 1 or 2 Limerick.
Season: August (full moon or black waters).

189. *Dubbed Wren Tail*
Wings & Legs: Wren tail (hacklewise).
Body: Sable fur.
Ribbing: Pale yellow silk.
Hook: No. 0 Limerick.
 or:
Wings & Legs: Wren tail.
Body: Plain orange, or plain yellow silk.
A standard pattern.

190. *Black Caterpillar*
Wings: Jay.
Body: Black Ostrich herl.
Legs: Black hackle.
Hook: No. 2 Limerick.
Season: May and June.

191. *Large Whirling Dun* or *Bloa*
Wings: Starling.
Body: Blue and orange silk ribbed alternately.
Legs: Partridge neck feather.
Hook: No. 2 Limerick.
A standard pattern. Considered the best of the duns by Wade.

192. *Little Violet Fly*
Wings: Blue or Black Cap (upright).
Body: Purple and crimson silk ribbed alternately.
Legs: Dark blue hackle.
Hook: No. 0 Limerick.
Season: May and June.

193. *Large Fly*
Wings: Dusky Woodcock.
Body: Orange silk, dressed thin.
Legs: Woodcock's neck or head hackle.
Hook: No. 2 Limerick.
    and:
Small Fern Fly
Wings: Yellowish-red feather from the Redwing or Thrush.
Body: Dusky orange fur from a Fox's head.
Legs: Pale dun hackle.
Standard patterns.

194 & 195 *Green and Grey Drakes*

196. *Oakfly* or *Downlooker* or *Canon Fly*
Wings: Yellowish-brown hen (short and flat).
Body: (Under wings) Hare's ear fur; (middle) orange and yellow; (tail) brownish dun.
Legs: Thin red hackle.
Hook: No. 3 or 4 Limerick.
Season: April, May and June.

197. *Stonefly*
Wings: Whalebone slips.
Head: Peacock herl, or India rubber.
Legs: Outside Woodcock under-wing.
Feelers: Two bear hairs.
Body: Yellow silk, wrapped over with clear strip of India rubber.
Whisks: Two strands of Woodcock's feather.
Hook: Long Mayfly size.

198. *Woodcock*
Wings: Woodcock.
Body: Brown Spaniel's ear and a little Squirrel's fur mixed, and dressed tapering with orange silk.
Legs: A red hackle.
Whisks: Two strands copper Mallard feather.
Hook: No. 1, 2 or 3 Limerick.
Season: May to August.

199. *Evening Bloa*
Wings: Light Jay.
Body: White mohair or silk.
Legs: Pale dun hackle.
Head & Tail: Brown silk.
Whisks: Light dun hackle-fibres.

200. *Common Fly*
Wings: (Spare and short) Starling.
Body: Black silk.
Ribbing: Silver twist.
Legs: Dark grizzled hackle.
Hook: No. 2 Limerick.

201. *Cocktail*
Wings: Inside Teal.
Body: Mole's fur.
Legs: Hackle like the wings.
Whisks: Two fibres white cock's hackle.
Hook: No. 0 or 1 Limerick.

202. *Captain*
Wings: Tail feather from a hen Grouse or Woodcock.
Body: Dull orange mohair.
Legs: Partridge hackle.
Hook: No. 2 Limerick.

Night Flies

White Moth
Wings: Mealy feather of a white Owl (large, broad, and the length of the body).

Body: White Peacock herl *(sic)*, or white Hare's fur.
Legs: Soft white hackle.

Brown Moth
Wings: Mottled Brown Owl.
Body: Fur of Weasel's tail, yellow Marten, and brown Spaniel's ear, well mixed.
Legs: Bittern's hackle.
Head: Peacock herl, or silver twist.

Cream-Coloured Moth
Wings: Yellow Owl (deep cream colour).
Body: Fur from a white Weasel's tail, or straw-coloured silk.
Head: Peacock herl.
Legs: Yellow hackle.

Black Clocker
Wings: Rook, or any black bird.
Body: Black Ostrich herl.
Legs: Black cock's hackle, rather full.
Hooks for Night Flies, No. 6 Limerick, or according to fancy.

H. S. HALL
188?

1. *Olive Dun*
Wings: Dark Starling.
Body: Olive or Gosling green silk.
Ribbing: Fine gold wire—optional.
Tag: Gold—optional.
Legs: Dull brown olive hackle.
Whisks: To match.
Hook No. oo or ooo.

2. Same dressing as above except:
Body: Quill dyed olive with or without gold tag.

3. Same dressing as 1 except
Legs: Light brown Hare's ear.

4. *Rough Spring Olive*
Same dressing as 1 except
Body: Leveret's fur dyed olive.
Ribbing: Fine gold wire.

5. *India rubber bodied Olive* (Detached body)
Wings & Hackle to match brown-olive body. In summer and autumn, horsehair instead of India rubber bodies are preferred.

6. *Hare's Ear*
Wings: Dark Starling.
Body: Hare's fur.
Ribbing: Gold.
Legs: Picked-out fibres of body.
Hook: 0 or 00.

7. *Red Quill*
Wings: Dark Starling.
Body: Undyed quill.
Legs: Red hackle.
Whisks: Red hackle.
Hook: No. 0 or 00, usually 00.

8. *Grey Quill*
Same dressing as 7 except
Legs: Grey hackle.

9. *Ginger Quill*
Same dressing as 7 except
Legs: Ginger hackle.
Whisks: To match.

10. *Iron Blue*
Wings: Waterhen's breast, or Great Tit's tail.

Body: Dark blue quill (violet shade) or mauve silk with
   Mole's fur.
Legs: Dark honey dun hackle (natural fly has yellow tips to
   dusky blue legs.)
Whisks: To match.
Hook: No. oo or ooo.

11. *Little Marryat* (Pale Watery Dun)
Wings: Medium Starling.
Body: Very pale buff Opossum fur spun on light yellow silk.
Legs: Palest buff Cochin-China cockerel hackle.
Whisks: To match.
Hook: No. o or ooo.

12. *Red Spinner* (Detached Badger)
Wings & Legs: Badger hackle dressed buzz (rusty grey almost
   black in centre with bright golden tips).
Body: Detached—Reddish-brown horsehair.
Hook: No. o or oo.

13. *Wickham's Fancy*
Wings: Dark Starling (or for variety, Landrail).
Body: Gold tinsel.
Legs: Red cock hackle, ribbed to tail.
Hook: Nos. oo to 1 or 2.

14. *Flight's Fancy*
Wings: Light Starling.
Body: Pale primrose floss.
Ribbing: Fine flat gold tinsel.
Legs: Pale buff or honey dun hackle.
Whisks: To match.
Hook: No. oo or ooo.

15. *Black Gnat*
Wings: Quite flat pike scale.
Body: Longish, with black Ostrich herl stripped.
Legs: 2 or 3 turns of Starling hackle.
Hook: No. oo or ooo.

16. *Silver Sedge*
Wings: Landrail.
Body: White floss.
Ribbing: Silver.
Legs: Buff or light red hackle worked all down the body.
Hook: Nos. oo to 1.

17. *Red Sedge*
Wings: Ruddy Landrail.
Body: Red fur from a Hare's face, or Fox's ear, or reddest part of Opossum.
Ribbing: Gold thread.
Legs: Red hackle, tail to head.
Hook: No. oo or 1.

18. *Big Sedge* (or Cinnamon)
Same as Red Sedge on No. 2 hook, except
Wings: Under covert feather of a Pea Hen faintly mottled with darker shades of brown.

19. *Alder*
Wings: Tail of hen Pheasant, or red Partridge tail for variety.
Body: Bronze Peacock herl.
Legs: Black hackle, or black hackle with red points.
Hook: No. 2.

20. *Brown Quill*
Wings: Medium Starling.
Body: Light quill dyed in Judson's light brown, or bleached Peacock quill.
Legs: Ginger hackle.
Whisks: To match.
Hook: No. oo.

21. *Indian Yellow*
Wings: Under wing feather of a young Grouse (bluish shade).
Body: Delicate brown silk ribbed with bright yellow silk.
Legs: Rich buff hackle.
Whisks: To match.
Head: 2 turns of dark orange silk.
Hook: No. oo.

22. *Blue-Winged Olive*
Wings: Distinctly blue (as in 21).
Body: A delicate greenish-olive.
Legs: A pale watery olive hackle.
Whisks: To match.
This fly sets up and rides cockily on the water. No satisfactory pattern yet devised.

23. *Little Sky Blue*
Wings: Delicate pale blue from Jay's wing.
Body: Pale straw colour (silk, quill or fur).
Legs: Light honey dun hackle.
Whisks: To match.
Hook: No. oo or ooo.

24. *Red Tag*
Body: Fat and short—Peacock's herl.
Tag: Red floss, wool, or Ibis (wool for preference).
Hackle: Dark rich red.
Hook: No. o, oo or ooo.

25. *Jenny Spinner* (Transformation of Iron Blue Dun)
(a) Wings: Two hackle points of very pale blue dun cock, almost white.
Body: (Detached) White horsehair whipped with 2 turns of mulberry silk to fasten whisks. Whip on with mulberry silk to show head and thorax of that colour.
Hook: No. oo or ooo.
(b) Dressed buzz with a pale grizzled hackle.

26. *The Intermediate*
A summer fly. Made with detached horsehair bodies of pale delicate shades with hackles and wings to match—honey duns, light buff, light olive etc.

T. C. HOFLAND
The British Angler's Manual
1839

1. *The Chantrey* (Sir Francis Chantrey)
Wings: Partridge, or brown hen, or Pheasant tail.
Body: Copper coloured herl.
Ribbing: Gold twist.
Legs: Black hackle.
Hook: No. 9 or 10.
 (Test: Stockbridge)

2. *Hofland's Fancy*
Wings: Woodcock's tail.
Body: Reddish dark brown silk.
Legs: Red hackle.
Whisks: Two or three strands of red hackle.
Hook: No. 10.

3. *March Brown* (or Dun Drake)
Wings: Partridge tail.
Body: Hare's ear fur.
Ribbing: Olive silk.
Legs: Partridge hackle.
Whisks: Two or three strands of Partridge feather.
Hook: No. 8 or 9.

4. *Blue Dun*
Wings: Starling.
Body: Water-rat's fur.
Ribbing: Yellow silk.
Legs: Dun hen's hackle.
Whisks: Two strands grizzle cock's hackle.
Hook: No. 10.

5. *For Carshalton and Test*
Wings: Starling, dark, spare, and short.
Body: Black silk.
Ribbing: Silver twist.
Hook: No. 10.

6. *Carshalton Cock Tail*
Wings: Teal's wing (inside).
Body: Light blue fur.
Legs: Dark dun hackle.
Whisks: Two fibres of white cock's hackle.
Hook: No. 9 or 10.

7. *Pale Yellow Dun*
Wings: Lightest (young) Starling.
Body: Yellow mohair, or Martin's pale yellow fur tied with yellow silk.
Hook: No. 12.

8. *Orange Dun*
Wings: Starling.
Body: Red Squirrel's fur.
Ribbing: Gold thread.
Whisks: Two fibres red cock's hackle.
Hook: No. 9.
   (Test and southern streams)

9. *Coachman*
Wings: Landrail.
Body: Copper-coloured Peacock herl.
Legs: Red hackle.
Hook: No. 8.

10. *Cowdung Fly*
Wings: Landrail or Starling.
Body: Dull lemon-coloured mohair.
Legs: Red hackle.
Hook: No. 8 or 9.

11. *Hare's Ear Dun* (Hampshire)
Wings: Starling.
Body: Hare's ear fur.
Whisks: Two fibres from the brown feather of a Starling's wing.
Hook: No. 10.
For variety, omit whisks.

12. *Edmondson's Welsh Fly*
Wings: Woodcock, or tail of a hen Grouse.
Body: Dull orange mohair.
Legs: Partridge back.
Hook: No. 8.

13. *Kingdom* or *Kindon* (Hampshire)
Wings: Woodcock.
Body: Pale yellow silk.
Ribbing: Crimson silk.
Legs: Black hackle.
Hook: No. 9.

14. *Brown Shiner*
Wings & Legs: Grouse hackle.
Body: Peacock herl twisted—spare.
Wales; rivers and lakes of Cumberland.

15. *Gravel Bed* or *Spider Fly*
Wing: Partridge rump.
Body: Water-rat's fur.
Legs: Black hackle.
Hook: No. 10 or 11.

16. *Iron Blue*
Wings: Tomtit's tail, or American Robin's tail.
Body: Water-rat's fur.
Hook: No. 12 or 13.

17. *Great Red Spinner* (March Brown)
Wings: Light Starling.
Body: Hog's wool, red and brown mixed.
Ribbing: Gold twist.

Legs: Bright red cock's hackle.
Whisks: Three strands red cock's hackle.
Hook: No. 7.

18. *Black Gnat*
Wings: Starling.
Body: Black hackle or Ostrich herl, tied with black silk.
Hook: No. 13.

19. *Wren-tail*
Wings & Legs: Wren's tail feather used as a hackle.
Body: Orange silk.
Hook: No. 12.

20. *Bracken Clock*
Wings: Pheasant's breast.
Body: Peacock herl.
Hook: No. 9 or 10, or for lake fishing, No. 6 or 7.

21. *Red Ant*
Wings: Light Starling.
Body: Peacock herl, full at tail, spare towards head.
Legs: Red or ginger cock's hackle.
Hook: No. 9 or 10.

21a. *Black Ant*
Same as 21, substituting Ostrich herl for Peacock herl, and black hackle for red.

22. *Sandfly*
Wings: Landrail.
Body: Fur from a Hare's neck, twisted on silk of the same colour.
Legs: Ginger hen hackle.
Hook: No. 9.

22a. *Sandfly* (hackle)
Wings & Legs: Ginger hen hackle.
Body: As last.
Hook: No. 12.

23. *Stone Fly*
Wings: Dark Mallard.
Body: Hare's ear fur mixed with brown and yellow mohair—yellow colour towards the tail.
Ribbing: Yellow silk.
Legs: Brownish red hackle.
Whisks: Two or three fibres of mottled Partridge feather.
Hook: No. 6.

24. *Alder Fly*
Wings: Brown speckled Mallard.
Body: Peacock herl tied with dark brown silk.
Legs: Coch-y-bonddhu hackle.
Hook: No. 8.

25 & 26. *Green and Grey Drakes*

27. *Black Palmer*
Body: Black Ostrich herl.
Ribbing: Silver twist.
Wings & Legs: Black cock's hackle.

28. *Soldier Palmer*
Body: Red mohair, or Squirrel's fur.
Ribbing: Gold twist.
Wings & Legs: Red cock's hackle.

29. *Governor*
Wings: Light Pheasant.
Body: Copper Peacock herl.
Ribbing: Gold twist.
Tag: Scarlet twist.
Legs: Red or ginger hackle.
Hook: No. 9.

30. *For Loch Awe*
Wings: Pheasant's tail.
Body: Orange mohair.
Legs: Ginger hackle.
Hook: No. 8.

31. *Second Fly for Loch Awe*
Wings : Waterhen.
Body: Copper Peacock herl.
Legs: Black hackle.
Hook: No. 7.

32. *For the Dee* (Hackle Fly)
Wings & Legs: Hackle from the neck of a pale dun hen.
Body: Dull yellow mohair.
Hook: No. 9.

33. *Another Fly for the Dee* (Hackle Fly)
Wings & Legs: Dark dun hen's hackle (rather full).
Body: Peacock herl.
Hook: No. 9.

34. *Fly for Llyn Ogwyn*
Wings: Dark copper-coloured Mallard feather.
Body: Peacock herl.
Legs: Black hackle.
Hook: No. 8.

35. *Coch y Bonddhu*
Wings & Legs: Coch-y-bonddhu (red and black) hackle.
Body: Peacock herl.
Hook: No. 8 or 9.

36. *Yellow Sally*
Wings: White hackle dyed yellow.
Body: pale yellow fur or mohair ribbed with fawn-coloured silk.
Legs: A ginger hackle.
Hook: No. 9.

37. *Ginger Hackle*
Wings & Legs: Ginger hackle.
Body: (Short and spare) Yellow silk.
Hook: No. 8 Kendal Sneck.

38. *Grouse Hackle*
Wings & Legs: Grouse hackle.
Body: Peacock herl, or orange silk etc.
Hook: Nos. 8 to 12.

39. *Dotterel Hackle*
Wings & Legs: Dotterel.
Body: Yellow silk.
Hook: Nos. 6 to 12 Kirby Sneck.

40. *For the Conway*
Wings & Legs: Dark dun hen's hackle.
Body: Dun orange mohair.
Hook: No. 11.

41. *Second Conway Fly*
Wings & Legs: Bright dun hen's hackle.
Body: Yellow mohair.
Hook: No. 10.

42. *Third Conway Fly*
Wings & Legs: Wren's hackle.
Body: Peacock's herl.
Hook: No. 9.

43. *Grannom* or *Greentail*
Wings: Pheasant or Partridge.
Body: Hare's face fur.
Tag: Green silk.
Legs: Grizzled cock's hackle.
Hook: No. 9.

44. *Water Cricket*
Legs: Peacock's topping (or a black cock's hackle will do), wind round the body and snip off fibres.
Body: Orange floss, tied on with black silk.

45. *Bluebottle Fly*
Wings: Starling.
Body: Dark blue floss, tied with brown silk.
Legs: Black cock's hackle.
Hook: Nos. 9 to 12.

46. *Housefly*
Wings: Starling.
Body: Ostrich herl (fullish).
Legs: Black hackle.
Hook: No. 12 or 13.

JOHN JACKSON
The Practical Fly-Fisher
1854

March

1. *Dark Bloa*
Wings: Dark feather from inside of Waterhen's wing.
Body: Red-brown silk.
Legs: Black cock hackle.
Whisks: Two fibres black cock hackle.

2. *Olive Bloa*
Wings: Starling, dyed onion.
Body: Light olive silk.
Legs: Olive stained hackle.
Whisks: Two small hairs from a Rabbit's whiskers.
Vary by using feather undyed, or Snipe's wing.

3. *Red Clock*
Wings & Legs: Red hackle, or cock Pheasant's neck feather.
Body: Brown Peacock herl.
Silk: Bright red.

4. *Little Brown*
Wings: Inside Woodcock or hen Pheasant wing.
Body: Red-copper coloured silk.
Legs: Brown hackle.

5. *Alder Fly*
Wings: Landrail or Throstle.
Body: Blue and brown Squirrel fur.
Ribbing: Lead-coloured silk.
Legs: Grizzled hackle (dark).

6. *Blue Midge*
Wings: Waterhen's neck or Landrail's back.
Body: Lead-coloured silk.
Legs: Grizzled hackle.

7. *Red-tailed Spinner*
Wings: Landrail.
Body: Red silk ribbed with gold twist.
Legs: Red hackle.
Whisks: Three strands of same.

8. *Great Brown*
Wings: Short hen Pheasant's quill.
Body: Copper coloured silk, ribbed with olive silk.
Legs: Olive stained hackle.
Tail: Two strands of same feather as wings.
   or, for early part of the season:
Wings: Ruddy grey feather from Partridge tail.
Body: Red silk, ribbed with olive silk.
Legs: Grey feather from a Partridge's back.
Whisks: Two strands of same.
   or, in heavy, cold weather:
Wings: Outside Woodcock's wing.
Body: Olive silk.
Ribbing: Gold tinsel.
Legs: Red hackle.
Tail: Two strands of same.
   or, late in April:
Wings: Light Pheasant stained in yellow dye.
Body: Hare's face, ribbed with yellow silk.
Legs: Greenish-yellow hackle.
Tail: Two strands wing feather.
   or:

Wings & Legs: Inside Woodcock's wing, hackled on.
Body: Orange silk.
  or:
Wings & Legs: Ruddy grey feather from Partridge's back, hackled on.
Body: Copper-coloured silk.

9. *Cowdung Fly*
Wings: Landrail.
Body: Gosling's down, or buff Berlin wool, or buff Ostrich herl.
Silk: Yellow.
Legs: Yellow hackle.

10. *Brown Clock*
Wings & Legs: Starling's neck, hackled on.
Body: Peacock herl and brown silk.

11. *Yellow-legged Bloa*
Wings: Inside Dotterel or Teal, or light Starling.
Body: Straw-coloured waxed silk.
Legs: Greenish-yellow hackle.
Tail: Two strands of greenish-yellow hackle.

12. *Water Spaniel*
Wings & Legs: Pewit's topping, or Tomtit tail feather, hackled on.
Body: Orange and lead-coloured silk.
  Snip off part of fibre.

April

13. *Grey Gnat*
Wings: Grey feather from Partridge's back.
Body: Orange silk.
Legs: Grizzled hackle.

14. *Pigeon-Blue Bloa*
Wings: Feather of blue Pigeon's or Waterhen's neck.
Body: Brimstone flame coloured silk.
Legs: Yellowish dun hackle.
Tail: Two strands yellowish dun hackle.

Head: Strand from the tail of cock Pheasant.
If you use Waterhen's feathers for wings, take the tips of two, and do not divide the wings.

15. *Yellow Midge*
Wings: Lightest Throstle wing.
Body: Pale yellow silk.
Ribbing: Orange silk.
Legs: Yellow hackle, or down from the root-end of a feather.

16. *Great Spinner*
Wings: Dark Starling.
Body: Brown silk.
Ribbing: Gold tinsel.
Legs: Red hackle.
Whisks: Three strands red hackle.
N.B. Jay's quill is more transparent.

17. *Black Midge*
Wings: Starling quill.
Body: Black silk or black Ostrich herl.
Legs: Black hackle.

18. *Spider-legs*
Wings: Rusty feather from Fieldfare's back.
Body: Lead-coloured silk.
Legs: Dark grizzled hackle.

19. *Sandfly*
Wings: Inside hen Pheasant's ruddy, mottled feather, dressed full.
Body: Reddish Hare's neck.
Ribbing: Light brown silk.
Legs: Ginger hackle.

20. *Greentail*
Wings: Inside Pheasant, dressed full.
Body: Lead-coloured silk.
Tag: Knot of green Peacock herl.
Legs: Ginger hackle.

21. *Downlooker*
Wings: Inside Woodcock.
Body: Orange and lead-coloured silk, neatly ribbed.
Legs: Hackle of Woodcock or hen Grouse neck.

22. *Stone Midge*
Wings: Pewit's breast.
Body: Heron herl wrapped on sky-blue silk.
Legs: Blue dun hackle.

May

23. *Little White Spinner*
Wings: Light blue feather from inside Pigeon's wing.
Body: Orange silk extremities, white silk for middle.
Legs: Pale blue dun hackle.
Whisks: Three long strands pale blue dun hackle.
  or, hacklewise:
Wings & Legs: Pale dun hackle.
Body & Whisks: As above.

24. *Grey Midge*
Wings: Woodcock's breast.
Body: Pale yellow silk.

25. *Yellow Sally*
Wings: Pale yellow dyed feather.
Body: Yellow silk ribbed with fawn silk.
Legs: Yellow hackle.

26. *May Brown*
Wings: Ruddy grey feather from a Partridge's back.
Body: Olive coloured silk.
Ribbing: Light brown silk.
Legs: Olive hackle.
Whisks: Three strands olive hackle.
  Spinner of same:
Wings: Starling.
Body: Same as above.
Legs: Purple hackle.

27. *Pale Blue Bloa*
Wings: Blue feather from outside of a Sea Swallow's wing.
Body: Pale yellow silk, ribbed with sky-blue silk.
Legs: Pale yellow hackle.
Whisks: Two strands pale yellow hackle.

28. *Yellow Fly*
Wings: Yellow dyed feather.
Body: Yellow silk.
Legs: Yellow hackle.
Whisks: Two strands yellow hackle.
Head: Green Peacock's herl.

29. *Little Stone Bloa*
Wings: Inside Swift's wing.
Body: Brown silk.
Legs: Brown hackle.

30. *Barm Fly*
Wings: Outside Brown Owl's wing.
Body: Orange and ginger silk.
Legs: Ginger hackle.

30a. *Oil Fly*
Wings: Outside Brown Owl's wing.
Body & Shoulder: Black Ostrich herl, and dark red silk for tail.
Legs: Black hackle.

31. *Great Alder Fly*
Wings: Landrail or Snipe.
Body: Dark mulberry silk towards the head, bright red silk at tail.
Legs: Brown hackle.

32. *May Fly* (Stonefly)
Wings: Inside Grey Goose wing.
Body: Two strands of yellow and one of drab Ostrich herl neatly ribbed and tied with brown silk.
Legs: Brown hackle.
Horns & Tail: Rabbit's whiskers.

(33 & 34. Green and Grey Drakes)

June

35. *Soldier*
Wings: Outside red hackle, inside Jay's quill.
Body: Light red silk, ribbed with brown silk.

36. *Hawthorn Fly*
Dress as No. 17 but larger (Black Midge).

37. *Light Silver Horns*
Wings: Thrush or Landrail, with four strands of Grey Mallard to make the white spots.
Horns: Two strands grey Mallard.
Body: Light brown and lead-coloured silk.
Legs: Sooty dun hackle.

38. *Black Silver Horns*
Wings: Outside Waterhen's wing, with two strands grey Mallard to make the white spots.
Body: Black Ostrich herl, ribbed with olive silk.
Legs: Black hackle.
Horns: Two fibres grey Mallard.

39. *Little Dark Bloa*
Wings: Inside Waterhen's wing.
Body: Lead-coloured silk.
Legs: Yellowish dun hackle.
Whisks: Two small hairs from Rabbit's whiskers.
 also:
Pale Blue Bloa
Wings: Light Starling.
Body: Pale yellow and fawn-coloured silk.
Legs: Pale yellow dun hackle.
Whisks: Two strands pale yellow dun hackle.

40. *June Dun*
Wings: Dotterel's back, or cock Sparrow's wing, hackled on.
Body: Blue Rabbit's fur and drab silk.

41. *Twitch Bell*
Wings: Lightest Starling inside.
Outside & Legs: Brown hackle.
Body: Brown Peacock herl—as in Soldier No. 35, but much less.

42. *Jumpers*
(a) Tomtit's tail hackled on.
Body: Yellow silk.
(b) Golden Plover, hackled on.
Body: Yellow silk.

43. *Little Olive Bloa*
Wings: Starling dyed onion.
Body: Lead-coloured silk, ribbed with yellow silk.
Legs: Dun hackle stained same as the wings.
Whisks: Two small Rabbit's whiskers.
The Spinner is made with red legs and whisks, body of brown silk ribbed with yellow silk.

44. *Black Ant*
Wings: Blue-cap's tail.
Body: Black Ostrich herl, small in middle.
Legs: Brown hackle.

45. *Red Ant*
Wings: Sparrow or Lark.
Body: Herl of cock Pheasant's tail.
Legs: Red hackle.

46. *Little Blue Bloa*
Wings: Bullfinch tail.
Body: Dark blue silk.
Legs: Dark blue or black hackle.
Whisks: Two strands blue hackle.

August

47. *August Brown*
Wings: Young Partridge back, Grey Goose breast, or bright hen Pheasant wing.

Body: Light brown silk.
Legs: Grizzled hackle.
Whisks: Three strands grizzled hackle.
Spinner: smaller and lighter than No. 7, *q.v.*

48. *Cinnamon Fly*
Wings: Yellow hen, Landrail, or Owl, near colour of cinnamon.
Body: Orange and straw-coloured silk.
Legs: Ginger hackle.

49. *Light Bloa*
Wings: Inside of Snipe's wing.
Body: Light drab silk.
Legs: Grizzled hackle.
Whisk: Grizzled hackle.
Spinner is too transparent to imitate.

50. *Dark Bloa*
Wings: Inside Swift or Waterhen wing.
Body: Reddish-brown silk.
Legs: Brown hackle.
Whisks: Brown hackle.

51. *Orange Stinger*
Wings: Starling.
Body: Head brown silk, tail orange silk, dressed small in the middle.
Legs: Furnace hackle.

52. *Grey Grannom*
Wings: Dark grey from Nighthawk or Brown Owl.
Body: Red Squirrel's fur, ribbed with fawn silk.
Legs: Ginger hackle.
Tag: Dark green to represent eggs.
Appears about the 12th. August.

53. *Nankeen Spinner*
Wings: Light Starling.
Body: Nankeen or fawn-coloured silk.
Legs: Honey dun hackle.
Tail: Three long strands of same.

54. *Shining Black Silver Horns*
Wings: Dark shining cock Pheasant's neck, or outside Rook's wing.
Body: Lead-coloured silk.
Legs: Dark grizzled hackle.
Horns: Two strands dark grizzled hackle.

September

55. *Light Olive Bloa*
Wings: Inside Dotterel, or Sea gull quill.
Body: Pale French white silk.
Legs: Pale blue hackle.
Whisks: Pale blue hackle.

56. *Dark Olive Bloa*
Wings: Inside Waterhen's wing.
Body: Lead-coloured silk.
Legs: Dark olive, or black hackle.
Whisks: Three small Rabbit's whiskers.

57. *Small Willow Fly*
Wings & Legs: Inside Snipe wing or small grizzled hackle.
Body: Light brown silk, or Mole's fur and yellow silk.

58. *Large Willow Fly*
Wings: Inside Woodcock.
Body: Mole's fur spun on yellow silk.
Legs: Brown hackle.
  or, hacklewise:
Wings & Legs: Grizzled hackle of copperish hue.
Body: As above.

October

59. *Bluebottle*
Wings: Jay's quill.
Body: Green Peacock herl, or purple silk.
Legs: Pewit's topping ribbed neatly down body, and fibres then snipped off, except under the wings.

60. *Housefly*
Wings: Lark's quill.
Body: Light brown silk, ribbed with drab Ostrich herl.
Legs: Grizzled hackle.

61. *Small Olive Bloa*
Wings: Starling stained onion.
Body: Yellow silk.
Legs: Olive stained hackle.
Whisks: Two strands olive stained hackle.

62. *Dark Grey Midge*
Wings: Dark grey feather of Partridge.
Body: Brown or olive silk.
Legs: Grey Partridge, or grizzled hackle.

63. *Red Palmer*
Greenish Peacock herl, tied with red silk and ribbed with gold tinsel, with a red hackle over all.

64. *Black Palmer*
Body: Dark Peacock herl or Ostrich herl, tied with green silk, and ribbed with gold tinsel.
Hackle: Black, brown, or red, over all.

64a. *Palmer for Spring*
Body: Green Peacock herl, tied with green silk, ribbed with gold tinsel, with a greenish stained or grizzled hackle over all.
b. Body: Green Peacock herl and yellow silk, with a mottled hackle from Grouse neck over all.
c. Body: As above, with Golden Plover hackle, or Tomtit's tail, over all.

ALEXANDER MACKINTOSH
The Driffield Angler
1806

February

1. *Palmer Fly* or *Plain Hackle*
Wings & Legs: Dark red cock hackle.
Body: Black Hog's wool.
Silk: Dark red.
Hook: No. 6.

2. *Gold Hackle*
Wings & Legs: Dark, black, red, or tinged cock hackle.
Body: Black Spaniel's ear, ribbed with gold twist.
Silk: Dark yellow.
Hook: No. 6 or 7.

3. *Blackwing Hackle*
Wings: Light Starling.
Body: Black water dog's fur—thin and neat.
Legs: Black hackle.
Hook: No. 6 or 7.

4. *Dark Brown Fly*
Wings: Light Starling.
Body: Brown hair from the flank of a brindled calf collected in Spring.
Legs: Small tinged hackle.
Silk: Dark red.
Hook: No. 7.

March

5. *Whirling Dun*
Wings: Starling.
Body: Bottom fur of a Squirrel's tail, mixed with a little light blue Hog's wool or mohair.
Silk: Dusty yellow.

6. *Early Bright Brown*
Wings: Mottled hen Pheasant wing.
Body: Dark red Spaniel's ear.
Legs: Very small tinged hackle.
Hook: No. 7.

7. *Little Bright Brown*
Wings: Light Jay.
Body: Light brown Spaniel's ear, mixed with yellow mohair.
Silk: Yellow.
Whisks: 2 forks.
Hook: No. 9.

8. *Whitest Dun*
Wings: Light grey hen Pheasant.
Body: Roots of Camel's hair.
Silk: Ashen colour.
Hook: No. 9.

9. *Later Bright Brown*
Wings: Woodcock or brown hen.
Body: Bright copper mohair.
Silk: Red.
Legs: Tinged hackle.
Hook: No. 9.

April

10. *Small Bright Brown*
Wings: Light Starling.
Body: Squirrel's fur from point of the ear where much weather-beaten, with a yellow cast.
Silk: Copper.
Hook: No. 9.

11. *The Great Whirling Dun*
Wings: Pale grey Mallard.
Body: Down of Fox cub, ash coloured at roots.
Silk: Yellow.

12. *Grouse Hackle*
Wings & Legs: Reddish brown neck of cock Grouse.
Body: Dark olive mohair and fine gold-coloured Hog's wool mixed.
Hook: No. 7.

13. *Brown Partridge*
Wings: Partridge Tail (not red).
Body: Sable fur and gold-coloured Hog's wool well mixed.
Hook: No. 7.

14. *Sooty Dun Hackle*
Wings & Legs: Sooty dun cock all down body.
Body: Lead-coloured mohair.
Silk: Ash colour.
Hook: No. 7.

May

15. *Dun Cut*
Wings: Dun feather from a Kite's wing.
Body: Bear's hair with a little blue and yellow mohair.
Silk: Yellow.
Whisks: 2 forks from a foulmart's tail.

16. *Green Drake*
Wings: Grey Mallard dyed yellow.
Body: A little fine wool from a ram's testicles (a beautiful dusty yellow).
Ribbing: Copper coloured silk.
Legs: Dark Bittern.
Whisks: 2 hairs of Fitch's tail.
Head: Brown Peacock's herl.
Hook: No. 5 or 6.

17. *Grey Drake*
Wings: Grey Mallard mixed with Jay or Widgeon.
Body: Light Camel's hair with a little light blue Hog's wool well mixed.
Silk: Ash colour.
Legs: Small bluish grizzled cock's hackle.
Whisks: 2 hairs from a Foulmart's tail.
Hook: No. 5 or 6.

18. *Yellow Hackle*
Wings: Mallard dyed yellow.
Body: As for Green Drake.
Ribbing, Tail & Head: As for Green Drake.
Hook: No. 6.

19. *Stone Fly*
Wings: Kite or Woodcock.
Body: Bear's dun hair with brown and yellow Camlet well mixed (browner towards wings and yellow towards tail).
Legs: Black hackle.
Silk: Copper and yellow.

20. *Black Silver Hackle*
Wings & Legs: Black cock's hackle.
Body: Black Ostrich herl.
Ribbing: Silver twist.
Hook: No. 8.

21. *Woodcock Fly*
Wings: Woodcock.
Body: Brown Spaniel's ear and a little Squirrel's fur well mixed.
Legs: Small tinged hackle (one side taken off) lapped neatly to tail.
Whisks: Brown Mallard.
Hook: No 8 or 9.

June

22. *Grizzle Hackle*
Wings & Legs: Dark grizzled cock.
Body: Feather from a Pheasant's tail (a dark reddish brown).
Silk: Red or copper coloured.
Hook: No. 8.

23. *Golden Sooty Dun*
Wings: Starling.
Body: Dark brown wool of a black Lamb (weather-beaten).
Legs: Body picked out.
Hook: No. 9.

24. *Little Blue Fox*
Wings: Starling.
Body: Fox's blue fur with a little light camel's hair and light straw mohair, well mixed.
Whisks: Monkey (fine ash colour).

25. *Purple Hackle*
Wings & Legs: Blood-red cock's hackle.
Body: Spaniel's fur on dark red silk.
Hook: No. 8.

26. *Owl Fly*
Wings: Whitey-grey Mallard.
Body: Very light yellow or almost white mohair and a very light yellow silk.
Head: Brown Peacock herl (small).
Hook: No. 7.

27. *Ant Fly*
Wings: Starling.
Body: Amber mohair mixed with a little black Spaniel's fur and small brown silk.
Legs: Blood-red cock's hackle.
Hook: No. 11.

28. *Green Grasshopper*
Wings & Legs: Light red cock's hackle.
Body: Green and yellow mohair well mixed.
Ribbing: Fine green silk and green Peacock herl twisted together.
Hook: No. 6.

29. *Dun Grasshopper*
Wings & Legs: Dun Smoky hackle.
Body: Dun Bear's hair and a little dark dun mohair.
Hook: No. 5 or 6.

July

30. *Badger Fly*
Wings: Sad grey feather from a hen Pheasant's wing.

Body: Badger's skin from Skinners' pits twisted on small red silk, with a dark red head.
Hook: No. 9 or 10.

31. *Orange Fly*
Wings: Black Crow's or Rail's wing.
Body: Dark orange mohair and small gold twist.
Legs: Small orange hackle.

32. *Wasp Fly*
Wings: Grey feather from Mallard.
Body: Dark Brown Bear's hair and black Rabbit's fur and a little yellow mohair well mixed.
Ribbing: Yellow silk.
Hook: No. 7 or 8.

33. *Shell Fly*
Wings: Starling.
Body: Fine yellow Hog's wool or mohair mixed with dark fur of Hare's ear.
Silk: Lead coloured.
Hook: No. 9 or 10.

34. *Little Dun*
Wings: Jay's light blue feather.
Body: White mohair on ash-coloured silk, raised under wing with a needle.
Hook: No. 9 or 10.

35. *Mealy White Moth*
Wings: White Owl.
Body: Soft white Hare or Rabbit's fur.
Hackle: Soft white hackle from head to tail.
Hook: No. 4 or 5.

36. *Mealy Cream Moth*
Wings: Yellow Owl (deep cream colour).
Body: Fur of a white Weasel's tail on straw-coloured silk.
Head: Brown Peacock herl.
Legs: Yellow hackle.
Hook: No. 4 or 5.

37. *Mealy Brown*
Wings: Mottled brown Owl.
Body: Fur of a Weasel's tail, a little yellow Marten's fur, a very little brown Spaniel's fur from ear, well mixed.
Legs: Bittern.
Head: Brown silk or silver twist.
Hook: No. 4 or 5.

August

38. *Fern Fly*
Wings: Dark grey Mallard.
Body: Hare's or Rabbit's neck of the colour of wintered fern.
Hook: No. 9.

39. *Harry Long Legs*
Wings & Legs: Smoky brown hackle.
Body: Bear's dun and blue mohair well mixed (long and slender).
Hook: No. 5 or 6.

JAMES OGDEN
On Fly-Tying
1879

1. *Red Fly or Old Joan Fly*
Wings: Soft quill feather of a Peahen—flat and full, and long enough to cover the bend of the hook.
Body: Ruddy Sheep's wool with equal quantity of the reddest part of Squirrel's fur, with a turn of light claret-coloured wool at the tail.
Legs: Two turns rather dark claret hackle.
Hook: No. 2, or smaller.
In Devonshire, a buzz pattern is used:
Wings & Legs: Brassy dun or grizzle cock's hackle.
Body: As above.

2. *The Hare's Ear Blue Dun* or *Cock Wing*
Wings: Starling (with or without onion dye), set on full and very upright.
Body: Hare's ear or face (with or without olive fur from Monkey's neck, or olive Berlin wool), spun on fine yellow silk.
Tag: Fine gold tinsel.
Legs: Dubbing picked out.
Whisks: Red cock's hackle.
For a change, use a body of yellow silk only, and Hare's ear hacklewise for legs. For variety, rib Hare's-ear body with fine gold tinsel or twist, and wing with Woodcock.
Hook: No. 2.

3. *Blue Dun*
Wings: Dark Starling, very upright.
Body: Water-rat's fur spun on primrose silk.
Legs: Dark dun hen's hackle.
Hook: No. 2, or smaller.
(Dressed in numerous shades)

4. *March Brown*
Wings: Hen Pheasant, reddish brown, very upright and full.
Body: Hare's ear with a little yellowish-olive mohair spun on yellow silk well waxed.
Ribbing: Fine gold tinsel, or twist, or yellow silk.
Legs: Brown Partridge back hackle.
Whisks: Three strands Partridge tail feather.
Hook: (not given).
Another pattern (Usk):
Wings: Dark freckled Partridge tail feather.
Body: Hare's ear with a little red fur from the Hare's neck.
Ribbing: Olive silk, not waxed.
Legs: Wren's tail.
Another pattern as the season advances:
Wings: Marbled part of a hen Pheasant's wing.
Body: Pale olive mohair.
Ribbing: Fine gold twist.
Legs: Honey dun hackle.

5. *Iron Blue Dun*
Wings: Two feathers from the breast of a Water-rail, or Tomtit's wing.
Body: Smallest possible pinch of Mole's fur, tied with reddish purple silk waxed with white wax.
Legs: Two turns yellow dun hackle.
Whisks: yellow dun hackle.
Hook: No. 0.

6. *Red Spinner*
Wings: Dark Starling, broad and upright.
Body: Ruddy brown floss.
Ribbing: Fine gold twist.
Legs: Dark red cock's hackle.
Whisks: Three strands red cock's hackle (long).
Hook: Nos. 1 to 2.

7. *Ogden's Fancy*
Wings: Bright Starling, broad and upright.
Body: Bright yellow silk.
Tag: Fine gold tinsel.
Legs: Bright red cock's hackle with black roots.
Whisks: Bright red cock hackle.
Hook: Nos. 0 to 5 or 6.
Use a blood-red or mahogany hackle for variety.

8. *Cowdung Fly*
Wings: Landrail (flat).
Body: (Short and full) Yellow wool mixed with a little dingy brown wool, spun on brown silk.
Legs: Ginger hackle slightly stained in copperas.

9. *Yellow Dun*
Wings: Young Starling (upright).
Body: Yellow silk, well waxed.
Legs: Yellow dun hackle.
 or:
Wings: Young Starling, very upright.
Body: Fine yellow silk, waxed with white wax.
Legs: Two turns of a good yellow dun hackle.

Whisks: Two strands honey dun hackle, rather long.
  or, buzz:
Wings & Legs: Yellow dun hackle (sparingly).
Body: As last above with small portion of yellow wool.
  or:
Wings & Legs: Dotterel hackle.
Body: As last above.

10. *Alder*
Wings: Hen Pheasant centre tail feathers, full and long.
Body: Bronze Peacock herl (with reddish brown tying silk) made full.
Tag: Dark claret mohair.
Legs: Dark brassy dun hackle, or black cock's hackle, or, best, a good furnace hackle.
Hook: No. 4, or smaller.

11. *Golden Dun Midge*
Wings: Young Starling, very upright.
Body: (Fine) Light olive floss.
Ribbing: Narrow gold tinsel.
Legs: Rather light dun hackle.
Silk: Very fine primrose, waxed with white wax.
Hook: No. 1, not larger.
(April to June on Wandle, Test, Itchen, Usk and Monow)

12. *Black Gnat*
Wings: Light Starling.
Body: Black horsehair.
Legs: Starling or black hen's hackle.
  or, buzz:
Wings & Legs: Two turns glossy Starling's hackle.
Body: Black horsehair.
Tag: Silver tinsel.

13. *Coch y Bonddhu*, or *Marlow Buzz*
Legs & Wings: Furnace hackle.
Body: Peacock herl dyed magenta (not too long).
Silk: Orange, waxed with white wax (showing two or three wraps at the head).
Tag: Fine gold tinsel.

14. *Oak Fly*, or *Downlooker*
Wings: Woodcock (flat).
Body: Bright orange floss.
Silk: Lead-coloured, showing at the head and shoulders.
Legs: Good furnace hackle ribbed down the body and snipped off except enough for the legs.
Hook: No. 2 or 3.

15. *Furnace Fly*
Wings: Starling (upright).
Body: Bright orange tying-silk.
Legs: Two turns furnace hackle.
Hook: No. 2.

16. *Tinkler's Dun* (Invented by Captain Tinkler)
Wings: Starling (upright).
Body: White purse silk, well twisted and wrapped close; tied with pale primrose silk waxed with white wax.
Legs: Ginger hackle.
Whisks: Three strands red cock's hackle.

17. *Wren's Tail*
Wings & Legs: Wren's tail.
Body: Light red Hare's neck fur spun on brown silk.
Ribbing: Fine gold twist.
Hook: No. 1 or 0.

18. *Little Orange Fly*
Wings: Water-rail or hen Blackbird (flat).
Body: Deep orange floss.
Legs: Dark furnace hackle.
Hook: No. 1.

19. *Stone Midge*
Wings & Legs: Two or three turns Starling hackle.
Body: Strand from Heron's wing.
Hook: No. 0 or smaller.

20. *Whirling Blue Dun*
Wings: Dark Starling (upright).

Body: Reddish brown fur from a Squirrel's legs, spun on yellow silk waxed with white wax.
Legs: Pale ginger hackle.
Whisks: Three strands red cock hackle.
Hook: No. 2.

21. *Palmers*
(a) Hook: No. 6 Long.
Body: Spare with narrow bronze Peacock herl.
Ribbing: Gold thread.
Hackle: Bright red cock, or furnace.

(b) *The Middle Hopper*
Hook: No. 4.
Body: Bright orange floss.
Ribbing: Magenta Peacock herl.
Hackle: Honey dun, or brassy dun, or grizzle dun with or without gold.

(c) *Black Palmer*
Hook: No. 4.
Body: Black Ostrich herl.
Ribbing: Rather narrow silver tinsel.
Hackle: Black cock.

22. *Bluebottle*
Wings: Two broad strips Starling (flat).
Body: Black Ostrich herl.
Ribbing: Blue tinsel.
Legs: Black hackle—cut off at top to let the wings lie flat.
Silk: Brown sewing silk waxed with white wax for head and shoulders.
Hook: No. 3 or 4.

23. *Housefly*
Wings: Two broad strips Starling (flat).
Body: Two or three strands freckled Turkey-tail feather wrapped close; short piece of light stone-coloured Berlin wool tied in at shoulder on each side.
Legs: Black hen, or glossy Starling.

24. *Small Willow* or *Needle Brown*

Male:

Hook: No. 1 long.
Body: Peacock quill, dyed orange at the tag-end.
Head: Black silk (round like a pin).
Wings: *Over,* hen Blackbird } Very flat and not at all broken.
       Under, Starling
Both sets of wings project beyond the end of the hook.
Legs: Half-inch grizzle hairs from side of the neck of a Badger, cut to proper length.

Female:

Body: Yellow silk with Peacock quill ribbed over, showing yellow silk between.
Wings: Under: Starling.
       Upper: Thrush.
Head: } As above.
Legs:

G. P. R. PULMAN
Vade-Mecum of Fly-Fishing for Trout
1841

1. *The Early Red*
Wings: Woodcock's wing-feather, to lie flat and be shorter than body.
Legs: Red hen's hackle.
Body: Body to be made thickly of the red part of the Squirrel's fur, or hair from a red sheep-skin door-mat, well broken up together before using.
Hook: No. 3, Kendal.*

---

*All hook sizes in this list are those of the Kendal Scale.

2. *The Blue Dun*
Wings: From Starling's wing-feather.
Legs: A blue hen's hackle.
Body: Fine blue fur from the Hare or Squirrel, ribbed with fine yellow silk thread.
Whisks: Two fibres from hackle of a blue cock.
Hook: No. 2 or 3.

3. *Another Blue Dun*
Wings: Starling's wing-feather, or Moor-hen's wing-feather.
Legs: Blue hen's hackle.
Body: Peacock's herl stripped of its down—the first turn or two at the bottom white, to form what is called a tag.
Whisks: To match the legs.
Hook: No. 3.

4. *The March Brown*
Wings: Woodcock's wing-feather dressed upright.
Legs: Brown-red hen's hackle.
Body: Brown fur from a brown sable muff or boa, ribbed with yellow silk thread.
Whisks: Two fibres hen Pheasant's tail-feather.
Hook: No. 4 or 5.

5. *The Sand Fly*
Wings: Landrail's wing-feather.
Legs: Light-red hen's hackle.
Body: Sand-coloured fur from a Hare's poll.
Hook: No. 3.

6. *The Grannam* or *Green-tail*
Wings: Wing-feather of a Partridge or hen Pheasant dressed flat.
Legs: Either small Partridge hackle, or fibres of body-fur picked out with a needle.
Body: Lower part of body is made of two or three turns of dark green floss silk, forming a tag, and the rest of the body of fur from a Hare's ear.
Hook: No. 3.

7. *The Hare's Flax (the Male Grannam)*
Wings: Woodcock wing-feather, dressed flat.
Legs: As for the Grannam.
Body: Either straw-coloured floss silk, or of fur from a Hare's ear, ribbed with yellow silk.
Hook: No. 3.

8. *The Whirling Dun*
Wings: Starling's wing-feather, dressed upright.
Legs: Blood-red hen's hackle.
Body: Blue fur combed with a tooth-comb from the roots of a Hare's or Squirrel's skin.
Whisks: Red cock's hackle fibres.
Hook: No. 2 or 3.

9. *The Cow-dung Fly*
Wings: Very light Starling's wing-feather, dressed flat, and not longer than the body.
Legs: Ginger hen's hackle.
Body: Yellow mohair mixed with red hair from a door-mat, wound rather thickly.
Hook: No. 3.

10. *The Yellow Dun*
Wings: Thrush or Starling's wing-feather, to stand erect.
Legs: A very fine light blue hen's hackle.
Body: Yellow Martin's fur, mixed with a little light blue fur from the Hare, Rabbit, or Squirrel, and ribbed with yellow silk.
Whisks: From a large yellow hackle.
Hook: No. 1.
This fly should be dressed very neatly and fine.

11. *Iron Blue Dun*
Wings: From the wing-feather of the Moor-hen or of the Skitty, to stand erect.
Legs: Blood-red hen's hackle.
Body: Water-rat or Mole's fur, ribbed with yellow silk thread.
Whisks: From a red cock's hackle.
Hook: No. 1.
This is, like the last, an exceedingly fine and delicate fly.

12. *Spider Fly*
Wings: Woodcock's wing-feather, dressed flat.
Legs: Black hen's hackle.
Body: Lead-coloured floss silk.
Hook: No. 2.

13. *The Stone Fly*
Wings: Woodcock wing-feather, made full and to lie flat.
Legs: A grizzle hackle—speckled blue and yellow.
Body: Brown fur from a Sable Boa, mixed with yellow Martin's fur, and ribbed with yellow silk thread.
Hook: No. 5 or 6.

14. *The May Fly*
Wings: Two dappled feathers, taken from below the wings or from the bottom of the neck of the Mallard, dyed greenish yellow, by boiling them in an infusion of the inner bark of the crab-tree or of the barberry tree, with a small piece of alum, to fix the colour. The plume part of the selected feathers are dressed back to back.
Legs: Ginger hackle.
Body: Straw-coloured floss silk or Martin's fur, ribbed with brown silk thread.
Whisks: Three stout black hairs, about half an inch long, taken from the Fitchet's tail or from a black Muff.
Hook: No. 6, Long May.

15. *The Grey Drake*
Wings: Two Mallard's feathers, not dyed, or two mottled feathers from the Widgeon, tied as above.
Legs: Dark blue hackle.
Body: White Ostrich herl, or white floss silk, ribbed with a black horse-hair.
Whisks: Three black hairs, longer than those for the May Fly.
Hook: No. 6, Long May, or Limerick of corresponding size.

16. *The Alder Fly*
Wings: Woodcock's wing-feather, dressed flat.
Legs: Black hen's hackle.
Body: Copper-coloured floss silk.
Hook: No. 4.

17. *The Red Ant*
Wings: Jay's wing-feather, dressed flat.
Legs: Very small red hen's hackle.
Body: Copper-coloured Peacock's herl, wound thickly for two or three turns at the bottom, to form a tuft or tag; the rest of the body dark red silk.
Hook: No. 1 or 2.

18. *The Black Ant*
Wings: Jay wing-feather, dressed flat.
Legs: Small black hen's hackle.
Body: Tuft or tag of black Ostrich herl; rest of body black silk.
Hook: No. 2.

19. *The Red Spinner*
Wings: Starling wing-feather, placed erect.
Legs: Red hen's hackle.
Body: Any fine red fur, or dark red silk, ribbed with fine gold twist.
Whisks: Two fibres red cock's hackle.
Hook: No. 2 or 3.

20. *The White Spinner*
Legs: White hen's hackle with a black list, wound thickly close to the head.
Body: Very light blue, nearly white, fur from a Rabbit's skin, ribbed with the finest silver twist.
Whisks: From a white cock's hackle.
Hook: No. 2.

21. *The White Moth*
Wings: The white part of a Magpie's wing-feather.
Legs: A white hen's hackle.
Body: White Rabbit's fur, wound very thickly.
Hook: No. 6, Long May.
Used only for late evening fishing in the height of summer.

22. *The Welshman's Button,* or *Hazel Fly*
Wings: Red feather of a Partridge's tail, short and dressed flat.
Legs: Black hen's hackle.

Body: Black Ostrich herl and copper-coloured Peacock's herl.
wound together, thickly.
Hook: No. 3 or 4.

23. *The Autumnal Dun*
Wings: From the wing-feather of the Snipe, Fieldfare, or Starling—very light.
Legs: Very light blue hen's hackle.
Body: Very light blue fur, or even the fur from an old white hat.
Whisks: From a very light blue hackle.
Hook: No. 1.

24. *The Red Palmer*
Legs: Blood-red cock's hackle wound from the bottom.
Body: Copper-coloured Peacock's herl, ribbed with gold twist.
Hook: Various.

25. *The Blue Palmer*
Legs: Blue cock's hackle wound from the bottom.
Body: Blue fur from the Rabbit, Hare, or Squirrel, ribbed with gold or silver twist.
Hook: Various.

26. *The Black Palmer*
Legs: Black cock's hackle, wound from the bottom.
Body: Black Ostrich herl, ribbed with gold or silver twist.
Hook: Various.

27. *The Partridge Hackle*
Legs: Mottled feather, nutmeg-brown, from the back of a Partridge.
Body: Light brown fur from a Sable Boa, ribbed with gold twist.
Hook: No. 3.
This is a favourite fly, as a dropper, for summer evening fishing. It is called by some the London Spider.

28. *The Coachman*
Wings: White part of a Magpie's wing-feather.
Legs: Red hen's hackle.
Body: Peacock's herl.
Hook: No. 4 or 5.

29. *The Walton*
Wing: Light wing-feather of the Woodcock.
Legs: Brown or yellow hen's hackle.
Body: Light brown fur from a Sable Boa, either ribbed or not with gold twist.
Hook: No. 3.

ROBERT SALTER
The Modern Angler
1811

1. *Blue Dun*
Wings: Starling (upright).
Body: Blue Fox fur mixed with a little yellow camlet. A paler body as the season advances (pale hedgehog).
 This fly is often made with a light dun hackle instead of a wing; but if used where a large one is required, it should have wings and a small hackle.
Season: March and throughout the season.

2. *Marlow Buzz*
Hackle: Pale red cock, black at the root; brighter as the season advances.
Body: Peacock herl. Often varied with black Ostrich herl, ribbed with silver twist until the middle of April; gold twist later.
Season: March and onwards.

3. *Camlet Fly*
Wings: Pale blue feather from under a Woodpigeon's wing.
Body: Yellow camlet.
Season: Mid-March.

4. *Stone Fly*
Wings: Peahen's feather (four wings).
Body: Brown Hare's ear fur with nearly the same quantity of yellow camlet.
Ribbing: Yellow silk.
Legs: A grizzle hackle, twice under the wings.
Season: Early March.
This fly is often made without wings.

5. *March Brown*
Wings: (Upright) Shaded part of a Partridge tail, or Brown hen's back.
Body: Brown Hare's ear fur mixed with a small proportion of lemon mohair.
Legs: On dull streams, when a large one is required it should have a Partridge hackle wrapped thrice around under the wings.
Season: Mid-March on for six weeks.
On small streams, it is used as a dropper with a Partridge back hackle without wings.

6. *Cowdung Fly*
Wings: Partridge wing (flat), or a small ginger hackle.
Body: Orange mohair, short and thick.
Season: March to early May.

7. *Peacock Fly*
Wings: Peahen's feather (upright), or brown hen feather.
Body: Peacock herl.
Legs: Three turns of a small dark dun hackle.
Season: Early April and on for six weeks, during cloudy warm weather.

8. *Sandfly*
Wings: Landrail.
Body: Brightest part of a Hare's neck.
Ribbing: Orange silk.
Season: Early April to mid-July.
May be made hacklewise with a ginger hackle or Wren's tail.

9. *Gravel Fly* (A small fly)
Wings: Peahen or brown hen's feather.
Body: Lead-coloured silk, a little waxed.
Legs: Three turns of a Plover's topping.
Season: End of April, for fourteen days.

10. *Down Fly*
Wings: Any soft white feather.
Body: White Rabbit's fur.
Legs: Two turns of a small white hackle.
Season: End of April.

11. *Orange Fly*
Wings: Fieldfare's tail; or, hacklewise, with a dark dun hackle.
Body: Orange silk.
Season: End of April to the end of July.

12. *Black Gnat*
Wings: Lightest Starling.
Body: Ostrich herl (black), short and thick.
Legs: A small light dun hackle.
Season: End of April to the end of July.

13. *Hawthorn Fly*
Wings: Palest Starling.
Body: Black Ostrich herl, long and slender.
Legs: Three turns of a Plover's top.
Season: End of April, continuing for three weeks.

14. *Iron Blue*
Wings: Hen Blackbird tail.
Body: Mole's fur.
Legs: A short dark dun hackle—three turns.
Season: Mid-May, continuing for three weeks.

15. *Willow Fly*
Wings & Legs: (Hacklewise) A yellow hackle.
Body: Yellow camlet.
Ribbing: Green silk.
Season: Mid-May.

16. *Orl Fly* (Four wings close on back)
Wings & Legs: (Hacklewise) A dark grizzle hackle.
Body: Bronze peacock herl.
Season: 20th. May to the end of June.

17. *Green Drake* } Ordinary patterns.
18. *Grey Drake*

19. *Oak Fly*
Wings: Woodcock's back.
Body: (Paler at the head than the tail) Bittern hackle.
Legs: A ginger hackle.
Season: Early June, lasting for about five weeks.

20. *Green Gnat*
Wings & Legs: (Hacklewise) A small black cock's hackle.
Body: (Very small) Green silk.
Season: Early June.

21. *Woodpecker Fly*
Wings: Pale green feather of a Woodpecker's back.
Body: Green silk.
Legs: A black cock's hackle.
Season: End of June and on for one month.

22a. *Brown Lady Fly*
Body: Brown Hare's ear fur mixed with darkest Otter fur.
Legs: A grizzle hackle.

22b. *Black Lady Fly*
Body: Black Ostrich herl.
Legs: A small bright red hackle.

23. *Yellow Palmer Fly*
Body: Yellow Camlet.
Wings & Legs: (Hacklewise) A ginger hackle.
Ribbing: (In large patterns) Gold twist.
Season: End of July to the end of September.

24. *Squirrel Fly*
Wings: Peahen.
Body: Red Squirrel fur.
Ribbing: Fine primrose silk.
Legs: Three turns of a grizzle hackle.
On clear streams, the hackle may be omitted.

25. *Blue Gnat*
Wings & Legs: (Hacklewise) A dark dun hackle.
Body: (Slender) Water-rat or Mole's fur.
Season: Mid-September to the end of October.

26. *Red Fly*
Wings: The red feather from a Partridge tail.
Body: Red Squirrel's fur.
Legs: Two turns of a ginger hackle.
Season: October.

27. *Miscellaneous Un-named Flies* (Hooks No. 10 for salmon-fly fishing).

(1) Wings & Legs: Mealy grey cock's hackle.
Body: Peacock herl.

(2) Wings & Legs: A small dun hackle.
Body: Silver twist.

(3) Wings & Legs: A ginger hackle.
Body: Yellow camlet.
Ribbing: Gold twist.

(4) Wings & Legs: Grouse back hackle.
Body: Hare's neck fur and orange mohair mixed in equal quantities.

(5) Wings & Legs: Dark red cock hackle.
Body: Gold twist.

(6) Wings & Legs: A bright red stained hackle.
Body: Peacock herl.

28. *Brown Night Fly*
Wings: Brown hen feather.
Body: Same colour (fur or mohair).

29. *White Night Fly*
Wings: White Owl.
Body: Same colour, and as big as a wheaten straw.
Hook: Medium worm hook.
Season: End of May to the end of June.

Hooks

On rapid streams, hook-sizes No. 9 or 10; on slow, deep streams, No. 5 or 6.

SHIPLEY AND FITZGIBBON
On Fly-Fishing
1838

January

1. *Red Brown Fly*
Wings: Starling or Dotterel.
Body: Dark brown mohair or red silk.
Hook: No. 2 Kendal.

2. *Blue Dun*
Wings: Old Starling.
Body: Straw-coloured silk.
Legs: Blue dun cock's hackle.
Hook: No. 3 Kendal.

3. *Light Blue Dun*
Wings: Old Starling.
Body: Greenish-yellow silk.
Legs: Soft, light blue dun hen hackle.
Hook: No. 2 Kendal.

4. *Golden Ostrich* or *Golden Palmer Fly*
Body: Black Ostrich herl ribbed with gold twist; dressed with orange or puce coloured silk.
Legs: Dark red cock.
Hook: No. 3 Kendal.

5. *Esterhazy Dun*
Wings: Fieldfare.
Body: Bright Esterhazy coloured silk.
Legs: Blue dun hackle.
Hook: No. 2 Kendal.

6. *Peacock Fly*
Hackle: Bluish dun.
Body: Peacock herl; dressed with greenish Pomona silk.
Hook: No. 2 Kendal.

February

7. *Dark Dun*
Wings: Fieldfare.
Body: Dark plum-coloured silk.
Legs: Blue dun hackle.
Hook: No. 2 Kendal.

8. *Plain Palmer*
Hackle: Red cock.
Body: Black Ostrich herl on red silk.
Hook: No. 3 Kendal.

9. *Red Fly*
Wings: Starling, or dun covert of Mallard.
Body: Dark red dubbing from hair in tan yards, dressed on orange silk.
Legs: Cock's hackle of same colour.
Hook: No. 2 Kendal.

10. *Another Blue Dun*
Wings: Starling.
Body: Yellow silk dubbed with Water-rat fur.

Legs: Blue dun hackle.
Hook: No. 2 Kendal.

11. *Red Dun*
Wings: Fieldfare.
Body: Esterhazy coloured silk.
Legs: Reddish dun hackle.
Hook: No. 2 Kendal.

12. *Furnace Fly*
Wings: Fieldfare.
Body: Orange silk.
Legs: Furnace hackle.
Hook: No. 2 Kendal.

March

13. *Another Blue Dun*
Wings: Light Fieldfare.
Body: Straw-coloured silk dubbed with Water-rat's fur.
Legs: Blue dun cock's hackle.
Hook: No. 2 Kendal.

14. *Dark Claret Fly*
Wings: Landrail.
Body: Deep claret silk.
Legs: Dark red cock's hackle.
Hook: No. 2 Kendal.

15. *Another Dark Dun*
Wings: Starling.
Body: Esterhazy silk.
Legs: Blue dun hackle.
Hook: No. 2.

16. *Winter Brown*
Wings: Fieldfare.
Body: Puce-coloured silk.
Legs: Dark furnace hackle.

17. *March Brown* or *Dun Drake*
Wings: Hen Pheasant's wing.
Body: Orange or straw-coloured silk dubbed with Fox-coloured fur from a Hare's poll.
Ribbing: Gold twist—optional.
Legs: Honey dun hackle.

18. *March Brown Dun Fly*
Wings: Hen Pheasant's wing.
Body: Hare's fur from back of the neck, spun on primrose silk.
Legs: Brownish dun hackle.

April

19. *Orange Dun*
Wings: Fieldfare.
Body: Orange silk.
Legs: Blue dun hackle.
Hook: No. 2 Kendal.

20. *Cowdung Fly*
Wings: Landrail.
Body: Yellow Lamb's wool and brown mohair mixed and spun on orange silk.
Legs: Ginger hackle.
Hook: No. 2 Kendal.

21. *Grannom* or *Greentail*
Wings: Hen Pheasant.
Body: Dark Hare's ear fur mixed with a little blue fur.
Tail: Green herl.
Legs: Pale ginger hackle.

22. *Light Blue Dun*
As in pattern No. 3, but on a No. 2 hook.

23. *Yellow Dun*
Wings: Feather from the Red-wing.
Body: Yellow silk.
Legs: Yellow dun hackle.
Hook: No. 2.

24. *Stone Fly*
Wings: Dark mottled hen Pheasant or Peahen—flat and not longer than the body.
Body: Dark Hare's ear fur with a little brown and yellow mohair.
Legs: Dark grizzled cock's hackle (long).
Whisks: Two Rabbit whiskers.
Hook: No. 4 Kendal.

25. *Sand Fly*
Wings: Landrail.
Body: Hare's poll spun on bright orange silk.
Legs: Ginger or light-red hackle.
Hook: No. 3 Kendal.

26. *Spider Fly* (Hacklewise)
Hackle: Woodcock.
Body: Lead-coloured silk.
   or:
Wings: Underside Woodcock's wing.
Body: Dark dun or lead-coloured silk, dressed very fine.
Legs: Black cock's hackle (long)—two turns.
Hook: No. 2 Kendal.

27. *Iron Blue*
Wings: Tomtit's tail.
Body: Water-rat or Monkey's blue fur on purple silk.
Hook: No. 2 Kendal.

28. *Another Dark Dun*
Wings: Under Waterhen's wing.
Body: Water-rat fur spun on yellow silk.
Legs: Blue dun hackle.
Hook: No. 2 Kendal.

29. *Another Palmer*
Body: Brown Peacock's herl on red silk.
Legs: Dark red hackle.

30. *Little Yellow Mayfly*
Wings: Fieldfare stained yellow.
Body: Yellow silk.
Legs: Light ginger hackle.
  or:
Wings: Dotterel's wing.
Body: Yellow Monkey's fur spun on lemon silk.
Hook: No. 2 Kendal.

31. *Silver Twist Hackle*
Hackle: Black cock.
Body: Black Ostrich herl, ribbed with silver twist.

32. *Fern Fly*
Wings: Palest Thrush.
Body: Brown fur from Fox's breast spun on orange silk.
Legs: Pale dun hackle.

June

33. *Green Drake*
Wings: Mallard from side under wing, dyed dingy yellow.
Body: Straw-coloured Ostrich herl.
Ribbing: Gold twist.
Legs: Ginger hackle.
Head: Two turns brown Peacock herl.
Hook: Up to No. 9 Redditch, or 3 Kendal.

34. *Grey Drake*
Wings: Sooty Mallard or Widgeon.
Body: Puce-coloured silk ribbed with silver twist.
Legs: Dark blue dun hackle.
Hook: No. 9 Redditch.

35. *Black Gnat*
Wings: Fieldfare.
Body: Green Plover's crest on dark purple silk.
Hook: No. 1 Kendal.

36. *Peacock*—No. 6 repeated.

37. *Light Mackerel Fly*
Wings: Light Grey Mallard.
Body: Light orange silk, ribbed with gold twist.
Legs: Light red hackle.

July

38. *Dark Mackerel Fly*
Wings: Darkish grey Mallard.
Body: Purple silk, ribbed with gold twist.
Legs: Dark furnace hackle.

39. *Ash Fly*
Wings: Woodcock.
Body: Orange silk.
Legs: Furnace hackle.
Hook: No. 2 Kendal.

40. *Orange Dun*
Wings: Fieldfare.
Body: Bright orange silk.
Legs: Light dun hackle.
Hook: No. 2 Kendal.

41. *Red Ant Fly*
Legs: Bright red cock's hackle.
Body: Light brown Peacock herl.
Hook: No. 2 Kendal.

42. *Black Ant Fly*
Wings: Fieldfare.
Body: Black Ostrich herl on dark puce silk.
Legs: Dark hackle.
Hook: No. 2 Kendal.

43. *Wren's Hackle*
Legs: Wren's tail.
Body: Light brown silk.

44. *Grouse Hackle*
Legs: Red cock Grouse hackle.
Body: Deep orange silk.

August

45. *Oak Fly*
Wings: Woodcock.
Body: Orange silk, ribbed with black Ostrich herl (thinly).
Legs: Dark red hackle stained a deeper colour.

46. *Little Whirling Blue*
Wings: Starling.
Body: Hare's fur from back of the neck mixed with a little yellow mohair—dressed on primrose silk.
Legs: Blue dun hackle.

47. *Summer Dun*
Wings: Young Starling.
Body: Greenish-yellow silk.
Legs: Soft, light-blue dun hackle—three turns.
Dress very delicately.

48. *Brown Fly*
Wings: Landrail.
Body: Fine yellow tying-silk.
Legs: Red cock hackle.

September

49. *Little Pale Blue*
Wings: Young Starling.
Body: Pale Water-rat's fur and fine fur dyed yellow spun on pale yellow silk.
Legs: A very pale olive hackle.
Dress very delicately.

50. *Willow Fly*
Wings: Fieldfare.
Body: Water-rat's fur, or Monkey fur, dubbed sparingly on yellow silk.
Legs: Dark blue dun hackle.

51. *Golden Dun*
Wings: Young Starling.
Body: Deep straw-coloured silk, ribbed with gold twist.
Legs: Honey dun hackle.

52. *Cinnamon Fly*
Wings: Pale reddish-brown feather of a hen.
Body: Dark brown fur—any sort.
Legs: Pale ginger hackle.

Night Flies

The White Moth
Wings: White Owl.
Body: White Ostrich herl, dressed with white silk.
Legs: A white cock's hackle.
Hook: No. 4 Kendal.

Brown Moth
Wings: Brown Owl.
Body: Dark brown bear's fur, dressed with dark brown silk.
Legs: A brown hackle.
Hook: No. 4 Kendal.

Cream-coloured Moth
Wings: Yellow Owl—of the deepest cream-colour.
Body: Of any fine cream-coloured fur.
Legs: A pale yellow hackle.

Black Clocker
Wings: Darkest fibres of a wild Goose's wing feather.
Body: Black Ostrich herl, thickly warped round the hook.
Legs: A large black hackle.

SAMUEL TAYLOR
Angling in all its Branches
1809

Standard Flies

1. *The Black Hackle*
Wings: Light Starling.
Body: Black dog's fur.
Legs: Black cock's hackle.
Hook: No. 5.

2. *Wren's Tail*
Wings & Legs: Wren's tail (all down the body).
Body: Sable fur and a little gold mohair (thin).
Hook: No. 5 or 6.

3. *Grouse Hackle*
Wings & Legs: Reddish-brown, mottled Grouse hackle, dusky towards the butt-end of the feather.
Body: Dark olive dusky yellow, and a little gold-coloured mohair.
Hook: No. 5 or 6.

4. *Smoky Dun Hackle*
Wings & Legs: Smoky dun cock's hackle (all down the body).
Body: Lead-coloured mohair.
Silk: Lead colour.

5. *Brown Rail*
Wings: Partridge tail (not the red feather).
Body: Sable fur and gold mohair (thin, except at shoulder).
Legs: None.

6. & 7. *Hare's Ear*
Wings: Starling.

Body: Hare's ear fur.
   or:
Wings: Rail.
Body: Hare's ear fur.
Hackle: Red.

8. *Red Hackle*
Wings: Starling.
Body: Light red mohair.
Hackle: Red cock.

February to April

1. *Dark Claret*
Wings: (Four) Upper: Partridge tail.
              Under: Starling.
Body: Dark claret and darkish Hare's ear fur.

2. *Dark* or *Blew Fox*
Wings: Starling.
Body: Fox's shoulder fur next to the skin, black Rabbit's tail, and a little straw-coloured mohair mixed.
Whisks: Two fine hairs from the skin of a Monkey, split.

3. *Dun Fox*
Wings: Starling.
Body: Fox fur next skin between throat and shoulder, and brass mohair mixed.
Whisks: Two fine hairs from the skin of a Monkey.

4. *The Ash Fox*
Wings: Starling.
Body: Fox's fur from throat next skin, and pale straw mohair.
Whisks: Two fine hairs from the skin of a Monkey.

5. *Light Fox*
Wings: Starling.
Body: Light Camel's hair, and lightest stone mohair.
Whisks: Two fibres from skin of Monkey.

April and May

6. *Brown Fly*
Wings: Partridge tail.
Body: Light brown Bear, high-coloured yellow mohair, and Hare's face.
Legs: Partridge.
Whisks: Dark Mallard.

7. *Greentail Fly*
Wings: Pheasant.
Body: Black part of Hare's fur, brown strip of feather from Peacock's tail as rib; a green bit of same at tail.
Legs: Grizzled cock's hackle.

8. *Spider Fly*
Wings: Inside Woodcock's wing, hacklewise.
Body: Lead-coloured silk.
Legs: Small black hackle.

9. *Yellow Cadow* or *Mayfly*
Wings: Grey Mallard dyed yellow.
Body: Fine Ram's wool, same colour.
Legs: Dark Bittern hackle.
Whisks: Two fibres Fitch's tail.
Head: Brown Peacock herl.
Hook: No. 4 or 5.

10. *Grey Drake* (Male)
Wings: Mallard mixed with Widgeon.
Body: Light Camel's hair.
Legs: Dark Bittern.
Whisks: Three Fitch's hairs.
Head: Brown Peacock herl.

Grey Drake (Female)
Wings: Grey Mallard only.
Body: Straw (oat).
Legs: Cuckoo cock.
Hook: No. 3, large.

June onwards

11. *The Grizzle Hackle*
Wings & Legs: Dark grizzled cock's hackle, half down the body.
Body: Brown Peacock herl, rib over.
Silk: Dark red.

12. *The Golden Sooty*
Wings: Starling.
Body: Dark mohair of a bright soot colour with a little gold mohair.

13. *Blue Blow*
Wings: Tomtit's tail.
Body: Mole fur with pale copper-coloured mohair.
Whisks: Two fibres Monkey.
Hook: Small and short shank.

14. *Green Caterpillar*
Hackle: Red or black cock's hackle.
Body: Green Peacock herl.
Ribbing: Gold or silver flat tinsel.

15. *Black Caterpillar*
Hackle: Black cock.
Body: Brown Peacock herl.

16. *The Lochaber*
Wings: Bright shining brown, or reddish brown, or dusky, mottled Grouse, hacklewise.
Body: Orange or yellow tying-silk.

17. *Green Bank Fly*
Wings: Starling.
Body: Mallow green mohair with a little yellow, thin and even.
Legs: Fine pale red hackle, ribbed down the body.

18. *The Cream Camel*
Wings: Yellow part of Owl or Thrush wing.

Body: Deepish cream Camel's hair, or fine Spanish wool and gold mohair.
Legs: Body-fibres picked out.

19. *Red Spinner*
Wings: Grey Drake feather tinged with reddish-yellow.
Body: Gold twist.
Legs: Red hackle all down the body.

20. *Ant Fly*
Red Ant:
Wings: Starling.
Body: Amber mohair.
Legs: Red cock's hackle.

Black Ant:
Wings: Lightest sky-blue feather with strongest gloss.
Body: Black Ostrich herl.
Legs: Black cock's hackle.

21. *Pale Blue Fly*
Wings: Lightest blue Sea Swallow.
Body: Bluest Fox-fur mixed with a very little yellow mohair or straw-coloured silk.
Legs: Fine pale blue hackle.
Hook: No. 6 or 7.

22. *Hare's Ear and Yellow*
Wings: Starling.
Body: Dark Hare's ear fur with a little yellow mohair.
Legs: Body picked out.

Night Flies

1. *Mealy White*
Wings: White Owl, mealiest feathers.
Body: White soft Rabbit's fur.
Legs: Soft white, downy hackle.
Hook: No. 4.

2. *Mealy Cream*
Wings: Deep cream-coloured Yellow Owl.
Body: Soft fur of the same colour as wing.
Legs: Pale yellowish hackle.

3. *Mealy Brown*
Wings: Soft Brown Owl.
Body: Lightish brown Rabbit fur.
Legs: Light brown Bittern.

MICHAEL THEAKSTON
British Angling Flies
1853

February

1. *Needle Brown*
Wings: (a) Bloa from under Judcock or Snipe wing; (b) Waterrail (brown); (c) Swift (brown); (d) Cock Pheasant (purple); (e) Fieldfare rump (blue grizzle), hacklewise.
Body: Fine bright orange or yellow silk, more or less waxed.
Legs: Work in a few fibres of fine fleshy grizzled hair or fur at the breast.
Season: All year. Dress very small, neat, and fine.

2. *Early Brown*
Wings & Legs: Woodcock underwing.
Body, Head & Shoulders: Orange silk waxed.
Legs: A few fibres of red-brown mohair worked in at the breast.
Season: Beginning of February to end of April.

3. *Little Early Brown*
Wings & Legs: Feather from under a Swift's wing.
Body: Orange silk, waxed.
Legs: A few fibres of red-brown mohair worked in at the breast.
Season: Beginning of February to end of April.

4. *Early Spinner*
Wings: Redwing.
Body: Yellowish-ashy silk.
Legs: Dark red-brown hackle.
   or:
Fashion hacklewise with a Redwing feather.
Season: February and all through March and April.

5. *Gravel Spinner* (Spider Fly)
Wings: (a) Starling; or (b), Blue Bloa of Crow.
Body: Lead or ashy-coloured silk.
Legs: A few fibres of dark brown mohair worked in at the breast.
   or, hacklewise:
Fashion with feather from a Starling or Crow.
Season: February, March and April.
May hatchings:
Wings & Legs: Woodcock wing feather (hacklewise).
Body: Lead-coloured silk.
Legs: (a) Black-red hackle; or (b), Water-rat fur spun on coppery coloured silk with a few fibres of red-brown mohair.
Dress smart and fine.

6. *Red Brown* (Red Fly of Ronalds; March Brown of Derbyshire)
Wings: (a) Landrail; or (b), Slightly broken feather of a brown hen; or (c) Brown Owl.
Body: Orange or yellow silk with a few fibres of mohair or Squirrel's fur at the breast for legs.
Season: Mid-February to end of April.

March

7. *Early Dun*
Wings: Old bronzed brown hen, or Brown Owl.
Legs: A few fibres of gingery Squirrel's fur or mohair.
Body: Copper-coloured silk tinged with Water-rat's blue fur.
Season: Early March, later afternoons and evenings of warm days.

8. *Blue Drake* (Blue Dun, Blue Upright, Olive Bloa of Jackson)
Wings: Starling.

Body: Orange silk tinged and dyed with Fox-cub down and two or three fibres of amber mohair.
Season: End of February and throughout the season.

9. *Orange Drake* (Red Spinner, *imago* of Blue Drake)
Wings: Orange or gold-tinged cock's hackle.
Legs: Orange or gold-tinged cock's hackle.
Body: Orange or yellow silk.
Walbran says that the body should be made *very* thin and slender with reddish-brown silk ribbed with fine gold wire.

10. *Golden-Legged Beetle*
Wings: Gilded feather of a Magpie's tail.
Body: A strand or two of same feather.
Legs: Fibres of honey or gold mohair.
Season: Throughout the season on fine days.
Probably analogous with Ronalds' Peacock Fly, Aldam's Little Chap, and the fancy Derbyshire Bumble.

11. *Tortoiseshell Beetle*
Wings: Rankly freckled feather of a Woodcock, Moorcock, or Snipe.
Body: Orange silk, or Magpie's gilded herl.
Legs: Amber mohair, or Squirrel's fur.
Season: All season.

12. *Heron Spinner*
Wings: Kingfisher (blue feather), or blue Titmouse.
Legs: Pale yellow mohair.
Body: Small pale-yellow silk.
Season: March and April.
Too small for practical use.

13. *Royal Charlie*
Wings: Partridge grey feather from side of the breast, tinged brown.
Body, Head & Shoulders: Orange silk, more or less waxed.
Legs: Freckled hackle of red or yellow dun hen.
   or:
Wings: Mottled tail feather of a Partridge.

Head, Shoulders & Body: Crimson silk.
Tag: Scarlet Macaw.
Legs: Black hackle.
Season: March, April and May.

14. *Cowdung* or *Lion Fly*
Wings: Landrail.
Legs: Yellow or ambry hen hackle.
Body: Orange silk with gold mohair and Squirrel's fur mixed.
Season: March and April, on windy days; and September to close.

15. *Brown Drake* (March Brown, Cob Fly of Wales, Great Brown of Jackson, Dun Drake of Yorkshire)
Wings: Under feather of a hen Pheasant's wing.
Body: Yellow silk.
Legs: A few fibres of light Hare's ear fur at the breast.
Season: Latter end of March and through Spring to Mayfly time.

16. *Amber Drake* (Great Red Spinner of Ronalds and Francis; Great Spinner of Jackson; Light Mackerel; *imago* of the Brown Drake)
Wings: Red or amber cock's hackle.
Body: Bright orange or yellow silk with eight or nine open turns of dark red-brown silk around it.
Legs: A few fibres of amber mohair worked in at the breast.
Season: A good evening fly during the season, especially after light showers.

17. *Light Brown* (Hacklewise)
Wings & Legs: Outside of Woodcock's wing.
Body: Orange silk.
Legs: A few fibres of mohair or Squirrel's fur.
Season: March, and on into summer.

18. *Black Fly* (or Midge)
Imitation similar to Housefly pattern, but much smaller in size. See pattern No. 20.

April

19. *Mottled Brown*
Wings & Legs: Partridge tail feather—red spotted with darker.
Body, Shoulders & Head: Orange silk.
Season: April and May.

20. *House Fly* (Hacklewise)
Wings & Legs: Blackbird's feather.
Body: Brimstone-coloured silk with a small portion of black hair or fur worked in.
Season: All season.

21. *Bluebottle* or *Flesh Fly* (Hacklewise)
Wings & Legs: Cock Pheasant's purple neck feather.
Body, Shoulders & Head: Light and dark blue shining silk, or Alpaca wool wound on the arming for the body, shoulders and head. Fasten at the head with orange or yellow silk.
Season: All season.

22. *Grannam* or *Greentail*
Wings: Hen Pheasant's wing, or Partridge wing.
Body: Coppery silk tinged with Water-rat's blue fur.
Legs: Mohair of a suitable colour.
Season: End of March and continues into May.
or, hacklewise:
Wings & Legs: (a) Landrail feather; or (b), a freckled light-brown hen hackle.
Remainder of dressing as above.

23. *The Spinner*
Wings: Partridge or hen Pheasant.
Body: Light-brown or fawn silk, or even woollen thread, tinged with a mixture of ash-blue and azure furs at the shoulders on a pale yellow bottom.
Legs: Black-brown cock's hackle.
Season: Very numerous in summer and autumn.

24. *Stone Fly*
Wings: (a) Wild Drake; or (b), Partridge; or (c) hen Pheasant.

Body: Yellow camlet with eight or nine open turns of dark-brown floss or camlet thread over it.
Head & Shoulders: Yellow camlet, darkened on the upper parts with brown bear's hair.
Legs: Hair, or a stiff hen hackle.
Season: Beginning of May, continuing three or four weeks.
Called "the May Fly" in parts of Yorkshire.

25. *Male Stone Fly*
Less in size and rather darker than the female. It shows more gold in the sun and is extraordinarily quick on its legs, but short in the wing.
Dress from the materials for the female pattern No. 24.

26. *Bee* or *Bank Fly*
Wings: Blackbird.
Body: Brown silk dubbed and tinged with yellow fleshy grizzle and hoary grey fine fur, or fur from a Fox-cub, Squirrel, etc.
Legs: (a) Red-brown mohair; or (b) hen hackle.

27. *Iron Blue Drake* (Little Iron Blue, or Iron Blue Dun; the Pigeon Blue Bloa of Jackson)
Wings & Legs: (Hacklewise) Water-rail or Waterhen's small leady breast feather.
Body: The two or three last joints, and the head and shoulders, dark-brown silk. Middle joints a light blue-grey.
Legs: A light blue-grey fur from a Fox-cub.
Season: Throughout season.

28. *Pearl Drake* (The Jenny Spinner of Aldam, Francis and Ronalds; the Little White Spinner of Jackson)
Wings & Legs: (Hacklewise) Glassy, silvery cock's hackle.
Body: Fine brown coffee-coloured silk, with white for the pearl parts.

29. *Spiral Brown Drake* or *Checkwing* (The Turkey Brown of Ronalds; the May Brown of Jackson)
Wings & Legs: (Hacklewise) Partridge back or shoulder—a freckled brown feather.

Body: Orange or yellow silk with a few fibres of Hare's ear fur worked in at the breast.
Season: Continues into October.

30. *Red Drake* (Great Spinner of Jackson; Great Red Spinner or Light Mackerel of Ronalds)
Wings & Legs: Red cock's hackle.
Body: Orange silk.

31. *Black Spinner* (or Gnat)
Wings & Legs: Starling's small feather.
Body: Black silk.

32. *Bloa Brown*
Wings & Legs: Snipe—the bloa feather from under wing.
Body: Yellow or orange silk, with a few fibres of amber-brown mohair at the breast.
Season: Early April.

33. *Little Dark Drake*
Wings & Legs: (Hacklewise) (a) Waterhen, or (b), Water-rail.
Body: Orange silk, waxed.
Season: Mid-April through summer.

34. *Little Red Drake*
Wings & Legs: (Hacklewise) Red cock's hackle.
Body: Pale orange or dim yellow silk.

35. *Hawthorn Fly*
Wings: A light neutral feather—Snipe or Starling.
Body, Head & Shoulders: Black silk with black Seal's fur or mohair twisted or wrought in.
Legs: Black hen's hackle.
Season: End of April, continuing for nearly a month.

36. *Red Brown Drake*
Wings: Partridge tail, mottled red feather.
Body: Orange silk.

Legs: Orange or amber mohair.
Season: End of April.

37. *Dark Amber Drake* (*Imago* of Red Brown Drake)
Wings & Legs: (Hacklewise) Deep orange hackle.
Body: Orange or yellow silk, more or less waxed.

38. *Sanded Dun*
Wings & Legs: (Hacklewise) (a) Landrail; or (b), Thrush, or (c) yellow-bronze brown hen; or (d), Brown Owl.
Body: Bright copper-coloured silk with or without a tinge of Water-rat's fur.
Season: April to October.

39. *Dark Drake* (Dark Watchet; Waterhen and Orange)
Wings & Legs: (Hacklewise) Waterhen or Water-rail's breast or from under the wing.
Body: Orange silk.
Season: End of April, continuing with variations to end of season.
A good general pattern of the Iron Blue Dun.

40. *Dark Red Drake*
Wings & Legs: (Hacklewise) Red cock's hackle.
Body: Orange silk.

41. *Plover Dun* (Hacklewise)
Wings & Legs: Freckled bloa feather from the Golden Plover.
Body: Copper-coloured silk tinged with Water-rat's blue fur.
Season: End of April and beginning of May.

42. *Freckled Dun* (Hacklewise)
Wings & Legs: Freckled feather from a Moorcock.
Body: Orange or copper-coloured silk.
  or, winged:
Wings: Moorcock.
Body: Orange or copper silk tinged with Water-rat's blue fur.
Legs: Moorcock's hackle.
Season: April to June; and again in September and October.

May

43. *Light Dun* (Alder)
Wings & Legs: (Hacklewise) (a) Landrail; or (b), Brown Owl; or (c), Dotterel; or (d), Brown hen, etc.
Body: Tawny or coppery silks of lighter or darker shades.
Season: April, May and June.

44. *Yellow Brown* (Yellow Sally of Jackson, Ronalds and Francis)
Wings & Legs: (Hacklewise) Small Canary or yellow Oriole.
Body: Yellow silk with a few fibres of yellow mohair or Hare's ear fur at the breast.
Season: May to the end of July; on fine days.

45. *Little Freckled Dun*
Wings: Rankly freckled feather from the Snipe or Judcock.
Body: Yellow silk tinged with blue fur.
Legs: Body-fur picked out.
Season: May and through summer.

46. *Least Dun*
Wings & Legs: (Hacklewise) Golden Plover hackle.
Body: Small copper-coloured silk.
Season: May to September.

47. *Light Drake* (Light Watchet)
Wings: Blue dun feather from a Tern or Sea Swallow.
Body: Yellow or straw-coloured silk.
Legs: A few fibres of amber fur from a Squirrel, at the breast.
Season: Early May, and through the season.

48. *Light Red Drake*
Wings & Legs: (Hacklewise) Fine small red cock's hackle.
Body: Amber silk.

49. *Fœtid Dun* (Fœtid Brown of Francis)
Wings: (a) Landrail; or (b), Light chestnut feather from a Cock Pheasant; or (c), Brown Owl.
Body: Copper-coloured silk tinged with Water-rat's blue fur.

Legs: A few fibres of light copper mohair, Squirrel, or Hare's ear fur.
Season: End of April through June.

50. *Dark Dun*
Wings: Dark feather from a Moorcock.
Body: Brown silk.
Legs: Dark brown hen hackle.
Season: Early May through June.

51. *Red Dun* (Possibly the Sedge Fly of Francis and the Bank Fly of Aldam)
Wings: (a) Landrail; or (b), Brown Owl; or (c), Red dun hen.
Body: Coppery or amber silk.
Legs: Red dun hen hackle.
Season: May, and again in autumn.

52. *Red Beetle*
Wings: Amber feather from a Cock Pheasant's breast.
Body: Orange or yellow silk, tinged with Mole or Water-rat's fur.
Legs: Orange and black fibres of mohair at breast, or a hen hackle.
Season: Early May, and through June.

53. *Mealy Brown Beetle*
Wings: Grey-brown Mallard.
Body: Orange silk tinged with Water-rat's fur.
Legs: Yellow-brown yellow-centred hen hackle.

54. *Brown Beetle*
Wings: Red-brown hen (of ambry transparency).
Body: Black floss.
Legs: Black hen's hackle, or mohair.
Season: Mid-May through June.

55. *Soldier Beetle* (Fern Fly of Ronalds and Francis)
Wings: Small amber feather with black top from a Pheasant's breast.

Body: Amber or yellow floss.
Legs: Orange mohair, or a hen's hackle.
Season: End of May into July.

56. *Oak Fly* or *Downlooker*
Wings: Woodcock or Partridge.
Body: Yellow or amber silk with open rounds of deep red-brown silk.
Shoulders: Tinged with Water-rat or Squirrel fur of an ashy colour.
May be dressed hacklewise with a Bittern hackle, or a yellow-brown freckled hen's hackle.
Season: Mid-May, through June.

57. & 58. *Spotted Spinner and Little Spotted Spinner*
Wings: Mallard or Teal, neutral ground rankly freckled.
Body: Dull yellow or fawn silk, tinged with fine blue fur.
Legs: Red hackle.
Season: Mid-May through June.

59. *Black Drake* (Darkest of the Drakes)
Wings & Legs: (Hacklewise) Coot or Waterhen, dark body feather.
Body: Red or crimson silk.
Season: Mid-May through June and July.

60. *Black-Red Drake*
Wings & Legs: (Hacklewise) Either (a), black-red cock's hackle; or (b), the purple feather from a cock Pheasant's neck.
Body: Orange silk.

61. *Grey Spinner*
Wings: Woodcock, or hen Pheasant wing.
Body: Fawn or amber-coloured silk, or Alpaca woollen thread tinged with blue dun fur.
Legs: A black-red hackle.
Season: Beginning of May into July.

62. *Green Drake* (Hacklewise)
Wings & Legs: Light coloured mottled feather from the wild Mallard, stained the ground colour of the wings of the natural fly.
Body: Pale yellow-green smooth woollen thread, warpt with eight or nine open rounds of darker shade.

63. *Grey Drake* (Hacklewise)
Wings: A black cock's hackle.
Body: Light cream-coloured smooth woollen thread, warpt with eight or nine open rounds of brown floss silk.
Legs: Fibres of red-brown hair.

64. *White Drake*
Too small for angling purposes.

65. *Black and Yellow Spinner*
Wings: Woodcock.
Body: Yellow silk marked and warped with black.
Legs: Dark red cock's hackle.

66. *Black Spinner*
Wings: Swift, Coot, or Waterhen.
Body: Dark brown silk.
Legs: Black-red cock's hackle.
Season: End of April through September.

67. *Blue Spinner* (or Gnat)
Wings & Legs: (Hacklewise) Either (a), Cock Pheasant's neck; or (b), Starling hackle; or (c), Rook.
Body: Light ashy-blue silk.

68. *Brown Dun*
Wings: Brown hen or Owl.
Body: Coppery silk tinged with Water-rat's blue fur.
Legs: Brown mohair, or a brown hen's hackle.
   or, hacklewise:
Wings & Legs: A brown hen's hackle.

69. *Sailor Beetle*
Wings: Amber feather tipped with black from a cock Pheasant's breast.
Body: Orange silk.
Legs: Fibres of orange mohair.
See Soldier Beetle, pattern No. 55.

June

70. *Horned Dun*
Wings: Snipe or Dotterel—bloa brown feather.
Body: Copper-coloured silk tinged with Water-rat's fur.
Legs: Light gingery hen's hackle, or mohair.

71. *Jumper Beetle* (Jumper of Jackson, Wrentail of Ronalds)
Wings: Amber part of cock Pheasant's breast.
Head: Black silk.
Body: Bright orange or yellow silk.
Legs: Light red-brown hen's hackle.

72. *Tufted Dun*
Wings: Landrail, or red or yellow dun hen.
Body: Copper-coloured silk tinged with Water-rat's fur.
Legs: Cream-coloured hen hackle, or light Hare's ear fur-fibres.

73. *Vermilion Drake*
Wings & Legs: (Hacklewise) Small white pinky cock's hackle.
Body: A small straw or lemon silk.

74. *Dark Pied Dun*
Wings: Blackbird with reddish underside.
Body: Coppery silk, tinged with Water-rat's fur.
Legs: A hen's hackle, or Hare's ear fur-fibres.
Season: June into August.

75. *Black Dun*
Wings: Waterhen, Coot or Crow.
Body: Dark leady brown silk.
Legs: A few fibres of dark brown mohair.

76. *White Dun* (or Bustard)
Wings: White or broken feathers of a yellow or Screech Owl.
Body: Light tawny woollen thread.
Legs: A tawny hen's hackle.
Season: Mid-June through July.

77. *Red Ant Fly*
Wings: Snipe or Starling.
Body: Peacock herl with small red or amber silk.
Legs: A few fibres of red-brown mohair.

78. *White-Legged Dun*
Wings: Dark broken feather of a Moorcock, or Snipe.
Body: Slaty, ashy silk.
Legs: Light gingery hackle with a black stripe down the middle.

79. *Dotterel Dun* (Hacklewise)
Wings & Legs: Dotterel.
Body: Copper-coloured silk slightly tinged with Water-rat's fur.
or, winged:
Wings: Dotterel.
Body: As above.
Legs: A few fibres of mohair of Hare's ear fur.

80. *Black Ant*
Wings: Silvery grizzle cock's hackle.
Body: Dark blood-red or black silk.
Legs: A few fibres of dark red mohair.

July

81. *Spotted-Whisk Drake*
A. *Subimago:*
Wings & Legs: (Hacklewise) Snipe, Tern or Sea Swallow bloa feather.
Body: Orange silk, well waxed.
Legs: A few fibres of light-red mohair, or Squirrel's fur.
B. *Imago:*
Wings & Legs: (Hacklewise) A small red cock's hackle.
Body: Orange silk, waxed at the shoulders.

82. *Fringed Dun* (Hacklewise)
Wings & Legs: Dotterel, or Sandpiper.
Body: Copper-coloured silk with a few fibres of Hare's ear fur or Squirrel's fur at the breast.

83. *Orange Brown*
Wings: Landrail.
Body: Bright orange silk.
Legs: A few fibres of mohair or Squirrel's fur.
Season: July till October.
  or, hacklewise.
Wings & Legs: Landrail.

84. *Light Pied Dun*
Wings: Landrail, or bronzy yellow-brown hen.
Head: White.
Body: Coppery silk, slightly tinged with purple.
Legs: Yellow-white hen's hackle, or Hare's ear fur.

85. *Grey Dun*
Wings: Light freckled Mallard.
Body: Copper silk tinged with Water-rat's fur.
Legs: Yellow dun hen's hackle.

86. *Coral-Eyed Drake*
Wings: Light blue bloa or blue dun feather from the Water-rail or a Sea Swallow.
Body: Pale amber silk, with a round of the red part of a small strand in the eye of a Peacock's feather.
Legs: A few fibres of Squirrel's fur, or mohair.
  and, in the spinner state:
Wings & Legs: (Hacklewise) A fine amber cock's hackle.

87. *Pale Blue Drake* (Little Pale Blue Dun of Ronalds)
Dun:
Wings & Legs: Light blue dun Tern's feather, hacklewise.
Body: Light ashy-blue silk.
  and, in the spinner state:
Wings & Legs: Light blue cock's hackle.

88. *Bronze Beetle*
Wings: Old bright bronzy yellow-brown hen—a slightly broken feather.
Body: Black silk.
Legs: A few fibres of mohair, honey shade.

89. *Little Brown Dun* (Brown Silverhorns of Francis; Light Silverhorns of Jackson)
Wings & Legs: (Hacklewise) Small slightly freckled Moorcock.
Body: Deep coppery silk, waxed.
Legs: A few fibres of red-brown fur at the breast.

90. *Late Black Spinner* or *Gnat* (Fisherman's Curse)
Wings & Legs: (Hacklewise) Starling, or cock Pheasant's neck feather.
Body: Black silk.

JOHN TURTON
The Angler's Manual
1836

1. *March Brown* (March and April)
Wings: Wing feather of Partridge, red mottled, top of tail or rump feather.
Legs: Wren's tail feather.
Body: Brown down from Fox's ear, twisted on orange silk.
Silk: Orange.
   and, in summer:
Wings & Legs: Feather from the outside of a Woodcock's wing, which is grey mottled and grey at the end.
Body: Dark brown tammy dubbing spun on Devonshire brown silk.
An excellent fly in dark waters.

2. *Barm Dun* (March and April)
Wings & Legs: A cock's hackle, tinged a barm colour.
Body: Dark red-brown dubbing from Fox's ear, close to the black part.
Silk: Red.
It gets darker towards the end of April, and is called the Black Red or Furness Fly, and kills all season: made with red silk; body, black silk at tail, and a lap or two of green Peacock feather close under the wing; a black-red cock hackle feather, red at the edges, and a black list up the middle; sometimes in black waters the body is quite black, and a dark furness feather, reddish at the underside only, and made with black silk and black dubbing.

3. *Brown Watchet* or *Orange Brown* (All season)
Wings & Legs: Wren's tail feather (applied as a hackle).
Body: Bright, light orange silk.
Head: Green Peacock's feather.
Silk: Light orange.
A little brown bear's down is used at the spring of the year, twisted round the silk. In dark waters, a little green Peacock's feather under wing.

4. *Hawthorn Fly* (March and April)
Wings: Lightest or bottom part of a Starling's quill feather.
Body: Black Ostrich herl.
Legs: Black hen, from neck. (Sometimes red legs in summer).
Silk: Black.
In May, use the Jay's wing quill feather for wing: this will be the Black Caterpillar Fly. In June, the sea-swallow's feather, for wing, makes it the Black Ant Fly.

5. *Whirling Dun* (Early April)
Wings & Legs: The middle dun of cock's hackle feather, tinged at the edges.
Body: Down of a Fox's cub, ash-coloured at roots, twisted thinly round the yellow silk, so that the ribs may be seen.
Silk: Yellow.
Some use a pale dun Mallard feather; it comes on towards the end of June, after rains.

6. *Dun Drake* or *The Old Man* (March and April)
Wings: The dark shaded feather under Woodcock's wing.
Body: Brown down from Fox's ear, ribbed with yellow silk.
Legs: Dark grizzled dun cock hackle feather.
 or:
Wings: Dark grey mottled Mallard feather.
Body: Bright ash-coloured silk.
Legs: Light ginger-coloured cock hackle.
A large fly, and kills the largest fish.

7. *Cock-up*, or *Upwinged Dun* (All season)
Wings: Starling's wing quill feather.
Body: Bright ash-coloured silk, having a shade of green in it, ribbed with a black horse-hair, and two black horns.
Legs: Lightest ginger cock hackle feather that can be got. It changes colour as the weather alters, sometimes having red and at other times yellow legs. This fly is the surest killer that is thrown on the water: too much cannot be said in its praise.

8. *Red Spider Fly* (March and April)
Wings & Legs: Red mottled Partridge rump feather.
Body: Hare's ear, dark coloured at bottom and grey at top.
Silk: Yellow.
In summer, for dark water, yellow dubbing is used. A very good fly, and often wanted.

9. *Brown Spider Fly* (End of April and May)
Wings: Large brown feather outside Woodcock's wing.
Body: Bright lead-coloured silk.
Legs: Black hen's feather from neck.
A good fly, and found on sand-beds by the river side; by some called the Sand Fly.

10. *Stone Fly* (End of April and early May)
Wings: Very dark grey Mallard's or Pheasant's wing quill feather.
Body: Bear's dun fur, with brown and yellow mohair mixed, most yellow underneath and toward tail; ribbed with yellow silk.

Legs: Brown moor game, out of neck.
Silk: Yellow.
Kills large fish late at night; also in strong streams, and on rough windy days. Comes on a second time in July.

11. *Orl Fly* (May and June)
Wings & Legs: A dark grizzled cock hackle feather.
Body: Copper-coloured Peacock's herl.
Silk: Red.
A good fly.

12. *Down Looker* (May till end of August)
Wings & Legs: Brown feather outside Woodcock's wing (hacklewise).
Body: Light, bright orange silk, ribbed with a thick black horse-hair; made small at tail; dark brown down from Fox's ear under wing.
Silk: Orange.
In discoloured waters, this is as good a killer as can be used, and takes the largest fish.

13. *Primrose Dun* (May and June)
Wings: Light Starling's quill feather.
Body: Bright, primrose silk.
Legs: Brimstone-coloured mohair (picked out with needle).
Silk: Primrose.
A good fly in clear water.

14. *Black Gnat* (June)
Wings & Legs: The small light Starling's under-wing feather.
Body: Black Ostrich and Pewit's cap feather.
Silk: Black.

15. *Yellow Spider Fly* (June)
Wings & Legs: Light brown mottled moor-game's feather.
Body: Light yellow silk, and yellow marten's fur from the throat.
Silk: Yellow.
Good in clear low water.

16. *Green Drake* (End of June and all July)
Wings: A mottled Mallard's feather from the top side of the thigh, dyed a yellow-green.
Body: Pea-green dubbing, ribbed with yellow silk.
Legs: Yellow-green mohair.
Whisks: 3 black horns.

17. *Red Ant* (June and July)
Wings: The light or bottom part of a Starling's quill feather.
Body: Peacock's herl, made thick at tail, and thin in the middle of the body.
Legs: Ginger-coloured cock hackle.
Silk: Light orange silk.
An excellent fly, and used in September on bright sunny days.

18. *Orange Dun* (July)
Wings & Legs: The light dun feather under young moor-game's wing.
Body: Light bright orange silk, and orange mohair dubbing under wing.
Silk: Light orange silk.
Good in black or disturbed waters.

19. *Tail to Tail*, or *Knotted Midge* (July and August)
Wings & Legs: Pewit's topping or cap feather, headed with Magpie's green feather from tail.
Body: Hare's scut, a mazarine blue.
Silk: Purple.

20. *Bank Fly* (July to September)
Wings: A Corncrake's quill feather.
Body: Bright, light orange silk.
Legs: Wren's tail.
Silk: Orange.
Seldom takes before three or four o'clock in the afternoon; a good killer late at night, and in dark waters.

21. *Brown Shiner* (August)
Wings & Legs: Light brown mottled moor-game's feather from bottom of neck.

Body: Light orange silk at tail, and green Peacock's feather close under wing, headed with green peacock.
Silk: Light orange.
At particular times, especially after rains, it is made with mulberry-coloured silk, and dark brown tammy twisted upon the silk; wing, a Grouse's feather, nearly black. This is a great killer after rains and in black waters; by some anglers called Old Joan.

22. *Proud Tailor Fly* (August)
Wings: The darkest brown feather of a Landrail.
Body: Bright pale orange silk untwisted.
Legs: Brown cock hackle feather.
Silk: Orange.
A large fly, and kills in low clear waters.

23. *Purple Midge* (September and October)
Wings & Legs: The blue feather, shaded with green at edge, out of an old cock Pheasant's neck.
Body: Black down, twisted on purple silk.
Silk: Purple.

24. *Little Pale Blue Dun* (September and October)
Wings: Sea-Swallow's outside wing feather.
Body: Light blue Rabbit, and a little yellow fur mixed.
Silk: Ash-coloured.

25. *Red Palmer* (All season in strong waters)
Wings & Legs: Red cock hackle.
Body: Thick, of black Ostrich's feather.
Silk: Red.

26. *Great Red Palmer*
Wings & Legs: Red cock hackle feather.
Body: Black Ostrich's feather, ribbed with gold twist.
Silk: Red.

27. *Whirling Blue* (March and April)
Wings: Feather from under Water-hen's wing, hacklewise.
Body: Mole's fur spun thinly on yellow silk.

28. *Black with Red* (All season)
Wings & Legs: Black hen's feather from neck.
Body: Black silk at tail, and black down close under the wing. Tying-silk red.

29. *Green Tail* (April)
Wings & Legs: Light brown mottled Woodcock's feather from bottom of neck.
Body: Hare's ear, the brown part ribbed with brimstone-coloured silk; head green Peacock's herl; and tip of tail, dark green silk.
Silk: Orange.
A very good fly, but only lasts about a week.

30. *Snipe Dun* (April and May)
Wings & Legs: A full Snipe's underside wing feather.
Body: Blue Rabbit's down, twisted on yellow silk.
Silk: Yellow.

31. *Red Shiner Fly* (April)
Wings & Legs: Red Woodcock's feather from butt end of wing.
Body: Light bright orange silk, ribbed with green Peacock's herl; and Peacock herl at head.
Silk: Orange.
A good killer after rains. It changes these colours: if there be bright days, the red Owl's feather from butt end of wing is used for wings; if a dark day, the brown Owl's feather must be used from outside of wing; if low clear water, the Partridge's rump feather is best.

32. *Cowdung Fly* (May)
Wings & Legs: Feather from underside of Jay's wing.
Body: Pea-green mohair spun on tying silk.
Silk: Pea-green.

33. *Black May Fly* or *Silver Palmer* (May)
Wings & Legs: A black hen's hackle feather.
Body: Black Ostrich's feather, ribbed with silver twist.
Silk: Black.

34. *Oak Fly* (May)
Wings & Legs: Partridge's rump feather, without moon.
Body: Yellow silk, ribbed with a strong black horse hair, light brown down under wing.

35. *Iron Blue Fly* (May)
Wings & Legs: Outside or butt end of Merlin hawk's wing.
Body: Dark Water-rat dubbing, ribbed with yellow silk.
Silk: Yellow.
An excellent fly, and frequently comes on after showers of rain.

36. *Small Black Midge* (May)
Wings: Fieldfare's quill feather.
Body: Black Ostrich's feather.
Legs: Blue Starling.
Silk: Black.

37. *May Imp* (May)
Wings: The yellow feather out of a green Linnet's tail.
Body: Waxed yellow silk.
Legs: Yellow Plover's feather.
Silk: Yellow.
A good fly in brooks after rains; seldom taken in clear water. The Little Yellow Drake is made the same way, only with a bright yellow body.

38. *Yellow Legs* (May and June)
Wings: A Jay's wing quill feather.
Body: Bright brimstone silk.
Legs: Yellow Plover's feather.
Silk: Yellow.
Both trout and greyling take this fly well in coloured waters.

39. *Grey Drake* (June)
Wings: A blue shaded green feather from a white Grouse.
Body: Blue and yellow dubbing mixed, ribbed with black, and three horns.
Legs: A middle dun grizzled cock's hackle feather.
Silk: Yellow.

40. *Purple Gold Palmer* (June)
Wings & Legs: A red cock's hackle feather.
Body: Purple mohair, ribbed with gold twist.
Silk: Purple.
Takes large fish in rough streams and dark waters.

41. *Red Spinner* (June)
Wings: Starling's quill feather.
Body: Red-brown Squirrel's down, ribbed with gold twist.
Legs: Red cock's hackle feather.

42. *Small Red Spinner* (June)
Wings: Starling's quill feather.
Body: Yellow Marten's fur from the throat twisted on the silk.
Legs: Red feather from a cock's neck.
Silk: Yellow.

43. *Netted Fly* (June)
Wings & Legs: Light mottled Partridge's feather from out of the horse-shoe mark on the breast.
Body: Yellow silk, and the yellow Marten's fur close under wing.
Silk: Yellow.

44. *Gold-Coloured Dun* (June)
Wings & Legs: Yellow or golden Plover, from outside of wing.
Body: Gold-coloured mohair, twisted on the silk close under wing.
Silk: Gold-coloured.
Best early in a morning or late at night.

45. *Brown Gnat* (June)
Wings & Legs: Feather under Starling's wing.
Body: Lightest brown and violet down mixed, twisted on the silk.
Silk: Very light brown.
A good fly in clear water; made long and very thin. By some anglers it is called the Fern Fly.

46. *Small Ant Fly* (June)
Wings: Martin's wing quill feather.
Body: Bright reddish orange silk, headed with green Peacock's feather.
Legs: Wren's tail feather.
Silk: Orange.
Best on bright days, and in low clear water.

47. *Grasshopper* (June)
Wings & Legs: A red cock's hackle feather.
Body: Green and yellow dubbing mixed, ribbed with green silk.
Silk: Pea-green.

48. *Sky-coloured Blue* (June and July)
Wings: Starling's wing quill feather.
Body: Blue and yellow dubbing mixed.
Legs: Yellow mohair (picked out).
Silk: Sky-blue.
Most taken in clear water.

49. *Buff-coloured Dun* or *Stream Fly* (June and July)
Wings & Legs: A buff-coloured dun hen's feather.
Body: Buff-coloured mohair, and yellow dubbing mixed close under wing.
Silk: Buff-coloured.

50. *Blue Gnat* (June and July)
Wings & Legs: A pale blue cock's hackle feather, tinged at edge.
Body: Blue, Fox's cub and yellow down mixed, twisted on the silk.
Silk: Yellow.
A very good trout fly.

51. *Small White Moth* (June and evenings to end of season)
Wings: A white Duck's feather.
Body: White part of Hare's scut, ribbed with yellow silk.
Legs: White hen's hackle feather.
Silk: Yellow.

52. *Shade Fly* (July and on bright days to end of season)
Wings: Water-hen's underwing feather.
Body: Light brown and pea-green dubbing mixed, with about three laps of green Peacock's feather close under wing.
Head: Green Peacock.
Legs: Blue Starling's feather.
Silk: Orange.
An excellent fly, and kills either in clear or discoloured waters; good for all sorts of fish that take flies.

53. *July Blue Dun* (July)
Wings & Legs: Bluecap's tail, or a dark blue Pigeon's feather.
Body: Mole's and Marten's fur mixed, twisted on the silk.
Silk: Ash-coloured.

54. *Violet Midge* (July)
Wings & Legs: Jackdaw's neck.
Body: Pale pink silk, and Water-rat's down close under wing.
Silk: Violet.

55. *Stone Midge* (July)
Wings & Legs: Pewit's topping feather.
Body: Fibres of blue Heron's wing; a silver colour, headed with green Peacock's feather.
Silk: Sky-blue.

56. *Orange Black* (July)
Wings & Legs: Black hen's hackle feather.
Body: Bright orange silk.
Silk: Orange.

57. *Wasp Fly* (July)
Wings & Legs: Starling's underwing feather.
Body: Brown Bear's hair, ribbed with yellow silk.
Silk: Light brown.

58. *Black Palmer* (July to September)
Wings & Legs: Black hen's hackle feather.
Body: Copper-coloured Peacock's feather; after rains, ribbed with silver twist.
Silk: Dark orange.

59. *White Dun Midge* (July)
Wings & Legs: Blue dun Heron's feather.
Body: White mohair, very small.
Silk: White.
Taken early in the morning, and in the evening.

60. *Red Clock Fly* (July and August)
Wings: Red Partridge's tail feather.
Body: Large Peacock's and black Ostrich's feathers mixed.
Legs: Blue Starling.
Silk: Dark orange.
On some days, a red freckled Partridge's tail feather must be used for wings.

61. *Black Wood Fly* (August and September)
Wings: Blackbird's wing quill feather.
Body: Purple mohair, ribbed with black Ostrich's feather; head, green Peacock.
Legs: Black hen's hackle feather.
Silk: Red.

62. *Yellow Spider Fly* (August)
Wings & Legs: The large mottled feather of a Sandpiper or Snipe.
Body: Yellow Marten's fur, twisted on the silk.
Silk: Yellow.

63. *Mill Dun* (August)
Wings: Lightest Starling, bottom of quill feather.
Body: One rib pink and one purple silk; a little light brown down close under legging.
Legs: Light ginger cock's hackle feather.
Silk: Light orange.

64. *Small Black-clock Fly* (August)
Wings: A Yellow Throstle's wing quill feather.
Body: Peacock's and Ostrich's feathers mixed.
Legs: Blue Starling's feather.
Silk: Black.

65. *Stone Gnat,* or *Dark Watchet* (August and September)
Wings: Martin's wing quill feather.
Body: Dark Water-rat's down.
Legs: Dark, tinged at edge, dun hen's feather from top of neck.
Silk: Plum-coloured.
It is the best fly that can be used for trout and greyling in dark waters.

66. *Little Whirling Blue* (August and September)
Wings: Starling's quill feather.
Body: Blue and yellow dubbing mixed, twisted on the silk.
Legs: Red feather from a cock's hackle.
Silk: Yellow.

67. *Grey Dun Midge* (September)
Wings & Legs: Light Woodcock's feather under wing.
Body: Yellow silk; head green Peacock.
Silk: Yellow.
On some days, the outside wing feather of the Dotterel is used for wing.

68. *Willow Fly* (September and October)
Wings & Legs: A blue grizzled cock's hackle feather.
Body: Blue Squirrel's fur and yellow down mixed, twisted on the silk.
Silk: Yellow.
Best on cold stormy days.

69. *Winter Brown* (October and November)
Wings & Legs: Woodcock's under wing feather.
Body: Bright orange silk, headed with Magpie's tail green feather.
Silk: Orange.

CONTEMPORARY TROUT-FLY PATTERNS

The following list of contemporary trout-flies, while deliberately restricted in the matter of selection, provides a sound and reasonable choice. All patterns listed are favourite, well tried flies, and all, in season, highly effective and reliable. Hook-sizes given in the old enumeration throughout.

EPHEMEROPTERA

OLIVES *(Baetis)*

DRY-FLY PATTERNS
Olive Dun (Standard Dressing)
Wings: Feather from the primary of a Starling's wing.
Body: Seal's fur dyed to a medium olive shade.
Hackle: Cock's hackle dyed olive.
Whisks: Three fibres, same as hackle.
Hook: No. 14.

Greenwell's Glory (Hackle pattern)
Hackle: Furnace cock.
Body: Yellow silk waxed with cobbler's wax, ribbed with fine gold wire.
Whisks: Three fibres furnace cock.
Hook: No. 14 or 15.

Greenwell's Glory (Variant—Skues)
Wings: Pale to dark Starling.
Hackle: Greenish yellow-olive cock.
Body: Yellow or primrose silk, waxed with clear wax. Gold wire rib.
Whisks: Three fibres, same as hackle.
Hook: No. 15 or 16.

Large Dark Olive (Skues)
Wings & Legs: Sharp darkish blue cock, hacklewise.

Body: A mixture of green, yellow, orange, olive and crimson Seal's fur and fur from a Hare's poll, spun on yellow tying-silk, and ribbed with fine gold wire.
Whisks: Three fibres same as hackle from a cock's spade feather.
Hook: No. 14.

The Rough Olive (Skues)
Wings: Dark Starling.
Hackle: Gingery-olive cock.
Body: Heron herl, dyed brown olive, ribbed with fine gold wire.
Whisks: Three fibres from shoulder or saddle of a cock, same as hackle.
Hook: No. 14.

Olive Quill
Wings: Medium to dark Starling.
Hackle: Darkish olive cock.
Body: Peacock quill dyed to an olive shade.
Whisks: Three fibres same as hackle.

Blue Quill (Hackle pattern) (Skues)
Hackle: Pale honey dun.
Body: Peacock quill, undyed.
Whisks: Three fibres, same as hackle.
Hook: Nos. 14 to 16.

Gold-Ribbed Hare's Ear (Medium Olive)
Wings: Medium Starling. Pale Starling is also used.
Body: Fur from the root of a Hare's ear, fur from the Hare's face also being used on occasion, ribbed with flat gold tinsel.
Legs: Fibres of Hare fur spun on the tying-silk hacklewise.

SPINNERS

The Red Spinner
Wings: Starling.
Hackle: Deep red cock.
Body: Red-brown silk, ribbed with fine gold wire.
Whisks: Three fibres same as hackle.
Hook: Nos. 12 to 14.

Pheasant Tail
See under General Patterns.

Lunn's Particular
Wings: Two medium blue cock hackle-points dressed flat.
Hackle: Medium Rhode Island cock.
Body: Undyed hackle stalk of Rhode Island cock hackle.
Tail: Three or four fibres Rhode Island cock hackle.
Hook: No. 14.

Hackle Red Spinner (Skues)
Wings & Legs: Medium, slightly rusty, blue dun cock hackle.
Body: Crimson Seal's fur, spun on hot orange tying-silk, and ribbed with fine gold wire. Whisks of honey dun cock hackle.
Hook: Nos. 14 to 16.

WET PATTERNS

Greenwell's Glory (Tweedside pattern)
Wings: Hen Blackbird, tied in a bunch and split.
Hackle: Coch-y-bonddhu.
Body: Yellow tying-silk, waxed with cobbler's wax, and ribbed with fine gold wire.
Hook: Nos. 12 to 14.

Rough Olive
Wings: Dark Starling.
Hackle: Drab brown-olive hen, dark centre and yellowish points.
Body: Heron herl dyed a brownish-olive shade, and ribbed with gold wire.
Hook: No. 14.

Waterhen Bloa
See Pritt's list.

Olive Upright (West Country)
Wings & Legs: Cock's hackle dyed olive.
Body: Peacock quill dyed yellowish-olive.
Whisks: Same as hackle.
Hook: No. 14.

Blue Dun
For the traditional dressings, see the lists of the earlier authorities.

Blue Upright
See R. S. Austin's dressing.

PALE WATERY DUNS *(Centroptilum luteolum, C. pennulatum, Baetis binoculatus B. scambus.)*

DRY-FLY PATTERNS

Little Marryat
Wings: Palest Starling.
Hackle: Pale buff Cochin cock.
Body: Fur from the flank of Australian Opossum.
Whisks: Three fibres same as hackle.
Hook: No. 16 or 17.

Ginger Quill
Wings: Palest Starling.
Hackle: Pale brown ginger cock.
Body: Pale Peacock quill.
Whisks: Three fibres same as hackle.
Hook: No. 15, 16 or 17.

Blue Quill (Hackle pattern)
Wings & Legs: Sharp, bright pale blue cock.
Body: Undyed peacock quill.
Whisks: Three fibres, same as hackle.
Hook: No. 15 or 16.

No. 1. *Whitchurch*
Wings: Primary feather from wing of a young Starling.
Hackle: Honey dun or ginger cock.
Body: Yellow floss silk.
Whisks: Three fibres, same as hackle.
Hook: No. 15 or 16.

Lock's Fancy
Wings: Medium to pale Starling.

Hackle: Pale honey dun cock.
Body: Pale primrose silk, ribbed with fine gold wire.
Whisks: Three fibres, same as hackle.
Hook: No. 14, 15 or 16.

July Dun (Skues)
Wings: Starling primary, from a darkish bird.
Hackle: Light greenish olive cock.
Body: Two or three strands of thin Heron herl from the outer wing coverts dyed greenish-yellow olive, ribbed with fine gold wire. (Tying-silk: yellow).
Whisks: Three fibres light greenish cock hackle.
Hook: No. 15.

SPINNER PATTERNS

Pheasant Tail
See pattern under General Patterns.

Rusty Spinner
See under General Patterns.

Lunn's Particular
See pattern given under Olives.

Tup's Indispensable
See under General Patterns.

WET-FLY PATTERNS

Poult Bloa
See Pritt's list for the Yorkshire pattern.

Snipe Bloa (Light Snipe & Yellow)
See Pritt's list.

Dotterel Dun (Hackle pattern)
Wings & Legs: Light-tipped fawn-coloured feather from marginal coverts of the Dotterel's wing.
Body: Primrose or straw-coloured silk.
Hook: Nos. 14 to 16.

BLUE-WINGED OLIVE (*Ephemerella ignita, E. notata*)

DRY PATTERNS

The Orange Quill (Skues)
Wings: Medium Starling, double dressed, full and split.
Hackle: Bright red cock; no worse for being lightly dyed orange.
Body: Condor quill stripped and dyed a rich bright orange. Tying-silk: hot orange.
Whisks: Three fibres, same as hackle.
Hook: No. 14.

Spinner (Skues)
Wings & Legs: Rusty blue dun cock, sharp and bright.
Body: Deep rich chestnut-coloured Pig's wool—fine, ribbed with fine gold wire. Tying-silk: hot orange.
Whisks: Three strands of honey dun cock spade feather.
Hook: No. 14.
See also Pheasant Tail and Rusty Spinners.

THE IRON BLUE DUN (*Baetis pumilus; B. niger*)

DRY PATTERNS

Iron Blue Dun (Skues)
Wings: Starling dyed an inky blue.
Hackle: Rusty blue dun cock (darkish).
Body: Peacock's quill from the eye, dyed inky blue, or darkest Heron herl from a big secondary, ribbed with fine gold wire.
Tying-silk: Crimson or claret.
Whisks: Three white or palest blue cock.
Hook: No. 16.

SPINNER

Claret Spinner
Wings & Legs: Honey dun cock.
Body: Deep crimson Seal's fur spun on crimson tying-silk and ribbed with fine gold wire.
Whisks: Three same as hackle.
Hook: No. 14 or 15.

CONTEMPORARY TROUT-FLY PATTERNS

WET PATTERNS

Snipe and Purple—See Pritt's list.

Dark Watchet—See Pritt's list of North-Country Trout Flies.

THE AUGUST DUN *(Ecdyurus longicauda)*

DRY PATTERN

Spinner (Skues)
Wings: The speckled part near the root of the red feather from a Partridge's tail.
Body: Flat tawsy gut-ends, dyed red-orange, and tied in at shoulder and whipped over the bare hook to the tail and back to the shoulder. Tying-silk: Orange.
Hackle: Red cock.
Whisks: Honey dun cock.
Hook: No. 13 or 14.

WET PATTERN

August Dun (Walbran)
Wings: Cock Pheasant wing feather.
Legs: Brown hackle.
Body: Light brown floss silk, ribbed with yellow silk.
Whisks: Two Rabbit's whiskers.
Hook: No. 13 or 14.

THE MAY FLY *(Ephemera danica; E. vulgata; E. lineata)*

Mayfly patterns are given by nearly all authorities, and reference to the various lists, notably that of F. M. Halford, will afford a wide choice. The following additional patterns may be mentioned as being effective on occasion.

The Brown or *Green Champion* (Hammond)
Wings: Mallard breast, dyed brown or green olive. (Halford uses Rouen Drake for this purpose).
Body: Yellow chenille, ribbed with gold tinsel.

Hackle: Red down the body, and at the shoulder; with a front hackle from the Partridge breast.
Whisks: Rabbit's whiskers.
Hook: No. 12 or 13.

The Fore and Aft (Horace Brown)
Shoulder Hackle: Red cock.
Tail Hackle: Light badger cock.
Body: Raffia—natural colour.
Hook: No. 12.

Straddle-Bug (Skues)
Hackle: Ginger cock, wound over the body.
Body: Natural raffia, ribbed with fine gold wire.
Whisks: Three fibres brown Mallard.
Hook: No. 11.

THE MARCH BROWN *(Rhithrogena haarupi; Ecdyurus venosus)*

Innumerable patterns are mentioned in earlier lists, which should be consulted. The following additional patterns are worth noting:

Hackle March Brown (Raffit)
Hackle: Snipe rump feather, finished behind shoulder.
Body: Rabbit's poll fur, lightly dyed in red ant colour and spun on hot orange tying-silk, which is exposed at the tail.
Hook: No. 13.

Hackle March Brown (North Country)
Hackle: Dark Partridge.
Body: Dark Hare's ear fur mixed with a touch of claret mohair or wool, ribbed with yellow silk.
Hook: Nos. 12 to 14.

GENERAL SPINNER PATTERNS *(Ephemeroptera)*

Badger and Yellow
Hackle: Badger cock.

Body: Primrose or yellow silk.
Whisks: Three fibres honey dun cock.
Hook: No. 15 or 16.

Cinnamon Quill
Hackle: Ginger cock.
Body: Cinnamon quill (from the root of a Peacock quill).
Whisks: Three fibres, same as hackle.
Hook: No. 15 or 16.

Ginger Quill
Hackle: Light brownish ginger cock.
Body: Pale Peacock quill.
Wings: Palest Starling.
Hook: No. 15 or 16.

Pheasant Tail (Payne Collier)
Hackle: Honey dun cock.
Body: Dark herl of cock Pheasant tail, ribbed with gold twist.
Tail: Three fibres honey dun cock spade feather.
Hook: No. 14.

Pheasant Tail (Skues)
Hackle: Rusty, or honey, or sharp blue cock.
Body: Three or four strands of the ruddy fibres from the middle feather of a cock Pheasant's tail, ribbed with three or four turns of fine gold wire. Tying-silk: hot orange.

Red Quill
Wings: Medium Starling primary.
Hackle: Small sharp bright red cock.
Body: Stripped Peacock quill from the eye feather, either undyed or dyed claret or orange.
Whisks: Three fibres honey dun cock, or bright red cock.
Hook: Nos. 14 to 16.

Rusty Spinner (Skues)
Hackle: Rusty dun cock.
Body: Chestnut-coloured Pig's wool or Seal's fur, ribbed with fine gold wire. Tying-silk: hot orange waxed with clear wax.

Whisks: Three fibres honey dun cock spade feather.
Hook: No. 14 or 15.

Red Spinner (Skues)
Hackle: Bright blue dun cock.
Body: Crimson Seal's fur spun rather loosely on hot orange tying-silk, ribbed with fine gold wire.
Whisks: Three fibres from spade feather of a blue dun cock.
Hook: Nos. 14 to 16.

Tup's Indispensable (R. S. Austin)
Hackle: Gold-freckled blue cock.
Body: A mixture of wool from the scrotum of a Ram (washed), cream-coloured Seal's fur, lemon Spaniel's fur, and a few pinches of yellow mohair.
Whisks: Fibres from light blue or honey dun cock spade feather.
Hook: No. 16.
(G. E. M. Skues suggested substitution of crimson Seal's fur in place of mohair. The dressing may be varied to suggest a dun, or a nymph, as well as a spinner.)

TRICHOPTERA

CADDIS FLIES

Grannom
See Ronalds' list for a good early pattern.

Small Dark Sedge
Medium Sedge   } See Halford's list
Cinnamon Sedge

Half Stone (West Country)
Hackle: Darkish blue cock.
Body: Tail-half of yellow or primrose floss silk; upper half of Mole or Water-rat fur spun on yellow tying-silk.
Whisks: Three fibres blue cock hackle.
Hook: Nos. 12 to 14.
Many quite effective Sedge Fly patterns are given in the earlier lists of wet-fly patterns.

SIALIDAE

ALDER

Alder (Canon Chas. Kingsley's famous wet pattern)
Wings: From the secondary feathers of a dark freckled game hen, dressed almost flat over the body.
Hackle: Black hen, dressed in front of wings.
Body: Peacock herl, dyed magenta. Tying-silk: crimson.
Hook: Nos. 12 to 14.
See also earlier wet-fly lists.

PERLIDAE

Yellow Sally (Stone Fly)
Hackle: Very pale ginger cock, or white cock dyed greenish-yellow.
Body: Greenish-yellow wool or mohair, spun on primrose tying-silk.
Hook: No. 14.

Willow Fly
See Pritt's list for dressings of Brown Owl, Light and dark Needle flies, and the Winter Brown.

ANTS

The Red Ant (Skues)
Legs: Two turns of deep red cock's hackle.
Body: Chestnut-coloured Pig's wool, fine, tied on in two blobs, the larger at the tail, and trimmed to shape wth the scissors. Tying-silk: red ant colour.
Hook: No. 14 round bend.

The Black Ant
See earlier lists.

COLEOPTERA
BEETLES

Little Chap
Hackle: Hen with dark blue centre and ginger-red points.
Body: Peacock herl body dyed magenta.
Hook: No. 16.

Welshman's Button
Hackle: From the neck of a cock Pheasant.
Body: Peacock herl dressed on red silk.
Wing-cases: Landrail feather.
Hook: No. 14.

Coch-y-bonddhu
Body: Greenish-bronze Peacock herl dressed fat.
Hackle: Bright Coch-y-bonddhu cock.
Hook: No. 13 or 14.
See also earlier lists.

SUNDRY GENERAL FLIES

Pope's Nondescript
Wings: Medium Starling primary.
Hackle: Bright red cock.
Body: Bright green floss silk, ribbed with flat gold tinsel. Tying-silk: Claret, exposed at head and tail.
Whisks: Bright red cock's shoulder or saddle hackle.
Hook: No. 16.

Baigent's Brown (Variant)
Wings: Young Starling.
Hackle: Medium honey dun cock, long in the fibre.
Body: Yellow floss silk.
Hook: No. 3 Limerick.

Partridge and Orange
Partridge and Yellow
March Brown
} These, with other hackle patterns, are worthy of inclusion in any modern list, and are highly effective. For dressings, see the lists of Pritt and others.

Black Spider
Hackle: Black cock for a dry fly, black hen or Starling neck for a wet pattern.
Body: Either black silk or black Ostrich herl or black Seal's fur, ribbed with silver wire.
Hook: Nos. 14 to 16.
By varying the size, this pattern may be used to suggest any dark insect, from the Hawthorn Fly down to a Smut. It is sometimes tipped with orange at the tail.

Greenwell Variants
By using lighter wings, paler hackles, and unwaxed tying-silks for the body, a range of patterns can be produced to represent the summer Olives. These variants are frequently very effective.

Little Red Sedge (Skues)
Wings: Landrail wing, bunched and rolled, and tied in sloping well back over the tail.
Front Hackle: Deep red cock, five or six turns in front of wing.
Body Hackle: Long deep red cock, with short fibres, tied in at shoulder, and carried down to tail.
Body: Darkest Hare's ear, ribbed with fine gold wire. Tying-silk: hot orange.
Hook: No. 14.

For other flies necessary on occasions, such as the Cow Dung, Water Cricket, Oak Fly, Sand Fly, Gravel Bed, etc., a wide choice of patterns is provided by the earlier lists.

EPILOGUE

Having followed the long evolutionary path of the trout fly, from the *Treatyse* down to as close an approach to the present as is wise or permissible, it is interesting to observe the manner in which opinion concerning trout flies has swung between extremes. At one extreme, there is the deliberate restriction of patterns to the bare minimum; at the other, an extravagant number of every conceivable kind of trout fly. The swing of the pendulum of opinion represents reaction from either extreme and operates quite regularly. Today, there is a trend away from a surfeit of patterns, wet and dry, and even on the chalk rivers of the South, the use of a single nymph or dry fly—surely the ultimate in extremism—is being practised if not advocated as the modern approach. Yet, if history is to be believed, the current trend is but part of a cycle which has occurred all through the centuries; and, if history is to repeat itself, there will surely follow the inevitable reaction. Whether the pendulum is slowing down and will ultimately come to rest at a point mid-way between the extremes is an open question, but it is at some such point that greatest interest and pleasure in fly-making and fly-fishing is probable.

Whatever the trend of the times, the trout can be relied upon to upset and confound both the theories and the practice of the fly-dressing fisherman, as, indeed, he has always done; and this is good for the sport, and very good for the soul. Moreover, it is to be ever borne in mind by contemporary fly-dressers and fishermen that, apart from technical advances and refinements, there is very little that is really new in the arts of fly-making and fly-fishing that was not known to our forebears. Realisation that this is so detracts not a whit from pleasurable interest; rather does the resultant humility clear the vision and prepare the way for fresh endeavour. We look back in order to advance!

APPENDIX ONE
FEATHERS FOR FLY-DRESSING

(Note: Many of the birds listed are now protected by legislation.)

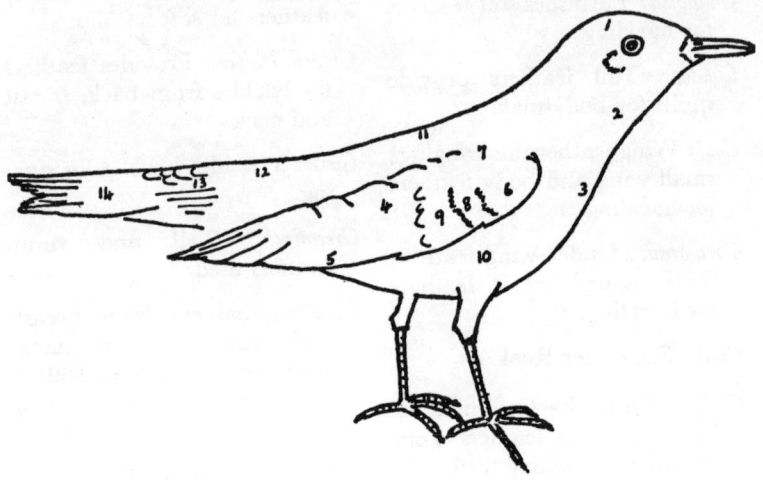

1. Crest.
2. Throat.
3. Breast.
4. Secondary Wing feathers.
5. Primary Wing feathers.
6. Lesser Wing Coverts.
7. Scapulars.
8. Median Wing Coverts.
9. Greater Wing Coverts.
10. Flank.
11. Back.
12. Rump.
13. Upper Tail Coverts.
14. Tail.

Blackbird: Primary and secondary wing feathers of the hen for winging; small wing and body feathers for hackling.

Bittern: Small feathers used for winging.

Bullfinch: Primaries and secondaries for winging.

Bunting: Primary and secondary wing feathers for winging.

Blackcock: Sickle feather from the tail provides herls for body-making. Breast of the hen (Grey Hen) furnishes hackles.

Bustard: Smaller feathers used for winging purposes.

Capercailzie: Feather from the wing of the hen for winging.

Canary: Feathers from the wing and tail used for winging.

Chaffinch: Furnishes soft feathers for hackling.

Condor: Tail feathers provide quills for body-making.

Coot: Wing feathers for winging; small wing and body feathers for hackling.

Cormorant: Under-wing feathers for winging; breast feathers for hackling.

Crow: See under Rook.

Curlew: Throat hackle is used for hackling. Also feathers from shoulder of a young bird.

Dipper: Primary and secondary wing feathers for winging; the breast for hackling.

Domestic Fowl: Cock hackles of high quality in the undernoted varieties and colours: Badger; black; blue; cinnamon; coch-y-bonddhu; cuckoo or creel; cream; furnace; ginger; honey dun; red; and white (for dyeing). Hen hackles in the same colours, and those of cockerels.
Spade feathers and saddle feathers from cocks for whisks.

Dotterel: Feathers from back and shoulders for hackling. Wing feathers for winging. Breast feathers for hackles also.

Dunlin: Wing and hackle feathers, but rarely used.

Fieldfare: Primary and secondary feathers for winging. Rump feathers also. Body feathers for soft hackles.

Golden Plover: Provides feathers for hackles from back, breast and neck.

Goose: Provides hackles for dyeing.

Greenfinch: Tail and rump feathers used.

Grouse: Feathers from breast, back and neck for hackling; also under-wing feather from poults. Secondary wing feathers used for winging.

Guinea Fowl: Breast feathers for dyeing; white feathers provide durable fibres for whisks.

Heron: Smaller wing feathers for winging; hackles from shoulders; fibres from large wing feathers for herls.

Ibis: Red breast feather for tags.

Indian Crow: Orange breast feather for tags.

Jackdaw: Neck and shoulders provide feathers for hackling; wing feathers used for winging.

Jay: Primary and secondary wing feathers for winging; feathers from under wing and from shoulder for hackling.

Landrail: Primaries and secondaries for winging; feathers from under wing and from shoulder for hackling.

Magpie: Tail feather used for herls.

Mallard: Small wing feathers for winging; brown speckled wing feather used for winging and whisks; blue white-tipped feather from wing used for winging loch flies; breast feathers used for winging mayflies.

Merlin: Wing feathers for winging; body feathers for hackling.

Nightjar: Feathers from back for hackling; wing feathers for winging.

Norwegian Crow: Feathers from neck and breast for hackling.

Ostrich: Tail or plumes provide herls for body-making.

Owl: Primary and secondary wing feathers for winging; also small coverts.

Partridge: Wing feathers and tail used for winging; brown feathers from back and grey breast feathers for hackling.

Peacock: Furnishes herls (bronze and green). Tail and sickle feathers provide quills for body-making. Peahen wing is used for winging.

Pewit: Crest feather, neck and breast feathers used for hackling.

Pheasant: Cock: neck feathers for hackling; breast feathers for tippets and occasional hackle; primary, secondary wing feathers and tail for winging; centre tail feather provides herls. Hen: Breast feathers for hackles; wing and tail feathers for winging.

Pigeon: Provides various feathers for hackling.

Redwing: Primary and secondary wing feathers for winging. For hackling, feathers from under the wing and from the shoulder.

Rook: Wing feathers for winging; various feathers from young birds for hackling.

Seagull: Feathers from wings for winging; smaller feathers for hackling.

Sea Swallow: Feathers from wings and body used for winging and hackling.

Sheldrake: Various feathers for winging.

Snipe: Primary wing feathers for winging. Feathers from under wing and shoulder for hackling.

Starling: Primary and secondary wing feathers for winging; tail also used for winging. Under wing and shoulder feathers for hackling.

Teal: Smaller wing feathers used for winging; also feathers from the side of the body.

Thrush: Wing feathers for winging; under wing and shoulder feathers for hackling.

Tit, Blue: Tail used for winging. *Great:* Tail used for winging and hackling.

Turkey: Tail feathers for winging and for herls for body-making.

Waterhen: Breast and under wing feathers for hackles; also outside wing feathers.

Water-Rail: Primary and secondary wing feathers for winging; breast feather also used. Shoulder feathers for hackling.

Widgeon: Wing feathers for winging; feather from side also used for this purpose.

Woodcock: Primary and secondary wing feathers for winging; small feathers from outside and under wing used for hackling. Feathers from back breast and neck also used.

Wren: Tail and secondary wing feathers used for hackling.

APPENDIX TWO
BIBLIOGRAPHY
OF BOOKS MENTIONED OR QUOTED

ALDAM, W. H. A quaint treatise on *Flees and the Art a Artyfichall Flee Making*. London, 1876. 4o.

AUSTIN, R. S. Manuscript book of *Dry-fly Fishing on Exe and other North Devon Streams*. n.d. (c. 1890).

BAINBRIDGE, G. C. *The fly-fisher's guide*. Liverpool, 1816. 8o.

BARKER, Thomas. *The Art of angling*. London, 1651. 12o.
Barker's delight, or the art of angling. London, 1657. 12o.

BEEVER, John ('Arundo'). *Practical fly-fishing*. London, 1849. 12o.

BERNERS, Dame Julyans. *A treatyse of fysshynge wyth an angle*. Westminster 1496. Fol.

BLACKER, William. *The art of fly-making*. London, 1843. 12o.

BOWLKER, Richard and Charles. *The art of angling*. Worcester. n.d. (? 1747). 12o.

CARROLL, W. *The angler's vade mecum*. Edinburgh, 1818. 8o.

CARTWRIGHT, Rev. Wm. *Rambles and recollections of a fly-fisher*. 1854.

CHETHAM, James. *The angler's vade mecum*. London, 1681. 12o.

COTTON, Charles. *The Compleat Angler, Part 2*. London, 1676. 12o.

CUTCLIFFE, H. C. *Trout fishing on rapid streams*. South Molton, 1863.

D(ENNYS) J(ohn). *The secrets of angling*. London, 1613. 8o.

DICK, St. John. *Flies and fly-fishing*. 1873.

DUNNE, J. W. *Sunshine and the dry fly*. London, 1924.

EDMONDS, Harfield H., and LEE, Norman N. *Brook and river trouting*. Bradford, n.d. (? 1916). 8o.

FRANCIS, Francis. *A book on angling*. London, 1867. 8o.

FRANCK, Richard. *Northern Memoirs*. London, 1694. 8o.

HALFORD, Frederic M. *Floating flies and how to dress them*. London, 1886.
Dry-fly fishing in theory and practice. London, 1889.
Dry-fly entomology. London, 1897.
Modern development of the dry fly. London, 1910.

HARDING, E. W. *The fly-fisher and the trout's point of view.* London, 1931.
HILLS, J. W. *A history of fly-fishing for trout.* London, 1921.
HOFLAND, T. C. *The British angler's manual.* 1839.
JACKSON, John. *The practical fly-fisher.* London and Leeds, 1854. 8o.
LAUSON, Wm. *The secrets of angling, by I. D. Esquire. Augmented with many proved experiments, by W. Lawson.* London, n.d. (? 1620). 8o.
MACKINTOSH, Alexander. *The Driffield angler.* 1806.
MARKHAM, Gervase. *A discourse of the generall art of fishing with the angle. Included in the second booke of the English husbandman.* London, 1614. 4o.
M(ASCALL) L(eonard). *A booke of fishing with hooke and line.* London, 1590. 4o.
MOTTRAM, J. C. *Fly-fishing: some new arts and mysteries.* London, n.d. (? 1916).
MOSELY, M. E. *The dry-fly fisherman's entomology.* London, 1921.
OGDEN, James. *On fly-tying.* Cheltenham, 1879. 8o.
PRITT, T. E. *Yorkshire trout flies.* Leeds, 1885. 8o.
North-country flies. London, 1886. 8o.
PULMAN, G. P. R. *Vade mecum of fly-fishing for trout.* London and Axminster, 1841. 12o.
RONALDS, Alfred. *The fly-fisher's entomology.* London, 1836. 8o.
SALTER, Robert. *The modern angler.* 1811.
SCOTCHER, George *The fly-fisher's legacy.* Chepstow, n.d. (? 1800). 8o.
SHIPLEY & FITZGIBBON. *On fly-fishing.* 1838.
SKUES, G. E. M. *Minor tactics of the chalk stream.* London, 1910.
The way of a trout with a fly. London, 1921.
Sidelines, sidelights and reflections. London, 1932.
Nymph fishing for chalk-stream trout. London, 1939.
Silk, fur and feather. London, 1950.
STEWART, W. C. *The practical angler.* Edinburgh, 1857. 8o.
STODDART, Thomas Tod. *The art of angling as practised in Scotland.* Edinburgh, 1835. 12o.
TAVERNER, John. *Certaine experiments concerning fish and fruite.* London, 1600. 4o.
TAYLOR, Samuel, *Angling in all its branches.* 1809.
THEAKSTON, Michael. *British angling flies.* 1853, Ripon.
TURTON, John. *The angler's manual.* 1836.

BIBLIOGRAPHY

VAVON, Antoine. *La truite et ses moeurs et l'art de sa pêcher.* 1927.
VENABLES, Robert. *The experienced angler.* London, 1662. 8o.
WADE, Henry. *Halcyon.* London, 1861. 8o.
WALTON, Izaak. *The Compleat Angler.* London, 1653. 8o.
WEBSTER, David. *The angler and the loop-rod.* Edinburgh & London, 1885. 8o.
WEST, Leonard. *The natural fly and its imitation.* 1912. 8o.
WHEATLEY, Hewett. *The rod and line.* London, 1849. 8o.
YOUNGER, John. *On river angling for salmon and trout.* Edinburgh, 1840. 6o.

INDEX

ARTIFICIAL FLIES

Adjutant Blue, 138
Alder Fly, 17, 76, 77, 148, 185, 203, 209, 227, 262, 274, 280, 284, 303, 309, 369
Alevin Fly, 164
Amber Drake, 334
Ant Fly, 29, 30, 197, 238, 298, 330
Artful Dodger, 150
Ash Dun, 233
Ash Fly, 323
Ash Fox, 327
Ash Palmer, 245
Ashy Dun, 229
August Brown, 290
August Dun, 84, 211, 220, 230, 365
Aunt Sally, 263
Autumn Brown, 188
Autumn Dun, 139
Autumnal Dun, 311

Badger and Yellow, 366, 367
Badger Fly, 45, 184, 264, 298
Badger Quill, 141
Baigent's Brown, 370
Bank Flee, 126
Bank Fly, 350
Barm Dun, 347
Barm-fly, 29, 228, 288
Bee, 200, 336
Big Dun, 124, 179
Big Sedge, 274
Black and Yellow, 265
Black and Yellow Spinner, 342
Black Ant, 45, 125, 148, 180, 196, 200, 228, 246, 279, 290, 310, 323, 330, 344
Black-Blue Dun, 30
Black Caterpillar, 49, 177, 257, 268, 329
Black Clocker, 271, 325
Black Drake, 79, 180, 341

Black Dun, 343
Black Fly, 27, 28, 45, 334
Black Gnat, 26, 29, 38, 45, 48, 73, 120, 123, 149, 158, 177, 185, 191, 209, 216, 224, 273, 279, 303, 314, 322, 349
Black Hackle, 30, 223, 245, 326
Black Harl Fly, 251
Black Headed Red, 177
Black Jack, 242
Black Lady Fly, 315
Black Louper, The, 15
Black May Fly, 352
Black Midge, 195, 286
Black Palmer, 21, 45, 57, 88, 198, 210, 220, 245, 280, 293, 305, 311, 356
Black Rabbit, 247
Black-red Drake, 341
Black Silver Hackle, 297
Black Silver Horns, 230, 289
Black Snipe, 120
Black Spider, 371
Black Spinner, 337, 342
Black Trooper, 264
Black Wing Hackle, 233, 294
Black with Red, 352
Black Wood Fly, 357
Bloa and Orange, 240
Bloa and Yellow, 240
Bloa Brown, 337
Blue Bloa, 241
Blue Blow Fly, 195, 200, 329
Blue Bottle, 85, 86, 218, 282, 292, 305, 335
Blue Drake, 332, 333
Blue Dun, 25, 38, 45, 46, 61, 139, 157, 192, 213, 222, 276, 301, 307, 312
Blue Gnat, 45, 54, 196, 221, 316, 355
Blue Midge, 201, 229, 284

Blue Palmer, 311
Blue Partridge, 117
Blue Quill, 138, 360, 362
Blue Spinner, 342
Blue Upright, 181
Blue-winged Olive, 142, 275
Blue-winged Olive Spinner, 364
Brachan Clock, 262
Bracken Clock, 179, 279
Breckan Clock, 247
Bright Bear, 36
Bright Brown, 25, 26
Bright Dun Gnat, 24
Bronze Beetle, 346
Brown Badger, 143
Brown Bear, 201
Brown Beetle, 340
Brown Caddis, 251
Brown Clock, 285
Brown Drake, 334
Brown Dun, 195, 252, 342
Brown Fly, 45, 46, 256, 324, 328
Brown Gnat, 29, 45, 354
Brown Lady Fly, 315
Brown Midge, 190
Brown Night Fly, 56, 316
Brown or Green Champion, 365, 366
Brown Owl, 110, 219
Brown Palmer, 57, 88
Brown Quill, 274
Brown Rail, 326
Brown Shiner, 261, 278, 350, 351
Brown Silver Horns, 230
Brown Spider Fly, 348
Brown Spinner, 215, 224
Brown Watchet, 115, 347
Buff-coloured Dun, 355
Buoyant Olive Dun, 162
Buss Brown, 39, 268

Caddis Fly, 45, 53, 218
Camel-brown Fly, 31
Camlet Fly, 29, 45, 312
Canon Fly, 45, 49, 73
Caperer, 228
Captain, 270
Carshalton Cock Tail, 277

Chantrey, 259, 276
Checkwing, 336
Cinnamon Fly, 84, 85, 119, 195, 212, 221, 230, 253, 291, 325
Cinnamon Quill, 142, 367
Claret Bumble, 145
Claret Spinner, 141, 219
Clock, 243
Coachman, 151, 231, 260, 277, 311
Coch-y-Bonddhu, 147, 217, 227, 263, 281, 303, 370
Cocktail, 270
Cock-up Dun, 348
Cock Wing, 301
Cockwing Blue, 206
Colour Olive Dun, 163
Common Fly, 270
Conway, 282
Coral-Eyed Drake, 345
Corkscrew, 146
Cow Dung Fly, 28, 45, 47, 63, 64, 148, 176, 193, 199, 213, 249, 277, 285, 302, 308, 313, 320, 334, 352
Cow Lady, 27
Crane Fly, 17
Cream Camel, 329, 330
Cream Coloured Fly, 193
Cream Coloured Moth, 271, 325
Creeper, 243
Crooked Back Dick, 248
Crossing Brown, 125
Cubdown Bloa, 118
Curlew, 118

Dark Amber Drake, 338
Dark Bloa, 111, 234, 239, 291
Dark Blue Dun, 123, 183
Dark Blue Quill Gnat, 182
Dark Brown, 25, 26, 45, 294
Dark Brown Tag Tail, 267
Dark Claret, 256, 259, 319, 327
Dark Drake Fly, 45, 338
Dark Dun, 259, 318, 319, 321, 340
Dark Fox, 256, 327
Dark Gold Twist, 182
Dark Grey Midge, 293
Dark Grouse, 235
Dark Loch Awe, 263

INDEX 385

Dark Mackerel, 79, 80, 258, 323
Dark Midge, 190, 239
Dark Olive Bloa, 292
Dark Olive Dun, 183
Dark Olive Quill, 136
Dark Olive Silver Horns, 188
Dark Pied Dun, 343
Dark Red Drake, 338
Dark Sedge, 150
Dark Silver Horns, 190
Dark Snipe, 111, 239
Dark Soldier, 244
Dark Spanish Needle, 113
Death Drake, 266
Dee Fancy, 262
Detatched Badger, 143
Detached Iron Blue, 138
Detached Olive, 135
Detached Red Spinner, 140
Dirty Dun, 187
Donne cutte, The, 15
Donne flye, The, 15
Dotterel, 115, 238
Dotterel and Claret, 249
Dotterel and Copper, 249
Dotterel and Olive, 249
Dotterel and Orange, 249
Dotterel and Pale Green, 249
Dotterel and Purple, 249
Dotterel and Scarlet, 249
Dotterel and Sky Blue, 249
Dotterel and Slate, 249
Dotterel and Yellow, 249
Dotterel Dun, 121, 344, 363
Down Fly, 314
Downhill Fly, 74, 209
Downlooker, 179, 287, 349
Dragon Fly, 44
Drake flye, The, 16
Drake's Extractor, 137
Dubbed Wren Tail, 268
Dun Cut, 27, 296
Dun Drake, 348
Dun Fly, 45
Dun Fox, 256, 327
Dun Grasshopper, 298
Dung Fly, 17
Dusky Green Parrot, 252

Early Bright Brown, 295
Early Brown, 331
Early Dun, 332
Early Red, 306
Early Spinner, 332
Eden Fly, 128
Edmead, 232
Edmondson's Welsh Fly, 261, 278
Emerald Fly, 201
Esterhazy Dun, 318
Evening Bloa, 270
Evening Moth, 200

Faren Fly, 201
February Red, 206
Fern Fly, 31, 53, 76, 77, 209, 217, 227, 248, 254, 300, 322
Fern-Owl, 244
Fieldfare, 252
Fieldfare Bloa, 110
Fire Fly, 202
Firey Clock, 243
Fisherman's Curse, 149
Flat Yellow, 179
Flesh-Fly, 29
Flight's Fancy, 137, 273
Foetid Brown, 228
Foetid Dun, 339, 340
Fog Black, 118
Fore and Aft, 366
Francis Fly, 231
Freckled Dun, 338
Fringed Dun, 345
Frog Hopper, 82, 83
Fry Fly, 164
Furnace, 145, 304, 319

Ginger Hackle, 281
Ginger Quill, 141, 272, 362, 367
Gold-coloured Dun, 354
Golden Dun, 139, 325
Golden Dun Midge, 67, 303
Golden Hackle, 233
Golden Midge, 190
Golden Ostrich Fly, 318
Golden Palmer, 56, 198
Golden Plover Hackle, 204

INDEX

Golden Plover, 242
Golden Sooty Dun, 264, 297, 329
Golden Wren, 255
Gold Eyed Gauze Wing, 81, 82
Gold Hackle, 294
Gold-Legged Beetle, 333
Gold-Ribbed Hare's Ear, 139, 360
Gold-Twist Hackle, 29
Goose Dun, 137
Governor, 151, 231, 262
Grasshopper, 21, 29, 30, 355
Grannom, 17, 45, 47, 68, 69, 147, 175, 185, 193, 208, 214, 225, 250, 282, 307, 320, 335
Grannom Larva, 147
Gravel Bed, 208, 224, 278
Gravel Fly, 45, 68, 69, 193, 250, 314
Gravel Spinner, 332
Great Alder Fly, 288
Great Blue Dun, 25
Great Brown, 284
Great Dark Drone, 63, 64
Great Dark Dun, 192, 247
Great Dun, 25
Great Red Palmer, 351
Great Red Spinner, 17, 65, 66, 196, 207, 223, 261, 278
Great Spinner, 286
Great Whirling Dun, 295
Green Bank Fly, 257, 329
Green-bodied Moth, 238
Green Body, 236
Green Caterpillar, 257, 329
Green Drake, 28, 29, 45, 77, 78, 123, 151, 152, 153, 179, 195, 210, 296, 322, 341, 350
Green Flesh Fly, 45
Green Gnat, 315
Green Gasshopper, 298
Green Insect, 146, 221
Green Midge, 190, 229
Greensleeves, 117
Green Tail, 36, 115, 122, 286, 352
Greentail Fly, 328
Greenwell's Glory, 157, 231, 359, 361
Greenwell Variants, 371
Green Woodcock, 178

Grey-Drake, 28, 45, 51, 78, 79, 195, 210, 296, 309, 322, 328, 342, 353
Grey Dun, 345
Grey Dun Midge, 358
Grey Gnat, 38, 188, 285
Grey Grannom, 291
Grey Housewife, 199
Grey-Legged Bloa, 264
Grey Midge, 116, 287
Grey Palmer, 198
Grey Partridge, 119
Grey Quill, 272
Grey Quill Gnat, 188
Grey Spinner, 216, 341
Grizzled Palmer, 245
Grizzle Hackle, 297
Grizzly Blue, 144
Grouse Brown, 254
Grouse Hackle, 178, 197, 203, 232, 281, 296, 324, 326

Hackle Blue Quill, 144
Hackle Hare's Ear Fly, 144
Hackle Iron Blue, 144
Hackle March Brown, 366
Hackle Olive Quill, 144
Hackle Red Ant, 147
Hackle Red Spinner, 143, 361
Half Stone, 147, 182, 368
Hammond's Adopted, 150, 229
Hare's Ear and Yellow, 330
Hare's Ear Blue Dun, 301
Hare's Ear Dun, 278
Hare's Ear Fly, 139, 158, 199, 255, 261, 272, 326, 327
Hare's Ear Quill, 136
Hare's Flax, 308
Hare's Flax Upright, 183
Hare's Lug, 237
Hardy Brown, 215
Harlequin, 151
Harry Long Legs, 31, 45, 193, 250, 300
Hauthorn Flie, 21
Hawthorn Fly, 45, 72, 194, 200, 216, 224, 251, 289, 314, 337, 347
Hazle Fly, 192, 247
Hearth-fly, 39

INDEX

Heron Dun, 266
Heron's Blue Body, 183
Heron Spinner, 333
High Tees Cocktail, 260
Hofland's Fancy, 231, 260, 276
Honey Dun Half Stone, 182
Horse-flesh Fly, 27
Horned Dun, 343
House Fly, 191, 228, 283, 293, 305, 335
Huzzard, 266

India-Rubber Olive, 135
Indian Yellow, 128, 142, 274
Intermediate, 275
Iron Blue Drake, 336
Iron Blue Dun, 71, 122, 138, 158, 178, 184, 202, 209, 214, 224, 272, 278, 302, 308, 314, 321, 364
Iron-Blue Fly, 45, 353
Iron Blue Spinner, 364

Jenny Spinner, 71, 72, 129, 143, 186, 224, 275
July Dun, 81, 119, 211, 229, 363
July Blue Dun, 356
Jumper Beetle, 343
Jumpers, 290
June Dun, 289

Kingdom, 261, 278
King's Fisher Fly, 44
Knop-fly, 37, 266
Knotted Grey Gnat, 265
Knotted Midge, 116, 237, 350

Large Ant, 119
Large Black Caterpillar, 126
Large Brown Grouse, 252
Large Dark Blue, 206
Large Dark Olive, 359, 360
Large Fly, 269
Large Red Ant, 54, 246
Large Red Spinner, 218
Large Whirling Dun, 268
Large Wickham, 151
Large Willow Fly, 292
Late Black Spinner, 346

Late Blue Gnat, 254
Later Bright Brown, 295
Least Dun, 339
Lesser Hackle, 24
Lesser March Brown, 175
Lesser Red Brown, 24
Light Bloa, 239, 291
Light Blue Dun, 317, 320
Light Brown, 27, 188, 334
Light Drake, 339
Light Dun, 124, 241, 339
Light Fox, 256, 327
Light Gold Twist, 182
Light Grouse, 235
Light Grouse Hackle, 204
Light Hare's Ear, 202
Light Mackerel Fly, 323
Light Olive Dun, 183
Light Orange Dun, 178
Light Pied Dun, 345
Light Red, 255
Light Red Drake, 339
Light Silver Horns, 289
Light Spanish Needle, 113
Light Spring Bloa, 235
Light Summer Dun, 189
Light Watchet, 113
Lilac Bloa, 248
Lion Fly, 225
Little Black, 109
Little Blue Bloa, 245, 248, 290
Little Blue Dun, 39, 226
Little Blue Fox, 298
Little Blue Midge, 252
Little Bright Brown, 295
Little Brown, 283
Little Brown Dun, 74, 75, 346
Little Brown Fly, 27
Little Castle Fly, 198
Little Chap, 122, 145, 177, 370
Little Coppered Blue, 253
Little Dark Bloa, 289
Little Dark Drake, 337
Little Dark Spinner, 74, 75
Little Dark Watchet, 112, 113
Little Dun, 27, 37, 299
Little Early Brown, 331
Little Freckled Dun, 339

Little Gosling, 200
Little Green Peacock, 265
Little Iron Blue, 49, 193, 250
Litgle Marryat, 142, 273, 362
Little Olive Bloa, 290, 293
Little Orange Fly, 304
Little Pale Blue Dun, 45, 86, 87, 351
Little Pale Blue Fly, 55, 258, 259, 324
Little Red Drake, 337
Little Red Sedge, 371
Little Sky Blue, 127, 275
Little Soldier Fly, 199
Little Spotted Spinner, 341
Little Stone Bloa, 288
Little Violet Fly, 269
Little Whirling Blue, 55, 259, 324, 358
Little White Dun, 30
Little White Spinner, 287
Little Winter Brown, 110
Little Yellow May Dun, 73
Little Yellow May Fly, 28, 194, 251, 322
Lochaber, 257, 329
Loch Awe, 263
Lock's Fancy, 362, 363
Lunn's Particular, 361

Mackerel Governor, 231
Mackerill, 38
March Brown, 17, 65, 111, 112, 129, 175, 184, 191, 207, 214, 223, 233, 276, 301, 307, 313, 320, 346
Marlow Buzz, 79, 80, 210, 312
Maure flye, The, 15
May Brown, 287
May Fly, 17, 20, 22, 50, 288, 309
May Imp, 353
Mealy Brown, 192, 300, 331
Mealy Brown Beetle, 340
Mealy Cream Moth, 299, 331
Mealy White Moth, 299, 330
Medium Olive Quill, 136
Medium Summer Dun, 189
Merlin, 176
Mid Blue, 221
Middle Hopper, 305

Midge Larva, 164
Mill Dun, 357
Moorish Brown, 36
Moorish Fly, 45
Moorpout and Orange, 242
Moorpout and Yellow, 242
Mottled Brown, 335
Mulberry Dun, 220
Mushroom Fly, 228
Mussel Shell, 244

Nankeen Spinner, 291
Needle Brown, 144, 225, 331
Needle Fly, 204
Netted Fly, 354

Oak Fly, 17, 20, 45, 196, 215, 226, 269, 304, 315, 324, 341, 353
Ogden's Fancy, 302
Oil Fly, 288
Old Joan, 300
Old Man, 348
Old Master, 116
Olive Badger, 143
Olive Bloa, 114, 283
Olive Dun, 17, 222, 271, 359
Olive Upright, 361
Orange Beck Fly, 265
Orange Black, 356
Orange Brown, 122, 345
Orange Bumble, 145
Orange Drake, 187, 333
Orange Dun, 124, 177, 178, 277, 320, 323, 350
Orange Fly, 30, 84, 85, 180, 192, 212, 249, 299, 314
Orange Grouse, 111
Orange Palmer, 217
Orange Partridge, 115
Orange Quill, 364
Orange Sedge, 150
Orange Stinger, 291
Orange Tag, 146
Orange Tawny, 266
Orl Fly, 45, 52, 216, 315, 349
Owl Fly, 29, 45, 257, 298

Pale Blue, 212, 330

INDEX

Pale Blue Bloa, 288, 289
Pale Blue Drake, 345
Pale Dun, 187
Pale Evening Dun, 80, 81, 186, 196, 227, 254
Pale Green, 234
Pale Olive Dun, 136
Pale Olive Quill, 136
Pale Summer Dun, 189
Pale Watery Dun, 273
Pale Yellow Dun, 277
Palmer Flie, 19
Palmer Fly, 22, 24, 27, 56, 57, 205, 225, 233, 294, 305, 318, 321
Palmer for Spring, 293
Palm-fly, 36
Partridge Hackle, 203, 204, 211, 232, 311
Partridge Tail, 235
Peacock-fly, 27, 29, 64, 65, 195, 223, 253, 258, 313, 318
Pearl Drake, 336
Pewit, 267
Pheasant, 234
Pheasant Brown, 236
Pheasant Tail, 367
Pigeon-blue Bloa, 285
Pink Wickham, 141
Pismire-fly, 39, 201
Plover and Yellow, 242
Plover Dun, 338
Pope's Nondescript, 370
Prime Dun, 35, 45, 232
Primrose Dun, 349
Proud Tailor Fly, 351
Pukshall Dun, 183
Poult Bloa, 116
Purple-fly, 38
Purple Gold Palmer, 354
Purple Hackle, 264, 298
Purple Midge, 351

Quill Gnat, 226

Red Ant, 45, 82, 83, 125, 148, 180, 197, 211, 219, 228, 279, 290, 310, 323, 330, 344, 350, 369

Red Beetle, 340
Red Brown, 23, 24, 317, 332
Red Brown Drake, 337
Red Clock, 112, 283, 357
Red Drake, 337
Red Dun, 241, 319, 340
Red Fly, 45, 60, 61, 181, 316, 318
Red Hackle, 244, 327
Red-Legged Blue Bloa, 248
Red Midge, 190
Red Owl, 117
Red Palmer, 21, 57, 88, 112, 198, 207, 244, 293, 311, 351
Red Quill, 140, 272, 367
Red Sedge, 274
Red Shiner Fly, 352
Red Spider Fly, 348
Red Spinner, 45, 53, 62, 140, 186, 217, 222, 246, 258, 273, 302, 310, 330, 354, 360, 368
Red Tag, 146, 187, 275
Red-Tailed Spinner, 284
Rough Olive, 135, 157, 158, 360, 361
Rough Spring Olive, 272
Royal Charlie, 333, 334
Ruddy Fly, 45, 176
Rusty Dun, 187
Rusty Spinner, 367, 368

Sailor Beetle, 343
Sally Fly, 45
Saltoun, 140
Sanctuary, 146
Sanded Dun, 338
Sand Fly, 67, 115, 196, 207, 216, 225, 236, 254, 279, 286, 307, 313, 321
Sand Gnat, 125, 178
Sandy-fly, 38
Sandy Moorgame, 117
Sandy-Yellow Fly, 45
Sea Swallow, 119, 246
Sedge Fly, 225
September Dun, 220
Shade Fly, 356
Shamrock Fly, 180
Shell Fly, 16, 30, 45, 265, 299

INDEX

Shining Black Silver Horns, 292
Shorn Fly, 45, 50
Silhouette Olive Dun, 163
Silk Fly, 178
Silver Dun, 220
Silver Horns, 82, 83
Silver Palmer, 352
Silver Sedge, 150, 274
Silver Twist, 182
Silver Twist Hackle, 322
Sky Blue, 76, 211, 218
Sky Blue Bloa, 239
Sky-coloured Blue, 45, 52, 355
Small Ant, 118, 355
Small Black-clock Fly, 357
Small Black Midge, 253, 353
Small Blue Bloa, 117
Small Bright Brown, 26, 295
Small Caterpillar, 126
Small Common Ant, 126
Small Olive Bloa, 293
Small Red Spinner, 207, 354
Small White Moth, 219, 355
Small Willow Fly, 292, 306
Smoke Fly, 119
Smoky Dun Hackle, 255, 326
Smut, 164
Snail, 254
Snipe Bloa, 114, 235
Snipe Dun, 352
Soldier, 289
Soldier Beetle, 340, 341
Soldier Palmer Fly, 198, 232, 262, 280
Sooty Dun Hackle, 296
Spanish Needle, 235, 236
Spent Gnat, 153, 154
Spider Fly, 48, 214, 236, 309, 321, 328
Spider-Legs, 286
Spinner, 335
Spiral Brown Drake, 336
Spotted-whisk Drake, 344
Spotted Spinner, 341
Spring Black, 175
Spring Bloa, 234
Spring Dun, 176
Squirrel Fly, 316

Starling Bloa, 118
Stone Bloa, 117
Stone Dun, 238
Stone Fly, 15, 17, 28, 29, 45, 47, 68, 179, 192, 199, 208, 226, 234, 269, 280, 297, 309, 313, 321, 335, 336, 348, 349
Stone Gnat, 358
Stone Midge, 116, 237, 287, 304, 356
Straddle-bug, 366
Stream Fly, 127, 355
Summer Dun, 128, 194, 251, 324

Tail to Tail, 350
Tailey Tail, 123
Tandy flye, The, 16
Thorn Fly, 37, 267
Thorn-tree Fly, 25
Tinkler's Dun, 304
Tortoishell Beetle, 333
Transparent Jenny Spinner, 163
Tufted Dun, 343
Tup's Indispensable, 186, 368
Twine Fly, 45
Twitch Bell, 290

Vermilion Drake, 343
Violet-fly, 26
Violet Midge, 356

Walton, 312
Wasp Fly, 16, 30, 264, 299, 356
Watchet, 237
Water Cricket, 62, 63, 109, 282
Water-Hen Bloa, 111
Water Spaniel, 285
Water Spider, 245
Watery Dun, 158
Welshman's Button, 45, 54, 148, 227, 310, 370
Whirling Blue Dun, 45, 86, 212, 304, 351
Whirling Brown, 202
Whirling Dun, 25, 201, 221, 230, 294, 308, 347
Whitchurch No. 1, 137, 362
White Drake, 342
White Dun, 344

INDEX

White Dun Midge, 357
White Gnat, 27
White Hackle, 31
White Legged Dun, 344
White Midge, 190
White Moth, 210, 219, 229, 270, 325
White Mout, 127
White Night Fly, 56, 317
White Spinner, 310
Whitest Dun, 295
Whitish Dun, 25
Whitterish, 267
Wickham's Fancy, 141, 231, 273
Willow Cricket, 268
Willow Flee, 127
Willow Fly, 45, 56, 86, 87, 180, 212, 221, 230, 314, 324, 358
Winter Brown, 110, 258, 319, 358
Woodcock, 270, 297
Woodcock and Orange, 240
Woodcock and Yellow, 241
Wren Tail, 197, 202, 211, 215, 229, 279, 304, 326
Wren's Hackle, 323

Yeasty Dun, 250
Yellow Brown, 339
Yellow Bumble, 145
Yellow Cadow, 328
Yellow Dun, 26, 36, 37, 70, 186, 193, 203, 208, 215, 217, 223, 238, 249, 302, 308, 320
Yellow Fly, 288
Yellow Flye, 15
Yellow Hackle, 297
Yellow-Legged Bloa, 114, 285
Yellow Legs, 237, 353
Yellow May Dun, 17, 38
Yellow Midge, 286
Yellow Palmer, 315
Yellow Partridge, 114
Yellow Quill, 185
Yellow Sally, 49, 74, 75, 115, 197, 217, 227, 254, 263, 281, 287, 369
Yellow Spider Fly, 349, 357
Yellow Summer Dun, 189
Yellow Watchet, 237

PERSONAE

Aldam, W. H., 60, 120 *et seq.*
Austin, R. S., 181 *et seq.*
Baigent, Dr. W., 160
Bainbridge, Geo. C., 59, 67, 191 *et seq.*
Barker, Thomas, 18, 19 *et seq.*
Berners, Dame Juliana, 132
Beever, John, 59, 175 *et seq.*
Blacker, Wm., 197 *et seq.*
Bowkler, Richard and Charles, 44 *et seq.*
Brown, Horace, 161
Carroll, W., 59
Cartwright, Rev. W., 206 *et seq.*
Chetham, Jas., 35 *et seq.*
Cotton, Charles, 23 *et seq.*, 39, 58
Cutcliffe, H. C., 60, 89 *et seq.*, 108
Davy, Sir H., 80
Dennys, John, 19
Dick, St. John, 213 *et seq.*

Dunne, J. W., 166, 167, 168
Edmonds, H. H., 165
Foster, David, 121
Francis, Francis, 222
Franck, Richard, 23
Halford, F. M., 133 *et seq.*, 160, 161, 165, 166, 167
Hall, H. S., 271
Hammond, John, 153
Harding, E. W., 168 *et seq.*
Hills, J. W., 120, 121
Hofland, T. C., 276 *et seq.*
Jackson, John, 60, 108, 110, 111, 283 *et seq.*
Lauson, Wm., 19
Lee, Norman N., 165
Mackintosh, Alex., 294 *et seq.*
Markham, Gervase, 18, 19
Marryat, G. S., 133, 134, 146
Mascall, Leonard, 18, 19

Mosely, M. E., 88, 89, 160, 165, 166
Mottram, J. C., 161 *et seq.*, 166, 168
Ogden, Jas., 120, 121, 300 *et seq.*
Ogden-Smith, Mary, 120
Pritt, T. E., 60, 108 *et seq.*
Pulman, G. P. R., 132, 306 *et seq.*
Ronalds, Alfred, 59, 60 *et seq.*, 108, 111, 132, 165
Salter, Robert, 312 *et seq.*
Scotcher, Geo., 59
Shipley and Fitzgibbon, 317 *et seq.*
Skues, G. E. M., 156 *et seq.*, 167, 168, 169
Stewart, W. C., 60

Stoddart, Thos. T., 60
Taverner, John, 19
Taylor, Samuel, 326 *et seq.*
Theakston, Michael, 59, 108, 132, 331 *et seq.*
Turton, John, 346 *et seq.*
Vavon, Antoine, 89
Venables, Robert, 23
Wade, Henry, 60, 232 *et seq.*
Walton, Izaak, 18, 23
Webster, David, 157
West, Leonard, 160
Wheatley, Hewett, 59
Wynkyn de Worde, 16
Younger, John, 60

Books by W. H. Lawrie

BORDER RIVER ANGLING
PRACTICAL ANGLING HINTS & RECIPES
THE BOOK OF THE ROUGH STREAM NYMPH
ANGLER'S QUIZ
BIG TROUT
SCOTTISH TROUT FLIES
ALL-FUR FLIES AND HOW TO DRESS THEM
ETC.

ENGLISH TROUT FLIES